CHILDREN OF THE REVOLUTION

GLOBALIZATION
IN EVERYDAY LIFE

Children of the Revolution

Violence, Inequality, and Hope in Nicaraguan Migration

LAURA J. ENRÍQUEZ

STANFORD UNIVERSITY PRESS
Stanford, California

STANFORD UNIVERSITY PRESS
Stanford, California

Printed in the United States of America on acid-free, archival-quality paper

Library of Congress Cataloging-in-Publication Data is available upon request.
ISBN 9781503613782 (cloth)
ISBN 9781503631281 (paperback)
ISBN 9781503631298 (electronic)

Cover design: Angela Moody
Cover image: Bettysphotos | Adobe Stock
Typeset by Newgen North America in 10/14.4 Minion Pro

Table of contents

Acknowledgments

The idea for this book started out as a joke. Andrea, one of the women whose story it tells, had related to me in a casual conversation over the telephone that she had spent time in a sanatorium in Nicaragua after being exposed to tuberculosis. Already being familiar with many aspects of her life, I responded that I had not yet heard that part of her history. I went on to say that she had experienced so much in her life that maybe I should write a book about her. We both laughed about the idea! But, after pondering it further over the following few months, I concluded that it would be a worthwhile endeavor. It seemed to make sense to broaden it to include all four of the women described in the following pages, though. I then formally broached the idea as a real undertaking to them. Hence, that joke was transformed from a spontaneous statement into a serious project of oral history.

I doubt that any of the four women imagined how much I would "pester" them with questions over the subsequent months and years, nor how long it might take for this enterprise to reach fruition. The depth of my gratitude to them for sharing their stories with me is hard to fully express. They were extremely generous in patiently answering my endless questions in their meager amounts of time off from work. Their willingness to cover both difficult and joy-filled terrain made the text that follows possible. I can only hope that having the opportunity to reflect back on their lives, as well as having this "memoir" of sorts that they can pass on to their children, is some small recompense. Thank you so very much, Andrea, Silvia, Ana, and Pamela.

Two colleagues and close friends—Nancy Jurik and Michael Burawoy—gave me the courage to begin this project, when I was timorous about making such a major shift from the topics I had previously researched to a study that had at its core the lives of a small group of immigrant women. Nancy called to my attention several wonderful books, including Mary Romero's *The Maid's Daughter*, that were organized in this way. And Michael reminded me about C. Wright Mills's famous aphorism that "sociology is the intersection of biography and history." Over time, both of them have listened to my quandaries about how best to present the women's stories in the form of a book that would be of interest to others, as well as reading parts or the whole of the manuscript and providing me with invaluable feedback.

Several other colleagues and friends also chimed in with their feedback at critical junctures. Beth Stephens and Elly Bulkin visited me in Italy while I was still engaged in interviewing there, and they dedicated part of their time to asking me important questions about the project and reading my first effort to put the women's stories in writing. Kyra Subbotin responded enthusiastically each time I discussed the book with her and helpfully brought her nonsociological perspective to a good chunk of the manuscript despite it being a very stressful time in her life. Nancy Moss also read and provided comments on several chapters early on in their development. Rose Spalding applied her precise analytical eye to a crucial piece of this project. And Marjorie Zatz kindly read the entire manuscript and made very constructive observations once I had a "whole" tome for someone to read.

I also received useful comments on several occasions, especially from the members of the Political Sociology and the Global South Working Group (PSGS) of the Department of Sociology at the University of California, Los Angeles, when I presented parts of this research. I am very appreciative of Carmen Brick, who gave me superb assistance in "tidying up" the whole manuscript, including the quotes. And Robert Enríquez converted my chicken-scratched, hand-drawn family trees into the pristine form they have taken in the volume.

I am also indebted to the anonymous reviewers that Stanford University Press called on to read the manuscript. They gave me extensive comments that have guided me in revising and strengthening the manuscript. And the enthusiasm of Marcela Cristina Maxfield, the editor who shepherded my book manuscript through Stanford University Press, made a real difference as I moved from my initial writing on the project to the completion of the final manuscript.

Funding for this project came from the Program on Comparative Studies of Societies at UC Berkeley. I am grateful for the support provided by the various grants I have received from the program.

Last, but certainly not least, my family has played a critical role in the evolution of this project. A family emergency took us to Italy at a time when I expected to be heading off for points south for my sabbatical. Fortunately, the emergency was resolved with time, but being "marooned" in Italy for a lengthy period of time was what made that joke become this project. My compañero, Maurizio Leonelli, loyally traipsed back and forth with me to my interviewing base in Milan during the months we were still living elsewhere in Italy in 2015. Then he and our son, Adriano Leonelli-Enríquez, joined me when I went to live in Milan to continue my research in 2016. The two of them happily helped me to host many gatherings of my "research group" (i.e., the four women) as the project moved forward. They both brainstormed with me about various aspects of the project, with Maurizio shedding particular light on Italy's NGO sector. And Adriano helped me to schlep my piles of books and interview materials back and forth from North America to Europe several times. Meanwhile, my brother, Robert Enríquez, has been a major source of stability in an otherwise constantly shifting landscape throughout this period of time, providing essential logistical and other kinds of support on an ongoing basis.

My gratitude to all of you is immense. Thank you for accompanying me on this journey.

CHILDREN OF THE REVOLUTION

1 | SITUATING THE STORIES OF ANDREA, SILVIA, ANA, AND PAMELA

Neither the life of an individual nor the history of a society can be understood without understanding both.

C. Wright Mills, The Sociological Imagination

THIS BOOK TELLS THE STORY OF FOUR WOMEN who came of age during a revolution. Andrea, Silvia, Ana, and Pamela were impoverished youth when the Nicaraguan revolution took hold in 1979.[1] They attained young adulthood while it blossomed and then withered away in the context of a war and profound economic crisis. Still, the Sandinista revolution gave them hope of a different future, if not for themselves, then for their children. While they initially envisioned themselves working to build that future in Nicaragua, over time it became clear to these women that it would be difficult to offer the next generation real social mobility through their labors there, as previously existing social equalities were only reinforced in the aftermath of the revolution. Hence, they eventually chose to emigrate to Italy to make their hopes realizable. Yet the network they relied on to arrive at their destination existed because of the revolution. And their work abroad paid off as their children, and now grandchildren, have alternatives they never had.

In telling their stories, this book describes the agency these four women engaged in as they sought a brighter future for their children. In fact, their life stories directly address the long-running discussion about the relationship between agency and social structure, the latter of which refers to

those patterns of social life that are not reducible to individuals and are
durable enough to withstand the whims of individuals who would change
them; patterns that have dynamics and an underlying logic of their own
that contribute to their reproduction over time. (Hays 1994: 60–61)

In recent years a number of scholars have furthered the conversation about
this relationship in ways that acknowledge the distinction between these two
phenomena and recognize that use of the term *agency*—which speaks to action that is oriented toward bringing about change—does not mean an assumption of unfettered possibilities in this regard. They do, however, suggest
that spaces can be found to promote change. Those spaces and opportunities
can lead to wholesale transformation—such as that brought about by some
revolutions—as well as small-scale modifications in the lives of individual
social actors. Yet even as social structures may enable agency in certain circumstances, agents' chosen actions "are *always socially shaped*" and are those
located "within the realm of structurally provided possibilities."[2] As they
contemplate those choices, they may look to the past, the present, or the future in gauging what might conceivably be achieved (Emirbayer and Mische
1998). Their options are also colored by their own social position, in terms of
their social class, gender, race/ethnicity, and other characteristics (Romero
and Valdez 2016).

In the cases of Andrea, Silvia, Ana, and Pamela, the formative, national
social structure in which they were positioned was that of Nicaragua. As
they grew up in the 1960s and 1970s, their lives were greatly shaped by being disadvantaged vis-à-vis multiple social inequalities that characterized
the country at the time. When the Sandinistas took power, their objective
was not only to rid Nicaragua of the Somoza dictatorship that had ruled
the country for more than forty years but also to alter the economic, political, and social structure to achieve social justice. That process of transformation brought about notable changes in each of those areas. It was greatly
weakened, though, by the late 1980s and ended when the Sandinistas left
office in 1990. The introduction of neoliberalism by the conservative government that took power and those that followed brought the economy and
society back into a full embrace of capitalism and, among other things, led to

an increase in poverty and inequality. Within this milieu, the aspirations of Andrea, Silvia, Ana, and Pamela were constantly challenged.

However, when these women eventually emigrated to Italy, the prevailing social structure there became the next context within which they might exercise some measure of agency. As immigrants, they were channeled into Italy's "care economy," whose existence and demand for their labor made their emigration possible. Their movement into the care sector was an expression of both the Italian social structure and the social positionality they embodied as immigrant women (Hondagneu-Sotelo 2001; Solari 2017). That sector expanded significantly in response to economic and demographic changes under way in much of the Global North, which are especially apparent in Italy (Solari 2017; Lutz 2011; Da Roit et al. 2013; Parreñas 2015). Moreover, the Italian government facilitated the incorporation of immigrants into its labor force as a way to address the social consequences of those changes, most especially that of the country's "care deficit."[3] Yet in so doing, these immigrants were relegated to a specific position in the country's social structure.

In spite of the inequalities generated by the Nicaraguan and Italian social structures, which subjected the four women to ongoing structural violence, they have been able to open up possibilities for their children that are distinct from what they had. In doing so, these women have contributed to the social mobility experienced by this next generation. Even as they work long and arduous hours to take care of members of Italian society, including the sick and elderly, they have made it possible for their children to attend college and assume professional jobs or positions that are in demand and can sustain them. And these women will not have to rely fully on their children in their old age, as their parents had to do with them.

In the chapters that follow, their stories unfold to show in stark relief these inequalities and additional social phenomena and dynamics. Principal among them is that of structural violence, which is defined as a situation in which the social structures in a society produce an unequal distribution of resources such that those disadvantaged by that distribution are unable to reach their full potential (Galtung 1969). Structural violence affects the better part of Latin America's population and is the predominant backdrop against which these women have sought to bring about change in their lives. We will see how that violence impacted them from their early childhood through well into their stay in Italy as middle-aged adults. That is to say, we will become acquainted with the ways in which structural violence was borne out in their lives before, during, and after Nicaragua's revolution.

Thus, this book offers a detailed longitudinal examination of structural violence while also capturing how the social change brought about by the revolution modified the nation's distribution of resources and opportunities for a period of time. In addition, it illuminates the ways in which the revolution and its aftermath contributed to the women's emigration, along a pathway and to a destination that were quite distinct from most south–north migration. The fact that it was only after long years of working in Nicaragua that they chose to emigrate in order to create an alternative future for their children will also be apparent. Importantly, the combination of that extended effort in their country of origin and their labors in their country of destination ultimately produced some measure of social mobility for the next generation. Hence, the lives of Andrea, Silvia, Ana, and Pamela have also embodied multiple expressions of agency, including having made this major life decision. But those expressions have been delimited by the structural violence that still characterizes the two societies of which they have formed a part.

My telling of their stories is based on oral histories that I developed with them in the course of numerous interviews between 2015 and 2018. I followed up those interviews with various forms of correspondence with them. The way to developing the necessary rapport for the interviews was opened by having known these women for an extended period of time—in one case going back more than thirty years—and being familiar with their lives in Nicaragua before their emigration. It is out of a conviction that their lives illuminate these multiple elements of Nicaraguan and Italian social history, as well as speaking to larger social issues, that I have put them to paper.

Before I recount their life histories, though, it is necessary to situate them within the relevant theoretical and historical discussions that can shed light on them. The remainder of this chapter is dedicated to that effort, as well as to describing my methodological approach in greater detail and presenting an outline of the book. In subsequent chapters, we turn to becoming better acquainted with these four Nicaraguan women.

RELEVANT THEORETICAL AND HISTORICAL DISCUSSIONS

The lives of Andrea, Silvia, Ana, and Pamela evolved in the context of a diverse array of social phenomena, including high levels of structural violence, political regime change, and the forging of new transnational labor systems. Although these phenomena are interrelated, we need to examine each in turn before we can identify the ways in which they were connected. Proceeding in this sequential fashion will allow us to understand the nature of each phenomenon and take into account what scholars have learned about it prior to grappling with the ways in which they may combine to produce even more complicated dynamics. The most overarching of these phenomena within the lives of the four women was that of structural violence.

Structural Violence

Various types of violence have impacted the lives of these four women, with structural violence being at the core of all of them. Each type will be discussed in the chapters that follow. But I will argue that, in comparison to other sources of violence, the structural violence deriving from class inequalities has been consistently present at each stage of their lives. Nonetheless, since the concept of structural violence is inclusive of various forms of violence, we begin this discussion with a brief exploration of what it consists of.

In 1969 Johan Galtung (168) introduced the concept of structural violence. Inherent in it is an understanding that the unequal distribution of vital assets, and especially the ability to decide how they will be allocated, means that certain members of the society in question are kept from reaching their full capability. Galtung (1969: 171) presents the example of people starving when it is objectively avoidable within a society. He uses the term *structural violence* to distinguish this type of violence from that of a personal nature. His concern is to ensure its incorporation into larger discussions of peace, which had been his starting point.

In the years since Galtung first described this phenomenon, others have joined the conversation about it. For example, Phillipe Bourgois (2001: 8) specified that structural violence is "historically entrenched political-economic oppression and social inequality." He also insisted on the need to broaden conception of it beyond individual societies to include "exploitative international terms of trade." The logic of this latter insistence is that this phenomenon contributes to its manifestation within national contexts. In speaking of extremely dire health care conditions in Haiti, Paul Farmer (2004) set forth structural violence as an explanatory factor in understanding them. He posited that analyzing such violence requires taking into account its historical emergence in examining any concrete instance of it. In addition, Farmer (2004) stated that it refers not only to inequality between classes but also to that between races and genders. Hence, the concept is broad enough to incorporate additional systems of inequality, including those stemming from racial hierarchies—or racial caste systems, and those stemming from sexual hierarchies—such as patriarchy.

Cecilia Menjívar (2011: 28–29) takes seriously the call to examine the ways in which gender, race, and class mediate the structural violence that impacts the poor Ladina women she studied in Guatemala. She focuses on the eastern part of the country, which was less directly affected by the last decades of that country's civil war, and analyzes everyday violence as it marks women's lives there. Drawing on the work of Arthur Kleinman (1997, as cited in Menjívar 2011: 1), she considers that violence to be a process "of ordering the social world," rather than an event. And Silvia Dominguez and Cecilia Menjívar (2014: 192) argue that various types of violence—including structural violence in its multiple manifestations, as well as symbolic, interpersonal, and gendered violence—combine to reproduce poverty among low-income women in what "amounts to a 'slow death.'"[4] Moreover, Kleinman (1997: 239) says that everyday violence "is all the more fundamental" because it is the hidden source "out of which images of people are shaped, experiences of groups are coerced, and agency itself is engendered."[5] That is, it underlies the social world.

In fact, the description of structural violence presented by Galtung, as well as those who have further elaborated this concept, is apt for the circumstances of the large percentage of Latin Americans who live in poverty. In 2019 poverty in all of Latin America affected 30.5 percent of the population, and extreme poverty affected 11.3 percent.[6] In the case of Nicaragua, poverty affected 44.4 percent of the population, and extreme poverty affected 8.9 percent in 2019 (FIDEG 2020: 11).[7] Inequality is the context out of which this poverty emerges. Latin America is the most unequal region in the world; it had an overall Gini index of .46 in 2019 (ECLAC 2021: 64). Moreover, in 2019 the wealthiest quintile of the population controlled approximately 51 percent of total household income, in contrast to the poorest quintile, which controlled just 5 percent (ECLAC 2021: 68). For Nicaragua, the Gini index was .495 in 2014 (ECLAC 2018: 72).[8] The wealthiest quintile of the population there controlled 48 percent of the country's income, and the poorest quintile controlled just 5 percent (ECLAC 2018: 36).

The implications of the structural violence these figures describe, at least in terms of class inequalities, typically extend throughout the life course. They begin even before the poor are born, with significant differences in prenatal care, broadly defined, for those located in distinct positions within the social structure. And in most cases, these implications continue to have an impact throughout their lives, given the relatively limited nature of social and economic mobility in the region. According to Florencia Torche (2014), both social and economic mobility data indicate a high persistence at the top of both of these hierarchies, which is consistent with what one would expect given the levels of inequality in Latin America.[9] However, data on shifts in occupational status suggest that there is even less economic mobility than social mobility. Unfortunately, data to assess mobility are limited to a few countries in the region, and Nicaragua is not among them. Nonetheless, given the general patterns, it seems safe to assume that the country's high level of inequality likewise extends to low levels of social and economic mobility.

The experiences of Andrea, Silvia, Ana, and Pamela illustrate how structural violence is expressed in each stage of a person's life. Yet the structural violence that affected their lives extended beyond class inequalities to include those generated by the racial caste system and patriarchy prevailing in Latin America, and the distinctions associated with immigration status in Italy.[10] That is, their experiences were also colored by racial discrimination, sexual harassment and violence, and discrimination stemming from their gender and immigrant status.[11] Through an examination of those experiences we can also see the ways in which several of these phenomena were and were not affected by the decade of social transformation that took place in Nicaragua, which sought to redress these exact forms of structural violence, as well as by the emigration from that country that escalated in the decades afterward. These features are two of the elements that distinguish this study from those describing structural violence in other contexts.[12]

A Brief Introduction to Nicaraguan History

The four women who form the centerpiece of this study lived through several decades of tumultuous change in Nicaragua. Given that aspects of the country's history affected their lives in diverse ways, a brief discussion of it is in order.[13]

Nicaragua came into the twentieth century with an agricultural economy, which the Liberal government in power was rapidly transforming by opening it to the world market largely through the production and export of coffee.[14] When that government was ousted by U.S.-backed political forces in 1909, a lengthy period of political turmoil ensued, which included more than twenty years of occupation by the U.S. Marines.[15] Shortly after the Marines finally withdrew in 1933, Anastasio Somoza García—the head of the National Guard established by the U.S. to substitute for its withdrawing forces—maneuvered himself into the presidency. The Somoza family then ruled over Nicaragua as if the country were its personal fiefdom from the mid-1930s until 1979.[16] Anastasio Somoza García had come from a middle-class family, and his most noteworthy previous employment had been as a used-car salesman. But by 1944, he was the owner of "fifty-one cattle ranches and forty-six coffee plantations" (Booth 1985: 67). He used various sorts of corruption and illegal activities to acquire his wealth,[17] a pattern carried on by his sons in the years they were in power. By the time the last Somoza to rule (Anastasio Somoza Debayle) fled the country in 1979, the family dynasty had significant financial holdings in construction materials, tobacco, meatpacking, fishing and fish canning, real estate development, the mass media, auto products, auto importing, the national airline, shoes, and vast agricultural properties (Booth 1985: 80).

During the reign of the Somoza family, the economy became more diversified, even as it remained overwhelmingly dependent on agricultural exports to fuel it.[18] Coffee, which was still important, was joined by cotton, sugarcane, and beef as the country's key exports. Some agro-industry was developed, especially associated with the production of the last three of these products. And a smattering of light industry, such as clothing production, emerged in Nicaragua under the auspices of the Central American Common Market in the 1960s. In terms of employment, agriculture remained a critical sector, even as the informal sector expanded exponentially in urban areas with the rapid growth of rural–urban migration between 1950 and 1979. Many of these new urban dwellers found employment in small workshops, in markets, and in providing services of all kinds.

Even putting aside the Somoza dynasty's self-enrichment, the economic growth that occurred during this period concentrated the country's wealth ever further, leaving most of the population living in poverty. For example, as was true throughout Central America, the expansion of cotton production for export in Nicaragua pushed smallholders out of the most productive areas in the regions where it was grown and onto more marginal land.[19] This dynamic almost inevitably undermined the ability of these peasant farmers to support themselves from their farm-generated income alone.

Politically, the country was characterized by the existence of multiple political parties that were played off against one another to keep the Somozas in power and by a repressive and corrupt state. Despite Anastasio Somoza García's assassination in 1956, each of his sons subsequently took a turn at running the country. And the National Guard sustained the regime until the very end.

Eventually, though, a broad swath of society—including students, peasants, businesspeople, and members of the informal sector—joined the effort to overthrow the dictatorship. The Sandinista National Liberation Front (Frente Sandinista de Liberación Nacional, FSLN), which had fought a political and military struggle against the regime since 1961, was at the forefront of the government that came to power in 1979.[20] Its goals went far beyond removing the last of the Somozas from power. They also included bringing about a social, political, and economic revolution aimed at creating a society that would be oriented toward the needs of the poor majority. The Sandinista government's early years were a time of hope among many of the country's poor. Not only was the repressive National Guard no longer a threat to daily existence, but achieving a more dignified life appeared to be a possibility. Nicaragua also became a beacon of inspiration beyond its borders, drawing many foreigners who came to work in a variety of capacities during this period.[21]

The Sandinistas initially succeeded in expanding the poor's access to social services and improving their livelihoods through new and enforced labor legislation and agrarian reform.[22] Moreover, agrarian reform and other

initiatives laid the foundation for a mixed economy that included cooperatives, a traditional private sector, and state enterprises, thereby providing
support for a wide array of economic actors.[23] The dynamism of this early
period was captured in the renowned Literacy Crusade of 1980—which mo-
bilized eighty thousand youth volunteers for five months to various parts of
the country to tackle the problem of illiteracy, reducing it from 50 percent to
12 percent nationwide—and in the construction of more than seven hundred
new schools in the first two years alone of the government.[24] The substantial
enlargement of the public health system—represented by the construction of
four new regional hospitals and a more than 25 percent increase in the number of health posts, especially in rural and other underserved areas—also
reflected this dynamism.[25] And the reshaped political system incorporated a
significantly broader range of participants than had been the case in the past.
The idea underpinning these changes was to develop an approach to problem solving that would address the needs of the majority of the population
through the activities of a diversity of organizations that were born and/or
strengthened within the economy and polity.

By the mid-1980s, though, an economic crisis had begun to make daily
life very difficult for most Nicaraguans. The crisis had its origins in the empty
treasury and huge foreign debt left to the Sandinistas when they took power,
the counterrevolutionary war waged by forces that were U.S.-organized and
-financed (the Contras), the U.S.-sponsored economic blockade, mistakes in
and mismanagement of economic policy by the inexperienced new government itself, and a lack of participation in the economy by certain parts of
the country's business sector.[26] The optimism of the early period of the Sandinista government receded, and aspirations for improved livelihoods were
replaced by the increasingly hard-to-attain goal of simply meeting one's basic
needs. The economic crisis, combined with the military draft imposed in
1983 to fight against the Contras, played a major role in the decision of voters
in the 1990 general elections to replace the Sandinistas with a coalition of
conservative forces.[27]

This coalition, headed by Violeta Barrios de Chamorro, was the first of
three conservative governments to preside over the country during the next
sixteen years. Together these governments implemented a neoliberal structural adjustment of the economy. The structural adjustment policies imposed

austerity on government spending—which reduced expenditures for social services, subsidies, employment, and so forth—and eliminated various kinds of supports that had been put in place to protect producers whose orientation was the local market.[28] This sector of producers tended to be more small and medium-size in scale and had gained substantial terrain during the Sandinista government in the 1980s. Hence, farmers growing food crops, as well as those producing other kinds of goods for Nicaraguan consumers, were hit by these measures. The objective was to expand export-oriented production, which would allow Nicaragua to repay its foreign debt. In the process, those producing goods for export were reprioritized and provided with access to various kinds of resources—land, loans, and so forth—to promote their production. Notable increases in poverty and income inequality were among the results of these economic policies.[29] The demobilization of social and political actors that had begun in the context of the economic crisis of the latter 1980s deepened as people found it necessary to focus more on their own and their family's survival when workplaces and organizations they had previously been part of could no longer come to their aid. This more individual orientation was also part and parcel of the neoliberal sensibility that was increasingly hegemonic worldwide.[30]

With the promise of better times ahead, a greatly changed Sandinista party was elected to govern once again in the national elections of 2006.[31] By then, though, Andrea, Silvia, Ana, and Pamela were all looking elsewhere for solutions for the challenges they were facing vis-à-vis their objectives of assisting their children in forging a life path different from their own and of aiding their aging parents. They had ceased to believe that the answer to their dilemma would be found in Nicaragua and were actively pursuing emigration options.

Structured Agency

The foregoing sketch of Nicaragua's recent history describes the multiple important changes that the country's social structure underwent before the emigration of the four women at the center of this study. First, the revolution that was initiated with Somoza's overthrow in 1979 opened up new forms of economic, social, and political organization. This process of transformation unfolded within the context of a small country with an agro-export-based economy that out of necessity had to continue to engage with the world market. The organizations and movement pushing the process of revolutionary change forward encountered opposition from some social forces within the country—especially those that felt they stood to lose ground—as well as those outside (e.g., the U.S. government). Yet they were able to draw on the support of a broad enough array of social groupings to make major modifications to the organization of society. As a result, the extremely concentrated access to economic and political resources that had prevailed until 1979 was diminished, and a greater diversity of actors were incorporated into decision-making bodies overseeing these spheres of social life.

Further alterations in the social structure were brought about with the right-leaning government's assumption of power in 1990, as it adopted a neoliberal orientation toward policy making. Despite the massive protests and resistance from certain societal sectors, by the mid-1990s significant changes had been wrought to open the economy to the international market, reduce the presence of the state within it, and reorient the society back in a strictly capitalist direction.[32] As a result, economic and political resources once again became increasingly concentrated.

The scale of these transformations sheds light on Sharon Hays's (1994: 61–62) conception of both structure and agency. She argued that social structures contain several key elements: (1) people create them and make their continued existence possible; (2) social structures enable as well as constrain agency—that is, they can provide the "tools" that make social change possible; and (3) the less profound the kind of change sought, the less resistance there will be to it and vice versa. Through their actions, most of the time people simply facilitate the reproduction of the social structure, which she terms "structurally reproductive agency" (Hays 1994: 63). Periodically throughout history, however, people have been able to take advantage of the tools she mentions to push forward change on a much larger scale, which Hays terms "structurally transformative agency" (Hays 1994: 64). A revolution would be one expression of the latter type of agency. It is critical to bear in mind, though, that there is a continuum of action between these two types of agency.

Mustafa Emirbayer and Ann Mische (1998) likewise see social change as being possible despite the constraining nature of social structures. They argue that agency is never entirely liberated from the constraints posed by the social structure, but neither is it entirely restricted by it. They also recognize the different scales of potential change. Emirbayer and Mische's (1998) contribution to this discussion has to do with the issue of temporality. That is, as people contemplate action of distinct types, their point of reference is one or more of the following: the past, the present, or the future. Although we all exist in the present, the present can be extended back (to the past) or forward (to the future). In looking at the past, actors may seek to return there or to move away from it. But what has occurred in the past also suggests what might be possible in the way of change. And in looking to the future, actors may seek to modify what lies ahead. Revolutionary movements, among others, are particularly oriented toward the future. Moreover, being immersed in contexts of change enables one to imagine alternatives to what presently exists. Hence, even after a situation of great flux—such as that set in motion by a revolution—has waned, those who have lived through it have had their imaginations opened up as to what is actually possible. In addition, Emirbayer and Mische (1998: 1007) hypothesize that the networks with which one interacts may give rise to distinct "agentic orientations," with the potential for innovative and resourceful reasoning and action increasing to the degree to which those networks offer exposure to different temporal outlooks and social relations. Here again, having lived through a change with the magnitude of a social revolution could well have entailed interacting with social groupings that would have fostered "multiple temporal" perspectives. Following their line of argument, such experiences would have opened up the possibility of thinking creatively when trying to find solutions to challenges being faced. This kind of creative thinking could, but need not necessarily, be geared toward agency directed at bringing about societal-level change. It could also be productive for individuals, such as these four women, if they are searching for answers to personal dilemmas.

Despite this relatively optimistic turn in the conversation about the relationship between structure and agency, another discussion in the literature calls to our attention the fact that certain groups have greater constraints imposed on their potential for agency arising from their social location within society. This literature is centered on the concept of *intersectionality*. In what is considered the opening salvo of this discussion, Kimberlé

Crenshaw (1989) makes the case that understanding discrimination on the basis of "single-axis" characteristics—such as gender or race—means that whole social groups within society (e.g., Black women) drop out of the analysis. That is, because of their position at the intersection of these two axes, Black women are impacted by discrimination in both spheres of inequality. Over the years since that salvo was fired, this concept has been broadened to consider a variety of additional axes: class, immigration status, sexuality, and so forth. This approach to analysis has been adopted to study topics as widely varying as entrepreneurship, social activism, and domestic service.[33] The principal point of the intersectional approach is that in analyzing any particular issue or topic, one must consider the multiple positionalities that members of a given group occupy, as each may have its own specific dynamics that are not entirely contained in any other. In the case of this study, we are concerned with how the interplay of structure and agency presented space for maneuver to a small group of poor Nicaraguan women who grew up and became adults in their country of origin and then emigrated to Italy for work. At a minimum, intersectional theory demands that we bear in mind the axes of class, gender, race/ethnicity, and immigration status in reflecting on their life stories.

Emigration from Nicaragua

In addition to coming of age during a revolution, Andrea, Silvia, Ana, and Pamela all eventually opted to emigrate from the country where that revolution took place, Nicaragua. In so doing, they expressed agency in their search for a way forward for themselves and their families.[34] They were not alone in doing so.

Emigration from Nicaragua is not a new phenomenon. However, particular periods have been characterized by greater movement abroad than others. The following discussion will describe three periods in the country's emigration history: prior to the ouster of Anastasio Somoza Debayle in July 1979; the years of revolutionary change (1979–1990); and the neoliberal era (1990–onward).[35] The four women whose life histories are the focus of this book went overseas during the latter two periods. Yet Nicaraguans have been leaving their homeland for much of the country's recent history.

As early as the 1960s, Nicaraguan immigration to the United States was noted by scholars working in this field (e.g., Zhao 2016). Undoubtedly, emigration from the country occurred before then, because of both the political dictatorship in place and economic changes that negatively affected certain sectors of the population. The Great Depression of the 1930s was a period of tremendous hardship for much of the population, but even the eras of relative economic boom—such as the 1950s and 1960s—advantaged certain sectors and disadvantaged others.[36] At the same time, the country's political situation fueled emigration to other Central American countries and elsewhere. The Somoza regime was established in 1936, and the political space for those who opposed it varied over the years but was mostly limited. Probably the greatest exodus stemming from the pre-1979 political situation occurred in the 1970s, as organizing against the dictatorship escalated and the latter responded with increased repression. According to Alberto Cortés Ramos (2006), "it is calculated that some 280,000[37] people left Nicaragua at that time, at least 80,000 headed for Costa Rica." This period culminated in the final insurrection of June–July 1979 and Somoza's departure (on July 17 of that year), which opened the way for the establishment of a new government.

The Sandinista period (1979–1990) brought about another exodus, of those closely associated with the Somoza regime and those who more generally opposed the political, economic, and social goals of the revolutionary government. But some who had fled the conflict in the late 1970s returned to Nicaragua after 1979. As the U.S.-sponsored Contra war took hold, the flow of people leaving grew.[38] Among those who left the country but stayed within Central America were approximately 19,500 Miskitus and Sumus who emigrated to Honduras and an estimated 100,000–125,000 Nicaraguans from across the country who went to Costa Rica (Cortés Ramos 2006). Total emigration for the 1980s was estimated by the government to be 155,000 (MIPLAN 1989, as cited in Funkhouser 1992: 1210). Yet by including data allowing for some estimation of undocumented emigration, Edward Funkhouser (1992: 1211) calculates that 400,000–450,000 Nicaraguans, or 10.7–12.0 percent of the 1989 population emigrated during this period. The United States and Costa Rica were the major recipients of these émigrés, with the former receiving more than the latter.

As discussed previously, the conservative government that came to power in 1990 put in place a new economic model based on a neoliberal framework. Given the major cuts in government spending required by that framework, economic inequality and poverty grew. This trend led to a surge of emigration.[39] Then, in the elections of late 2006, the FSLN won the presidency once again. After assuming office in 2007, its perennial candidate, Daniel Ortega, introduced a number of poverty reduction programs. His government did not, however, stray far from the larger economic model that had prevailed under the conservative governments of the previous sixteen years. Hence, emigration remained an option that many pursued to address their economic difficulties. In fact, approximately forty thousand people emigrated from Nicaragua each year during the first decade of this century (Andersen and Christensen 2009: 2). Given that remittances from the country's emigrants had come to constitute more than 10 percent of its GDP by the 2000s, labor has become one of Nicaragua's most important export "products."

The major destinations for Nicaraguan emigrants during this third period continued to be Costa Rica and the United States, although the order of importance between these two countries reversed after 1990. In Costa Rica, Nicaraguans worked on a temporary basis in the export harvests. Those who stayed on a more permanent basis found employment in the service (mainly women) and construction (mainly men) sectors. The UN Population Division[40] estimated them to number 350,854 in 2020. However, since the economic crisis of 2008, many Nicaraguans have continued their southward trajectory to Panama, as Costa Rica's economy has been unable to absorb them. Hence, Panama has become the second most important regional destination (Yarris 2017: 11). Meanwhile, the number of Nicaraguans in the United States was estimated to be 255,008 in 2020.[41]

Europe remained a more remote destination, although a relatively small number of émigrés also moved in that direction. The UN Population Division estimated the number of Nicaraguan émigrés in Europe to be 51,163, including Italy, where they estimated that 1,381 resided in 2020.[42] And although more women had emigrated from Nicaragua overall than men (53 percent/47 percent), this pattern was much more striking in Europe (71 percent/29 percent). All told, a sizable part of Nicaragua's population emigrates for at least some months of each year,[43] and women have a prominent presence in the pool of émigrés.

Even though not encapsulating their entire experience of immigration, as we will see in Chapter 4, these four women opted for what has been a less common path than that of most immigrants in the world today and of Nicaraguans historically speaking.[44] Given that history, the phenomenon of their compatriots emigrating would have been familiar to the women. But their choice to emigrate to Europe, and more specifically to Italy, reflected social and economic dynamics of the past several decades in that country and the region that contains it. And these women have been at the forefront of a shift in the direction of migration for Central Americans that seemed to be emerging by the end of the 2010s, as Europe appeared to be a more accessible destination than the United States (*New York Times* 2019; *The Guardian* 2019).[45]

Immigration to Italy

Italy has a long history of participation in global migratory flows. In the late 1800s, southern Europe became a region that sent migrants elsewhere in the world to look for work. Southern Europeans were forced into global population movements as they increasingly found supporting themselves in their home countries to be a challenge given the transformations that were under way in those economies. These migrants numbered in the millions (Calavita 2005: 3). After World War II, labor opportunities—especially factory jobs—increased in northern and central Europe, allowing southern Europeans to remain in that region instead of continuing the patterns established in the earlier period of emigration to far-flung places.

In the 1970s, the outward movement of people from southern Europe was reversed. At that point in time, this region joined northern Europe as a "receiving" area for migrants from elsewhere in the world. By way of illustration, between 1970 and 1990 the number of foreign-born people in Spain increased by close to 100 percent; in Italy, the number increased by more than 430 percent (calculated from Chell-Robinson 2000: 105). And in 2020, Spain and Italy were the 10th and 11th most important receiving nations in the world, respectively.[46] Finally, to give some comparative perspective, the percentage of the population that was foreign-born in 2019 was 15.4 percent for the United States, 13.1 percent for Spain, and 10.4 percent for Italy.[47] All of this is to say that immigration into southern Europe has become a major demographic, social, political, and economic phenomenon over the past forty to fifty years.

Where are the immigrants to southern Europe generally, and Italy in particular, coming from? In 2020, eastern Europe was the predominant origin region for the population of foreign residents in Italy, with Romania and Albania being the largest contributors from that part of the world.[48] The next largest contributors to Italy's pool of foreign residents were Morocco, China, the Philippines, and several other African and Asian countries. Among foreign residents in Italy coming from Latin America, Peruvians are the most important subgroup, constituting the 16th largest contributor to Italy's overall population of foreign nationals, followed by Ecuador, which is the 18th largest contributor. Hence, in several decades, Italy has gone from having an overwhelmingly native-born population to hosting immigrants from all over the world.

Several factors came into play to bring about this shift. On the one hand, as Italy's economy diversified and grew in the post–World War II period, fewer of its own people felt compelled to look for work elsewhere. Kitty Calavita (2005: 3) describes what occurred in this period as Italy's "economic miracle." Indeed, when the Group of Six (G6) formed in 1975, Italy was included in this organization of the world's major industrialized countries that were also considered leading democracies. In the period following the Great Recession, with the growth of unemployment in the country—especially among youth and particularly those from southern Italy—emigration to northern and western Europe accelerated.[49] Even with high levels of unemployment, though, Italy has remained one of Europe's most important receiving countries.

A number of dynamics allowed this attraction to continue. Victoria Chell-Robinson (2000: 105) argues that one of these dynamics was a "diversion effect," in that it became harder for immigrants from outside the European Union (EU) to gain entry to the countries in northern and western Europe that they had tended to go to earlier on as immigration regulations were tightened up there. Since they could still enter southern European countries, they migrated there. Yet Asher Colombo and Giuseppe Sciortino (2003) dispute this hypothesis. They document that immigration to Italy increased *before* regulations were imposed in northern and western Europe and showed no notable upsurge in the years immediately following the changed policies to the north. They do, however, highlight a significant increase in immigration to the country starting in 1980.

As importantly, Colombo and Sciortino (2003) speak in terms of migration systems, thereby calling to our attention that there are diverse streams of immigrants who have responded to distinct trends in Italy's society and economy at different moments in time. Among the trends that they mention are postcolonial migrations, as expressed, for example, in immigrants arriving from Tunisia and Eritrea following the end of Italian colonialism there. Another system is embodied in those immigrants who come to work in specific sectors of the economy, such as Tunisians and, eventually, other Africans, and eastern Europeans who have come to work in the country's agricultural sector on a seasonal basis; migrants from various parts of the world who have joined the domestic service sector; others from the Middle East and Africa who work in factories and mines; and high-level professionals who have been incorporated into business and the fashion and cultural industries. Several additional migration systems they point to are those of students and other youth, refugees, and migrants who come to establish businesses. Their objective is to demonstrate that Italy is not characterized by only one type of immigrant.

What these scholars and others make clear is that even in the context of the deindustrialization that has taken place in Italy since the 1970s, certain parts of its economy have continued to grow—most especially high technology and service—and have created a demand for foreign labor.[50] While not necessarily concurring precisely with Colombo and Sciortino's (2003) theses, Giovanni Campani (2010: 145) notes that new migrants to southern Europe—including Italy—are largely destined for work in specific niches within the economy, in what has come to be called the Mediterranean Model. As mentioned earlier, one such niche is that of domestic work. This niche has absorbed the better part of the immigrants from Latin America (interview, Italian scholar of immigration, June 28, 2016). And it was precisely this sector of Italy's economy to which Andrea, Silvia, Ana, and Pamela were attracted when they found their prospects for improving their incomes constrained in their home country, thereby limiting their ability to open up new options for their children.

Domestic Work

In his classic piece on the functions of immigration, Michael Burawoy (1976: 1051) reminds us that labor forces have to be "maintained and renewed." The former process refers to the day-to-day reproduction of laborers, while the latter refers, in the most basic circumstances, to ensuring that as workers move out of the labor force, new workers will enter it to fill their slots. Moreover, if the need for labor grows, then the "renewal" component in this equation must also expand. Systems of immigration are one way of addressing a "deficit" in the availability of new, local labor for renewal of the labor force.[51]

All over the Global North a dramatic influx of women into the labor force occurred starting in the 1970s and accelerated thereafter (Ehrenreich and Hochschild 2003). This influx was due to both changes in gender dynamics arising from second-wave feminism and the dropping value of salaries of male breadwinners. The latter phenomenon meant that it became substantially harder for those breadwinners to sustain their families at the standard of living they had previously attained on just one salary. So married women entered the labor force to add to the household income.[52] But then the question arose of who would perform the work these women had previously done in the home—in terms of taking care of the house and its family members. Given that shifting gender dynamics did not include an overhaul of the division of labor within the household (Ehrenreich and Hochschild 2003), another solution had to be found.

In the case of Italy, Europe overall, and to some extent the Global North more generally, an additional factor that increased the need for outside help for work in the home was the aging population. Moreover, the proportion of Italy's population that was older than 65—22.3 percent—was the highest in the EU in 2016.[53] Previously it had been Italian homemakers who had taken care of their elderly relations. As these women increasingly joined the paid labor force, however, they were no longer available to provide this care.

Hiring outside help has been the solution of choice, for those who could afford it, to resolve the dilemmas created by the incorporation into the labor force of women who had formerly minded the home and family.[54] In fact, Helma Lutz (2011) notes that domestic work is the largest labor market worldwide. Yet the unequal value placed on "productive" versus "reproductive" labor, which has its roots in the midnineteenth century and is interwoven with what have come to be their "gendered natures," still diminishes the status of the latter and what people are willing to pay for it. This dynamic has meant that local populations are less inclined to enter this sector of the economy in their search for work.[55]

Returning once again to Burawoy's (1976) analysis of migration systems, he highlights the role that states may play in the establishment of such systems. In fact, the formal and/or informal response of a number of governments in the Global North has been to look to immigrants to take care of their citizens' homes and families, including their elders. Italy's has been among these governments, with the number of immigrants among the care provider labor force putting this in clear evidence: according to Caritas-Migrantes (2008, as cited in Tognetti Bordogna and Ornaghi 2012), "of an estimated 774,000 family assistants, or care workers in Italy [in 2008] . . . 700,000 [were] foreign workers."

The overwhelming reliance on immigrants to fill this demand in Italy's labor market is in large part a reflection of the nature of the country's welfare system. Until the 1990s, Italy was characterized by having a well-developed "welfare state."[56] That is, it had a state that attended to the overall welfare of its population. But the state has been moving in a neoliberal direction since that time. In the Italian context, this trend has been manifested in several key forms: "deregulation and casualization of the labor market, specifically, and waning welfare state protections and individualization" (Molé 2010: 38).[57] Within this new political-economic environment, it makes more sense to permit the entry of immigrants to deliver these services than for the state itself to offer them. To the extent that its citizens can pay for immigrant domestic workers and caregivers, this policy saves the state from having to do so. For citizens who are unable to hire help, it makes more economic sense for the Italian state to furnish them with money transfers that they can use to obtain this care at home than to pay for them to be in an assisted living facility.[58] Given the tradition of in-home care for family members, which predated both the influx of women into the labor force there (as suggested earlier) and the country's neoliberal turn, the approach of the state in this regard has probably not seemed atypical.[59]

In order to enable the functioning of this type of immigration system, the state has been notably more generous toward migrant workers who seek employment in the care and domestic sector than those aiming to work in other sectors of the economy. This pattern has been most clearly expressed with regard to the issue of legalization of migrants' immigration status. According to Giuseppe Sciortino (2004: 120), "throughout the 1990s, nearly half of the scarce legal admissions of foreign workers were granted to domestic workers." Even when the right-wing government that was in power in 2001 imposed a much more restrictive immigration bill, it included an amnesty specifically for domestic workers and care providers.[60] Having legal documentation is important for immigrants because it provides them with the security of being able to remain in the country, as well as the prospect of garnering higher wages than the undocumented.[61] Therefore, the privileging of this sector of workers is a major statement of their perceived significance for the economy and/or society from the point of view of the state.[62]

In his analysis of migration systems, Burawoy (1976) also makes the case that states that facilitate their development typically seek ways of restricting the inflow of people so that it is only the laborer who is permitted entry. That is, the families of immigrant workers who come to fill particular gaps in the labor pool are often not permitted to accompany them. Part of the logic of this control is that, then, the wages of that immigrant labor force do not have to cover the needs of anyone besides the laborers themselves. Moreover, the fact that such immigrants have a home to go back to means that those who employ them in the receiving country do not have to fully sustain (in an integral fashion) even the lone worker who migrates to work there. Instead, family members who remain in the migrants' place of origin help to maintain the migrants' foothold there, along with ensuring at least a partial source of sustenance for them on their return. The result is that neither their complete incorporation into the receiving country, nor wages sufficient to provide for their reproduction, have to be guaranteed.

This combination of dynamics has meant that it is not uncommon for migratory systems to emerge that are highly gendered. For the migrants whom Burawoy (1976) was studying, who went to work in South Africa's mines and the United States' agricultural fields, it was men who predominated and it was women who remained behind to keep the household intact. In contrast, in the case of migrants destined for domestic work and caregiving, women have been the ones to travel, and men and children have been more likely to stay at home because this labor has been considered to be the domain of women for some time now.[63] For example, Barbara Ehrenreich and Arlie Hochschild (2003) speak of the high percentage of Filipino households in which the children have been left with grandmothers, aunts, and fathers when their mothers have gone overseas to work; in Lutz's (2011) study of domestic and care work in Germany, it was Polish women who migrated to provide this labor, and their husbands and families remained behind. Moreover, Annie Phizacklea (1998) and Floya Anthias and Gabriella Lazaridis (2002) describe the "feminization of migration" more generally.

These same gender patterns prevail in the case of migrants providing domestic labor and care in Italy. Within the overall population of immigrants to Italy, women constituted 51.75 percent at the start of 2020.[64] Going back to the data referred to earlier, identifying the eighteen most important sending countries for Italy's immigrant population, several of them have provided abundant labor to meet the demand for domestic workers and care providers. Within this subset of countries, women had an especially high profile in their migrant pools. For Italy's fifth most important sending country, Ukraine, women represented 77.37 percent of the documented migrants in 2020.[65] They have been arriving in Italy since the collapse of the Soviet bloc and the imposition of structural adjustment measures that followed it.[66] However, women from other parts of the world—including Asia and Latin America—started to flow into Italy's domestic sector even earlier, and they continue to be the majority within their national immigrant pools: for example, women represented 56.52 percent of the documented migrants from the Philippines (Italy's sixth most important sending country), 58.41 percent of the documented migrants from Peru, and 56.45 percent of the documented migrants from Ecuador in 2020.[67]

The relative contribution of the countries sending women to work in Italy's domestic and care sectors has shifted somewhat over time. Jacqueline Andall (2000: 124) notes that African women made up the largest group of foreign-born domestic workers at the national level in the period between

1972 and 1982. Philippine domestic workers have also had a presence there since the 1970s (Basa et al., 2017). Latin American migrant women started to arrive at least as early as 1968,[68] and their numbers grew as military conflicts and structural adjustment spread throughout that region. In sum, diverse groups of immigrant women together make up the bulk of the workers who provide these services.

One final issue should be raised with regard to the general topic of domestic workers and care providers in Italy: additional factors—beyond the mere existence of jobs—may draw migrants there to seek employment in this sector. Comparatively speaking, domestic workers and care providers receive better pay in Italy, Canada, and the United States, relative to other possible destinations (Parreñas 2015).[69] Given that economics are often the major element pushing migrants to go abroad for work, opting to go where wages are higher would be a logical choice. Moreover, Italy is one of only a few countries in the world (along with Canada and the United States) where these workers may eventually be able to obtain some kind of permanent residency status (c.f. Parreñas 2015). When this advantage is combined with the fact that once a migrant has submitted their application for legal documentation with the support of their employer, they are not obligated to remain employed by that particular individual, Italy becomes a country where an immigrant can think of staying in the medium to long term without being tied to any particular family beyond the time that they choose to be. Furthermore, in many parts of the world regulations that do exist vis-à-vis those who are employed in this sector do not provide them with rights as workers per se.[70] Italy is one of a limited number of countries that do. Italy's National Contract for Domestic Workers dictates a minimum wage (for both live-in and hourly workers), time off for rest and leisure, a month of paid vacation and a month of bonus salary for each year worked, and severance pay (c.f. Solari 2017). Both documented and undocumented workers are covered by this contract. And these workers find support from the country's unions in having their contract rights enforced.

In sum, domestic and care work *is* the principal option open for migrants like Andrea, Silvia, Ana, and Pamela, who are considered unskilled by Italy's standards.[71] It is an open option because native Italians prefer to work in other areas of the economy given this sector's low status and concomitant low pay. Moreover, as we will see from the experiences of these women, domestic and care work can be arduous and those employed in it often have to be available to provide their services many more hours a week than in most jobs in the Global North. Nonetheless, domestic and care workers in Italy are relatively advantaged vis-à-vis their counterparts in most other immigrant destination countries in terms of their prospects for attaining legal documentation to be in the country, higher pay, and various protections and benefits as workers. And they can and do turn to unions for assistance if their rights in any of these areas are not respected by employers.

Social Mobility as an Outcome of Emigration

Andrea, Ana, Pamela, and Silvia all went to work in Italy with the objective of helping their families back home to prosper.[72] For the first three of these women, being able to send their children to college was a major consideration in making the decision to emigrate.[73] For the fourth, Silvia, it was to be able to help support her elderly and ailing parents that she was motivated to leave her home country. However, once in Italy, she also assisted one of her younger sisters to attend college with her remittances. Because attending college held the promise of generating more employment options for their children and younger siblings than these women had, with all of the ramifications that would have in terms of their prospects for income generation, the women were determined to make pursuit of it a possibility for the next generation.

Other scholars have also found that being able to finance their children's education (especially college) and to support ailing parents were critical factors in the decision of migrants to work overseas. For example, among the Filipino families in Rhacel Salazar Parreñas's (2005) study, being able to provide for their children's education—both in private K–12 schools and in college—was the first priority driving the parents to work abroad. Lutz (2011) found that Polish emigrants in Germany had the same concerns. In contrast, Cinzia D. Solari's (2017) Ukrainian interviewees in Italy were preoccupied about the basic sustenance of their households back home, in addition to ensuring that there would be sufficient resources for other less essential objectives like providing for a college education. However, a major difference between Filipino, Polish, and Ukrainian immigrants and the women who are at the center of my study is that they often had professional backgrounds and high levels of education. Yet changes in the labor market—wrought by the structural adjustment of their economies—resulted in it no longer being possible to maintain the lifestyles they had previously in their nations of origin and to ensure that their children might also become professionals. This constraint was the case even if they were employed as professionals at home. Hence, they were not so much seeking social mobility for their children as to be able to sustain the middle-class status they had already attained.

Thus, we need to look beyond these relatively more advantaged groups of women to assess whether emigration improves the likelihood of social mobility for family members left in the sending country. According to Sanket Mohapatra and colleagues (2010), remittances that are received by sending-country families reduce poverty by raising income levels, stabilize income, and are disproportionately invested in human capital formation.[74] Although their paper does not speak directly to the issue of social mobility, the last of these effects certainly has the potential to contribute to it. Lykke E. Andersen and colleagues (2005) draw the link between remittances and social mobility more directly and positively, while also pointing to the dangers in relying too heavily on this source of income and on what they call "moral hazards" that can result from such income. A number of other studies are less sanguine. For example, Sylvie Démurger (2015) argues that the effects of migration for the family left behind are not necessarily uniformly positive. Having a parent overseas may lead to an increase in the likelihood of one or more of their children dropping out of school.[75] The outcome depends on the individual circumstances of the family. But Jody Heymann and colleagues (2009) found that the impact of migration depends on which family member migrates. That is, if family caregivers leave, this can have serious negative consequences in a variety of realms—including that of education—for the children left behind.[76] While obviously not an exhaustive review of the literature on this topic, this brief discussion suggests a number of the factors that must be taken into account when trying to gauge whether emigration can contribute to social mobility.

Andrea, Ana, and Pamela were all the principal caregivers for their children when they decided to emigrate. Through a close look at their lives, we will be able to observe how some of the potential risks for children when their parents' emigrate arose and were addressed. We will also see how individual circumstances made a difference in the extent to which these women's pursuit of their families' fortunes outside Nicaragua facilitated their attainment of a clear degree of social mobility for the next generation.

A BRIEF STATEMENT ABOUT MY METHODOLOGY

As mentioned earlier, the following account relies on oral histories conducted with these four women. I interviewed each of them on multiple occasions between September 2015 and July 2018. The interviews were structured in that I sought to obtain information about the same topics from all of them, to allow for comparisons. But they did not follow a set script, in terms of either wording or order of questions. Instead, given the objective of hearing their life history, the interviews moved along the paths their lives had followed. The interviews were conducted in Spanish, with some Italian interwoven into their comments. I recorded the interviews but simultaneously took copious notes so that I would have a road map that would allow me to transcribe the tapes selectively. I then translated the transcriptions I had completed, to be able to include them in this book.

Andrea, Silvia, Ana, and Pamela were very generous with their time, especially bearing in mind the limited opportunity they each had for being away from their jobs (e.g., Andrea had one day off a week), which was when we spoke. I had known each of these women for years before I undertook this project. I first met Andrea when my Nicaraguan household was looking for a live-out housekeeper. The several of us who composed the household were engaged in distinct endeavors in Nicaragua, but we were all living there for an indefinite period of time.[77] We went to the agency of Doña Juana, who is discussed in Chapter 2, looking to hire such a person. Andrea ended up being that person and she worked for us over several periods of time. Meanwhile, I kept in touch with her during the intervening periods and after her last stint of work with us. We corresponded when I was away; I would visit with her regularly in her home and she would come to mine when I was in Nicaragua during those intervening periods. I came to know many members of her family, including her parents, partner, children, siblings, cousins, and so on, and eventually her grandchildren as well. When this project commenced, we had known each other more than thirty years and I already knew many of the people her narrative would come to describe.

Among the members of Andrea's family whom I had met during our long acquaintance and evolving friendship was her sister, Silvia. We were introduced during her early years in Managua, although it was not really until she came to work for us for periods of time starting in the late 1990s that I would get to know her better. I likewise stayed in touch with Silvia even after she emigrated to Italy, visiting with her and Andrea when I visited Italy with my family.

Ana was a more recent acquaintance. She was recommended to us by some friends for whom she had worked as a live-out housekeeper and who were leaving Nicaragua to return to their home country, Germany. She was quickly absorbed into the daily routine of our household, becoming fast friends with Andrea, who was taking care of our young son at that point. Ana's own younger children also spent time in our home and our son in theirs, as they, too, became friends over time. Even after Ana had begun to work overseas, her children remained part of our lives in Nicaragua, and we visited with all of them once they had emigrated to be with her in Europe.

Finally, I came to know Pamela, as she worked in the office of the nongovernmental organization (NGO) where my husband worked. Although we spoke frequently on the phone during those years and I would chat with her when I stopped by the office, my familiarity with her family and home life came through the oral history I conducted with her for this book rather than through personal experience with them in the context of Nicaragua. Nonetheless, I now regularly visit with her when my life takes me to Italy, and she spends time with my husband and me when she returns to Nicaragua.

All of this is to say that by the time I proposed this oral history project to Andrea, Silvia, Ana, and Pamela, a long time had lapsed since we (or my husband) had an employer-employee bond with any of them, and my relationship with them had grown into a friendship such that they were comfortable accepting this proposal. In fact, they seemed to be genuinely pleased to have someone interested enough in their stories to put them to paper. In addition, I consciously steered clear of asking questions about their feelings or thoughts concerning their past work association with my family (or my husband). I took this approach so that they would not feel compelled to respond in any given way. At times, they did voice some opinions about it. While being appropriately responsive to the expression of those opinions, I did not pursue the topic beyond the comments they made on their own. Therefore, although it was that bond that introduced me to them, it was ultimately our enduring friendship that allowed me to gain their trust, which was critical for the writing of this book.

Most of my interviews with these four women were conducted face-to-face. However, three of my ten interviews with Andrea were by telephone. While I was writing up their stories, when I had further questions, I corresponded with them by email, text, and telephone.

As this project evolved, I also conducted interviews with scholars working on related topics, as well as with representatives from, or individuals who had worked with, NGOs that provide various types of assistance to immigrants. These organizations included the Ufficio per la Pastorale dei Migranti of the Catholic Church, Gruppo Abele, and Asociación Misericordia. Moreover, I myself went through the process—albeit, without a doubt more smoothly given the color of my skin, my country of origin, my profession, and my justification for the request—of obtaining a Permesso di Soggiorno (a permit to stay in Italy beyond the ninety-day limit allowed for tourists). In so doing, I became acquainted with the bureaucracy that each of these women had dealt with, at times quite painfully, in obtaining their legal documentation.

ORGANIZATION OF THE BOOK

In the pages that follow I present the life stories of Andrea, Silvia, Ana, and Pamela. In the process, we will become acquainted with the social structures that they confronted and the agency they employed to change their and their children's prospects. These social structures presented challenges to this group of women that began when they were quite young, continued through their adolescence and early adulthood, and eventually led to their emigration. Nonetheless, they tried to make their lives in Nicaragua until they were well into adulthood, by which time they concluded that if they stayed in their country of origin their children would be condemned to experience similar kinds of limitations to what they suffered. In introducing the reader to the entirety of their histories, I seek to paint a more inclusive picture of the multiple factors that ultimately coalesced to produce their decision to emigrate. In addition, I show what that decision has meant for them, in terms of their circumstances in Italy as well as for their families back home in Nicaragua.

Thus, Chapter 2 describes their lives from birth onward, illuminating the class inequalities inherent in the structural violence that so dramatically impacted them, as well as some situations in which these inequalities were compounded by gender (and more subtly, racial/ethnic) inequalities. We learn about how it affected their home lives, their schooling, their work trajectories, and their health. Yet the social structure that imposed these inequalities was not stable. The Sandinista revolution modified it—opening up opportunities for these women and their families—and then further alterations to the social structure occurred with the country's turn to the right starting in 1990. Therefore, the ways that each of these shifts affected them is part of their story.

Chapter 3 focuses on the sexual violence—an expression of the gender inequalities that are an integral part of structural violence—as well as on the physical violence that characterized the lives of Andrea, Silvia, and Ana. That is to say, sexual violence is a product of the gender inequalities that are the essence of patriarchy. Both sexual and physical violence were inflicted on them from a very young age. Despite being subjected to this violence, these three women also expressed agency by protecting themselves at a certain point, confronting the perpetrators, and removing themselves from the situation where they could be hurt. I will argue, though, that even after they left their parents' homes—where they had experienced the violence—signs of the lasting effects of this violence were evident for some time. Nonetheless, they acted consciously in doing their part to ensure that there would be no repetition of these patterns of violence in the lives of their own children.

As their children were getting older, Andrea, Ana, and Pamela found themselves in the position of having to figure out, alone, how to achieve their dream of seeing their children attend college. The fathers of their children had proven themselves unwilling or unable to contribute to their children's well-being, and these women realized that it would be their responsibility to do so. These dynamics were another manifestation of the gender inequalities these women experienced. Chapter 4 discusses the decision-making process each went through to arrive at the conclusion that going overseas was the best option available to them to fulfill this responsibility. Silvia went through this process as well, despite not having children of her own. As her parents aged, became infirm, and looked to their children for support, she too responded to family care demands by looking abroad for possibilities. This chapter also examines the network they relied on to emigrate, the jobs and legal situation that awaited them when they did, the social context they encountered in Italy, and their thoughts about where their future lies—in the country they emigrated to or back "home."

Since the major factor impelling three of these women to leave Nicaragua and travel across the globe to Italy for work was to improve the life chances of their children, Chapter 5 focuses on the diverse ways in which their children's lives have been distinct from their own. These differences defined the homes in which they were raised, the educational opportunities they had, and the fact that the next generation did not have to leave school to go to work. Moreover, children mostly came later for this next generation, their work options were unlike those of their parents, and they were protected from experiencing the sexual and physical violence that their mothers had faced. Although none of the women's children has yet to clearly move into the middle class, those who are working have found jobs that are stimulating, that they like, and that provide them with an income that, by and large, allows them to support themselves and their own children (for the several of this generation who have their own children). Hence, they have achieved a notable degree of social mobility from where their mothers were at that stage of their lives.

Finally, the Conclusion ties together the themes raised in the previous chapters and links the life stories of Andrea, Silvia, Ana, and Pamela with the array of arguments set forth in the present chapter. In essence, their stories poignantly illustrate the ways in which diverse elements of the social structure—of a class, gender, racial/ethnic, and migratory nature—play out in the lives of poor women from Latin America. However, given the country they were born in and the time period of their birth, their lives coincided with a societal effort to transform that social structure. Among the changes that the Sandinista revolution facilitated was the way these women thought about what was achievable for "people like them"—that is, in their social position, with its various facets.[78] That change in consciousness made them determined that they would find a way for the lives of their children to be different from their own.

Meanwhile, early on in the revolution certain material aspects of the lives and prospects of Nicaragua's poor had improved. But the economic crisis that engulfed the country in the latter part of the 1980s and the structural adjustment that was imposed following the assumption of power by the opposition in 1990 undermined many of those improvements. As a consequence, the distinctions—particularly of a class nature—that had previously been in place were reinforced. By the time Andrea, Ana, and Pamela had begun to contemplate their options for making sure that their children would be able to study and would have better employment opportunities than they had, the limits on what was possible within Nicaragua had become clear. The revolution had not succeeded in eliminating the constraints of class. The women were faced with scraping by to try to piece together something for their children, or emigrating. Yet the pathway that made their emigration possible was an unexpected result of that revolution. And while Andrea, Silvia, Ana, and Pamela ended up working in Italy's service sector, the circumstances of their arrival and employment were relatively advantaged. Moreover, the income from that employment has meant that their children have had better prospects than they had. In sum, within the constraints imposed by diverse elements of the social structure, the actions of these four women over the course of their lives have expressed agency. Ultimately, though, that agency was delimited by what was structurally possible.[79]

2 | CHILDHOOD AND COMING OF AGE IN NICARAGUA

Poverty is the worst form of violence.

Mahatma Gandhi

Once I started my work life, which I say started when I was two . . . wherever I went [to work] the [male] boss wanted something with me or his sons wanted something, or the [male] friends of theirs who arrived. That is to say, I always felt harassed.

(Interview with Andrea, September 24, 2015)

THE STORIES OF ANDREA, SILVIA, Ana, and Pamela paint a poignant picture of many aspects of life that are shared among poor women throughout Latin America. Structural violence, as embodied in their poverty among other ways, affects much of the region's population, and its overarching presence conditions every stage of the lives of those it touches. However, these four women came of age in the 1980s, during the Sandinista revolution. The revolution held out the promise of profound social transformation. Indeed, it did bring many changes to Nicaragua. For Andrea, Silvia, Ana, and Pamela, the changes were both material and nonmaterial. Nonetheless, these changes were ultimately not enough to overcome the constraints imposed by the women's poverty and the other kinds of inequalities to which they were subjected. Yet even as they let go of the illusion that their own trajectories would be fundamentally uplifted, the new horizons the revolution had opened in their thinking gave them hope that their children would have very different lives from their own.

This chapter recounts the early periods of their lives. In so doing, we will become acquainted with the ways in which their histories reflect the structural violence, especially that which arises from class and gender in-equalities, that is so prevalent in Latin America. Their lives were also deeply colored by Nicaraguan politics, and their histories illustrate the special ele-ments contributed by having lived through a revolution. Finally, their stories express the strength and resilience that led each of these women to search for a way out of that structural violence at various points in time, including in the wake of the revolution that many had hoped might sweep away the array of inequalities that generated that violence and kept much of the population from reaching their full potential.

COMING OF AGE IN TIMES OF CHANGE: THE STORIES OF FOUR WOMEN

The distinct periods of Nicaraguan history—simplified as prerevolution, revolution, and postrevolution—could be described in terms of an intensi-fication of already existing structural violence, a concerted effort to amelio-rate it, and a reintensification of it. The lives of the four women who are the focus of this book were buffeted by these shifts, even as the experience of some level of structural violence remained a constant for them. That violence affected their living situations, their access to education, their employment histories, and their health. In so doing, it has influenced their life courses. In the pages that follow we will examine the ways in which it played out in each of these areas.

Their Families and Abodes

Andrea and Silvia are sisters, and they were born in 1965 and 1972, respec-tively. Andrea spent most of her first ten years—and Silvia, her first few years—on one or the other of two cattle haciendas their father worked on, both of which were located in a relatively remote part of rural Chinandega, a department in north western Nicaragua.[1] As Andrea related:

> When I was born, my father was the administrator . . . on one of the haci-endas of Señor Guillermo. This farm, which was in La Concepción, was a large farm; it was huge, with many workers. My brothers were already . . . for example, my brother Eduardo was already working [there] at seven years old. . . . I was born there, on the hacienda . . . We lived on the haci-enda . . . It was a large house . . . the hacienda house.

I think we lived there about ten years. [The owner's] name was Guillermo Padilla. He was one of the richest men around. Just on the hacienda we lived on, that is, on that farm alone, there were three thousand cattle. I couldn't tell you how much land it had, but it was enormous. They say he was super rich.[2]

Given the extensive nature of cattle ranching in Nicaragua, the farm must have been quite large.

Then Andrea and Silvia's father quit his job, in an act of what Andrea called his "irresponsibility."[3] Among the things that he purchased with his severance pay was a plot of land of about three quarters of a *manzana*.[4] There, their father settled the members of his two families who were still living at home. While Andrea and Silvia each had twenty-six siblings and half siblings, they had grown up with twelve other children in their immediate

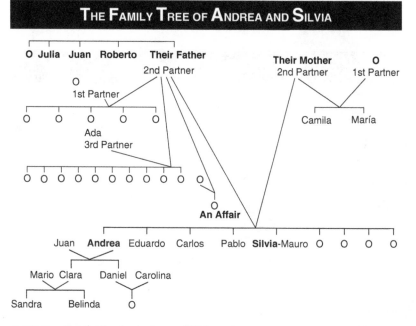

FIGURE 1. Family Tree for Andrea and Silvia
Note: The only names that are used on this family tree are those that appear in the text. Nonetheless, Andrea and Silvia had many other family members, as the tree shows. In order to acknowledge their other relatives, without burdening the reader with many additional names, I have used the symbol "o" to indicate these further family members.

household, five of whom were half brothers and sisters (see their family tree).[5] Their father's second family had come into their lives when Andrea was about two.[6] He had ten children with his other partner, Ada, and he brought their family to share that same plot of land with the household of Andrea and Silvia. However, because of the tiny size of the farm and the large number of people contained in these two households, it did not produce enough to support all of them. But there the two households remained and it would ultimately fall to the children to support the family.

Ana, who many years later would come to be a friend of Andrea and Silvia, was born in 1970. She, too, grew up in rural Chinandega, although in not quite as remote an area of the department as they did. Nonetheless, the situation of Ana's family was quite precarious and they moved around a lot as they sought a way to survive. Ana is the oldest of her mother's six children (see her family tree).[7] Until her stepfather came into their lives, they lived with her grandfather, who had a small farm (of 3 *manzanas* or 2.1 hectares) where they grew corn and beans and had a few cows. Before Ana was born, her mother

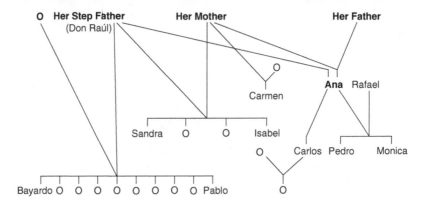

THE FAMILY TREE OF ANA

FIGURE 2. Family Tree for Ana
Note: The only names that are used on this family tree are those that appear in the text. Nonetheless, Ana had many other family members, as the tree shows. In order to acknowledge their other relatives, without burdening the reader with many additional names, I have used the symbol "o" to indicate these further family members.

had been a domestic worker in the city of Chinandega, which was also the capital of the department. Since it was up to her to support her newborn daughter,[8] she went back to this work after Ana's birth. But, as Ana recounted:

> She couldn't work as a live-in servant anymore because . . . she couldn't leave me by myself. My grandfather was alone, given that my grandmother had died, and she didn't have anyone to help her . . . She started to work in the rural areas close by, in Santo Tomás. She worked for people like her, poor people, who didn't have the possibility of paying her in money . . . they would give her food . . . My mom took me to work with her . . . even when she did farm labor, she took me with her . . . she picked sesame, cotton; she planted vegetables, tomatoes, squash, corn, wheat, and everything like that . . . to survive and support us.[9]

Thus, although the farm Ana's grandfather had was larger than that of Andrea's and Silvia's father, and fewer people lived on it, Ana's mother was still quite poor.

Then Ana's stepfather joined the family.[10] It was a boom period for cotton production in the department of Chinandega. As she recounted:

> At that time there was a lot of work in the cotton harvest in Nicaragua . . . in Honduras [where my stepfather was from] there wasn't a lot of work; that's also why he came here . . . and so he started to build a house to live in with my mom . . . on my grandfather's plot of land. He worked there [on my grandfather's land] some, but more off the farm . . . We survived from that and what he could earn off the farm . . . in the cotton harvest . . . We "survived." Sometimes [when there was little to go around] we'd have to share an egg between three of us . . . Life was difficult in the countryside.[11]

Despite there being enough work in Nicaragua to draw laborers from all over, including neighboring countries, the cotton harvest lasted only for roughly three months of the year. Those employed in it then had to find other ways to get by the remainder of the year. And getting by clearly continued to be a challenge for Ana's family. As part of that effort, Ana's mother and stepfather sought to attain some land to farm their own crops:

> After a few years, they decided to move . . . At that time, they were giv-
> ing land to poor people, you know. [Interviewer question: So this was
> in the 1980s?] No, it was before the '80s, when people occupied land,
> remember?[12]

That is, Ana's family organized with other landless families to take over land
that they then farmed until they were evicted.

Land invasions had taken place in Chinandega in the 1960s and early
1970s as cotton and sugarcane production expanded in this department. But
they escalated notably in 1977 and 1978, as the Agricultural Workers' Union
(ATC) was forming [see especially Gould (2014) and Collins (1982)]. The
first period of insurrection against the Somoza regime began in September
1978. So militant actions such as land invasions were occurring in rural areas,
alongside the growing rebelliousness in the country's urban areas.

When I asked Ana if her family and their fellow land occupiers succeeded
in staying on the land they took, Ana recalled:

> We did this for some time, but afterward, the Guardia [the National
> Guard] would arrive. We'd stay a little while, but then they'd throw us
> off the land, and burn down our house . . . and we'd leave, you know, like
> the "*sin tierras*."[13] We'd go here, and we'd go there . . . Over two or three
> years we were in various places. I remember, my mom was always with
> us, she'd take us along. We'd eat; we'd make huge pots of food, of rice.
> Everything was collective . . . everyone who arrived would eat, from the
> same huge cooking pot . . . For the kids it was fun because it was enter-
> taining. But for the adults, it wasn't entertaining, they lived in constant
> fear. [The Guardia] poisoned the water, poisoned the food, they'd burn
> the houses . . . we'd get word that the Guardia was coming that night to
> burn down our houses, and everyone would leave and sleep in the open.
> When we woke up in the morning, perhaps they hadn't come and we'd go
> back to our little houses. Our houses were built of bamboo and branches
> of coconut palm. That's how we lived for some years.[14]

Along with other children, Ana went begging for food on the banana plantations and other large farms.[15] To say that their existence was insecure is an
extreme understatement.

Things took a turn for the better for the family when Ana was around ten years old. By then the Somoza dictatorship had been overthrown:

> After that, we went and took some other land . . . that was at the beginning of the revolution. . . . It was nearby [the community we were from] . . . That I remember, because I was older then. And I already had Carlos [my son]. It was there that I got pregnant with him and that he was born. I believe we stayed there for perhaps four or five years . . . We had a house there and lived well. And then, one time it flooded, we lost almost everything . . .
>
> . . . We farmed there, we lived by farming . . . we worked collectively. It was a cooperative. The [Sandinista government] gave us a small plot of land to build our houses, and then there were lands away from [where our houses were located] that [the cooperative] worked communally, they cultivated communally . . . At the end of all this, we lived in this place that they had given us, and that got flooded, and I think my mom was afraid [to stay there]. We left there and went to live with my grandfather again. [The floodwaters had] entered [our house] . . . and we were left with practically nothing . . . I think that's why we left there.[16]

Hence, the revolution transformed Ana's family from being *"toma tierras"* (or squatters) to being legal members of a cooperative. That is to say, Ana's family, like tens of thousands of others, became agrarian reform beneficiaries once that process started in 1979.

Initially, the agrarian reform took the form of people who had been workers on the vast agricultural estates of Somoza and his close associates becoming workers on the state farms that were established following the confiscation of those estates when his regime fell. Aside from maintaining production on these more developed farms, the goal vis-à-vis their workers was to radically improve their living and working conditions. By August 1980, there were 1,200 such farms, which employed 35,358 workers (Kaimowitz and Thome 1982: 230). Where cooperatives had formed during the war against Somoza's regime, they were further developed such that by August 1980 there were 1,327 collective farming initiatives, with 13,402 members. In 1981 the Sandinista government enacted the Law of Agrarian Reform, which targeted unused land on other very large estates. With these farms

in hand, the government distributed additional land to peasants and agricultural workers who were willing to form cooperatives and farm them
collectively, resulting in the number of cooperative members continuing to
increase. In the mid-1980s the government extended the reach of the agrarian reform so that it included distribution of land to peasants who were disinclined to join a cooperative that entailed collective farming but who still
needed access to this key resource. This latter group of peasants received land
as members of noncollectively farmed cooperatives or as individual farmers. By 1987, state farms, distinct types of cooperatives, and farmers who received land as individuals together controlled almost a third of the country's
agricultural land.[17]

Ana's family eventually left the cooperative they had joined, as noted earlier. But while they were part of it, it gave them a measure of security and a
place of their own for a longer time than at any point since her stepfather had
joined the family.

Andrea, Silvia, and Ana would come to know Pamela some years after
they had moved to Nicaragua's capital city of Managua as young adults.
Pamela was born in Managua in 1966. Her family also moved around a fair
amount when she was a child. Although her father had grown up on his
family's land and they even had cattle, he had become a persona non grata
in his family and had moved to Managua before Pamela was born. Moreover, throughout Pamela's childhood and until her mother died in 2009,
her mother's was the more constant income in the household. Aside from
making and selling tortillas, she also earned money by washing and ironing
clothes for people. While these tasks represented dignified work, they did
not generate much in the way of earnings.

Because the income of Pamela's parents was limited, they and their four
children (see her family tree) could not afford a place of their own and initially lived with one of her uncles in Managua.[18] However, tensions with
the extended family led them to move to a rural area in the department of
Matagalpa (in the central mountain region) for several years. There they
lived with Pamela's maternal grandparents. Given the difficult situation in
that household, they returned to Managua. Once again, they lived at the
house of her uncle: "He gave us a place at the far end of his lot. It was at the
time of the [1972] earthquake. He gave my mom a place to put up a house

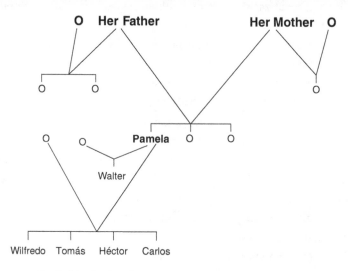

FIGURE 3. Family Tree for Pamela

Note: The only names that are used on this family tree are those that appear in the text. Nonetheless, Pamela had many other family members, as the tree shows. In order to acknowledge their other relatives, without burdening the reader with many additional names, I have used the symbol "o" to indicate these further family members.

of plastic . . . that's where we lived . . . after we came back from Matagalpa."[19] That is, they moved back into the plastic shack they had occupied earlier. When relations with the extended family deteriorated again, they rented a space elsewhere in Managua.

However, their fortunes improved when Pamela's mother was granted a lot in Managua in the wake of the devastating earthquake of 1972:

> What helped us out was, when [my mom] was helping to clear the streets [of rubble] in the center of Managua, they gave her a *canasta básica* [a basket filled with basic food supplies]. They gave it to everyone who was helping to clean up. And, aside from that, they gave us a lot [to build a house on].[20]

The earthquake, whose epicenter was in the central area of Managua, left eight thousand people dead, over 80 percent of the urbanized area in the city damaged, and the central core of the city in rubble (H. Williams, 1982: 274).[21] Moreover, "75 percent of the housing stock was destroyed or seriously damaged, leaving about 250,000 persons without shelter" (274). Both the public and private (for-profit and nonprofit) sectors were involved in the city's reconstruction, such as it was, and the building and repair of homes for those in need of them.[22]

As part of this reconstruction process, Pamela's family received their lot—which was located on land that had belonged to a private individual but was made available to them by the government[23]—and were finally able to build and live in a home of their own when she was about seven years old. This gave them a measure of stability and security that had been unknown to them until that time. Lack of official documents would eventually become a problem for Pamela's family, though. Because her parents were not given a title for the land when they received it, and because neither of them had ever been issued birth certificates, their children were stymied in trying to legally inherit that property after their parents passed.

Their Schooling

Pamela's urban upbringing made her education more feasible than was the case for Andrea, Silvia, and Ana, as that was where public elementary and secondary schools were concentrated at this point in the country's history. She completed primary and secondary school and received a technical degree in accounting, which she worked for while in secondary school.[24] Yet because of the family's restricted resources, Pamela had to attend a different shift at school from her sisters: "My sisters went to school in the morning, and I waited for them to come home at noon so that they could lend me the shoes they were wearing because those were the shoes in which I went to school in the afternoon."[25] Being in school also did not keep her from having to work. She began helping her mother with the latter's tortilla business when she was eight. Then, as she recounted:

> When I was ten or eleven years old, I had to go to the mill to have the corn ground [for the tortillas] in the morning—it was a walk of about four blocks—at four o'clock in the morning . . . Afterward, I came back home [with the ground corn]; at nine thirty I went out to sell the tortillas.[26]

Given these circumstances, it was impressive that she stayed in school.

Andrea, Silvia, and Ana had a harder time staying in school. For Andrea and Silvia, part of the problem was lack of access to a school. Where they lived during their father's long tenure as a hacienda administrator was quite far away from the nearest school. There were simply not a lot of schools in rural Nicaragua at the time they reached school age, as the educational infrastructure the Somoza dictatorship had developed in the countryside was minimal despite the fact that 51 percent of the population lived there.[27] Hence, rural-dwelling children found it much more challenging to make it regularly, if at all, to a school. This can be seen in figures about completion rates for elementary school:

> Of the approximately 7 percent of elementary school-age children who actually entered primary grades in 1976, over half dropped out within a year. Two thirds of the students enrolled were in urban areas. During the 1970s, official statistics revealed that in rural areas only 5 percent of those who entered primary school finished; in the cities the figure reached 44 percent. (Miller 1982: 245)

The result was very high levels of illiteracy: while illiteracy at the national level was 50 percent in 1979 (as mentioned in Chapter 1), it reached as high as 90 percent in some rural areas (Barndt 1985: 326).

In Andrea's case, she started school at age nine. As she noted:

> Where I grew up [on the hacienda] was about four kilometers away from the school . . . and you had to cross a river and a stream to get there. So they didn't send us to school when we were small . . . They sent all of us at the same time [the four oldest siblings] . . .
>
> [But] the problem was, there was only one teacher. She divided the room in two and some faced one direction and the rest faced the other . . .
>
> The room was full of kids . . . It went from first to sixth grade. So you could even find people, young men, with mustaches [in the classroom]. My brother, at thirteen, was already pretty big . . .
>
> It wasn't a school [per se]; it was a house . . . a house that functioned as a school. It had one blackboard on one side and another on the other. [The teacher] taught first through third grade together, even though she

divided us up, saying this is for first-graders, this is . . . I don't know how she did it . . . Profesora Jeny.

There were only classes in the morning . . . She lived there with her daughter, who we all admired because she was well dressed and had shoes. We only had flip-flops. Her mother gave her classes alongside us.[28]

The school had a dirt floor and tile roof. It did not have enough chairs for all the students, so those who arrived first got one and the rest sat on the floor.[29] Even if the teacher was a dedicated and capable educator, these were far from ideal circumstances for academic learning.

Neither Andrea nor Silvia (who also started first grade at age nine) was able to make it to school every day. Sometimes their parents kept them home so that they could contribute to the household's sustenance by working.[30] This was not because they were girls; their brothers probably lost more school time than they did in order to help out.[31] And sometimes, during the rainy season, the river that lay between their home and the school rose so high that they were unable to cross it. In order to ensure that the swollen river would not keep them from school too much their first year, Andrea and three of her siblings were sent to live with their father's "other" family:

> They sent all of us [my three siblings and I, who were studying] . . . For me, [it was like] they "tore us up by the roots"—to live with our stepmother who at that time lived at Las Palmas[. This was] the other hacienda . . . where our dad was also the administrator. Our dad had sent his other wife to live there.[32]

They would go home on weekends to see their mother. This arrangement enabled Andrea to finish first grade. But she did not like living with their father's other "wife" and their children, a state of affairs which further complicated her educational experience.

After three years of helping at home following first-grade, Andrea went back to school:

> I did second grade . . . I started it just before I turned twelve years old. At the end of 1977, [my parents] told me that the following year I would be going away [to school], they had given me as an *hija de casa* [an informally, adopted daughter] to this family, to Don Guillermo and Doña

> Emilia [the owners of the haciendas my dad was the administrator of] . . .
> I protested a lot, because I didn't want to go. I had only seen this family
> from far off . . . And for me, they were untouchable, with us so low down
> and them so high up . . . I was to help them and they would allow me to
> study and give me what I needed . . .[33]

Andrea's feelings vis-à-vis Don Guillermo and Doña Emilia reflected the
social relations of much of Nicaragua's countryside at that point in history.
Although elsewhere in Chinandega age-old patterns of patron-client relations were receding (as we saw earlier in the case of Ana's family), those feelings were still at least somewhat prevalent on the cattle haciendas. Within
those relations "loyalty to the *hacendado* (landowner)—with all his grandeur, warmth, intelligence, and authority"—brought some security that typically included access to a small parcel of land, often some foodstuffs, and,
perhaps, assistance in times of need (Gould 2014: 5). The position he held on
the hacienda would have situated Andrea's father between those at the bottom of this social hierarchy, who were seen as "ragged, dark-skinned, [and]
illiterate,"[34] and the hacendados he worked for. Nonetheless, his position was
clearly closer to those at the bottom than to his employer.

When Andrea went to live with Don Guillermo and Doña Emilia, the
school she attended had multiple classrooms, a paved floor, and a teacher for
each grade. But she found her "home" situation to be unbearable:

> I was there a year and then I escaped . . . When [my parents] told me I was
> going to help them out, they didn't say I was going to work . . . and how
> I worked! I worked *muchisimo*. They had a huge store, in addition to all
> of the storage areas within the house . . . I went to school in the morning,
> from seven o'clock to twelve o'clock, and I worked from twelve o'clock to
> nine o'clock at night. I was great with managing the prices and everything
> and so the work fell to me . . . I didn't study much; I didn't have time. They
> let me go home once a month; [it was] seven kilometers away . . . I felt as
> if I'd been given away . . . At work . . . it felt like forced work . . . without
> pay . . . I wasn't happy there.
>
> And every time I went home, the Señora would ask me if my mother
> had told me to steal things [from their store]. This only made me more
> resentful toward her, because she didn't know my mom. My mom always

said, "I know you handle a lot of money and other things, and this gives you all kinds of possibilities. But don't take a cent of it. If you need a notebook, ask for it. Don't even take a pencil. Because then they'll treat you like a thief." . . . So at the end of the school year I left and went home.[35]

While Don Guillermo and Doña Emilia may have felt they were doing Andrea and her parents a favor, allowing her to live with them and study, the long hours she put in working at their store and the distrust that characterized the relationship between them made it an ordeal for Andrea.

Then the final stages of the war against the Somoza dictatorship shut down the national school system in 1979. Andrea was fifteen years old before she went back to school. At that point, she tested into a fifth/sixth-grade class at night school and completed primary school while she worked full time as a maid.

Andrea's sister Silvia and their friend Ana had somewhat smoother paths through primary school. Silvia attended first through third grades in that same one-room schoolhouse where Andrea had studied and spent periods of time living with her father's other family to be able to attend school. Then she moved to Managua to live with Andrea and her family. She attended the rest of elementary school there. Ana started primary school on schedule and was able to stay at the same school all the way through it. The town she lived in most of the time with her mother, stepfather, and siblings had a school with three paved classrooms. The younger children attended in the morning, while the older ones attended in the afternoon.

Secondary school was a much bigger challenge for Andrea, Silvia and Ana, and none of them were able to complete it. Andrea had the hardest time:

At many times in my life I have been sorry that I wasn't able to study more. I finished . . . fifth/sixth grade. But I don't have my grades from it (my diploma). And I believe I never will have it. They gave them out, but in our house, everything got lost . . . When I finished sixth grade and wanted to register for the first year [of secondary school], in a commercial school, where I could study to be a secretary, they asked for my birth certificate. I said I'd go back [to my parents'] home and get it. When I went, I realized that my birth had never been registered . . . and [I] asked for [my parents'] help in getting me registered. My dad was always drinking, but I asked him to help me to get it . . . And my dad never went to get it.

So, I stopped going to school and . . . I just worked and hung out. I didn't have any plans about what I'd do with my life. Earlier on I did have plans, when I wanted to go to school. And then they said that I couldn't, as long as I didn't have a birth certificate. But I didn't have any idea how to resolve this problem . . . it didn't occur to me that I might go to a lawyer [to get it taken care of]. I've always had a desire to study, but I don't have any degrees [to show for it].[36]

Once Andrea moved to Managua and started working, some years later, she paid a lawyer to assist her with obtaining a birth certificate. However, not having had this crucial document when she first wanted to start secondary school meant that her comprehensive education stopped after she completed primary school. Later on, with help from her employers, Andrea completed several programs at a technical school. But she remained frustrated that her formal, general education had been cut so short. Moreover, it greatly limited the range of jobs she could apply for.

Silvia and Ana each made it part way through secondary school. After completing four years of secondary school, Silvia entered a private technical school, first to learn the skills of a cashier and much later on to study computer programming. Financial support from Andrea made her participation in and completion of these technical programs possible.

Meanwhile, Ana dropped out of secondary school at age thirteen, when she became pregnant with her first child. Although this pregnancy was the result of sexual violence, as will be discussed in Chapter 3, her mother made no effort to help Ana remain in school after her son Carlos was born. Because of her gender, the pregnancy and resulting child were considered her problem to handle. And she had no other way to provide for herself and her son besides working. So before Carlos was a year old, Ana was forced to find a job. Hence, structural violence, stemming from the conjoining of class and gender inequalities, kept Ana from being able to finish secondary school while she still lived at home. She eventually took some courses in manual skills once she moved to Managua, and she started secondary school once again there. But Ana's attendance ended with the birth of her second child, and she was unable to complete secondary school.

Their Ongoing Work Experiences

Even while they were in school, though, Andrea, Silvia, Ana, and Pamela contributed to their families' income generation efforts. As described earlier, Pamela helped her mother with her tortilla business from age eight onward. Andrea worked in Don Guillermo and Doña Emilia's store to earn her own keep when she was twelve years old. Yet Andrea and Ana had started working "in the fields" even earlier.

This was the heyday of cotton, and its production dominated the region where Andrea, Ana, and Silvia were born. Cotton transformed the national economy and it was the centerpiece of the boom the economy underwent between the 1950s and early 1980s. It also modified the landholding structure wherever it was grown.[37] Those who were pushed aside by cotton's expansion—peasant farmers who mostly produced food crops—increasingly found themselves forced to sell their labor during the cotton harvests in order to supplement their farm-earned income. The childhoods of Andrea and Ana were marked by these larger socioeconomic dynamics.

Andrea recalled going with her brothers to work in the cotton harvest as a young girl. She commented that "there was the heat, the dust, and the thorns that cut your hands. And you had to be careful not to dirty the cotton balls with your blood."[38] They were fortunate that they did not have to travel far or stay away from home for extended periods of time, because cotton was grown locally and so they were able to pick it in their own hamlet. Given that she was almost seven years younger than her sister Andrea, Silvia escaped this fate, as their family no longer participated in the harvest labor force by the time she was old enough to have done so. But Ana had also worked picking cotton as a very young child; she estimated that she was about five years old when she started going to the harvest.[39] The grueling conditions that characterized the cotton harvest[40] were an early introduction to what the world of work would be like for them.

Their participation in the cotton harvest labor force also put in evidence the difficult economic circumstances of their families. There were other signs as well, though, some of which were described earlier for Ana's family. And even though Andrea's and Silvia's father was a hacienda administrator, and therefore the family was entitled to live in one of the houses on the farm, his position did not ensure them economic well-being. Moreover, as Andrea recounted, for their mother, "all those years [on the hacienda] she had to sacrifice herself, because working in a place like that meant that she had to get up at three o'clock in the morning to fix food for the workers."[41] And Andrea, like at least one of her brothers (as mentioned earlier), started to work there before she was ten years old:

> There were many workers that my mom took care of on the hacienda . . . these workers, some of them, gave me clothes to wash . . . I washed and ironed them, and [the workers] paid me. One time, my pay was a piglet [a lot of laughter] . . . I'd then give the money to my mom. I didn't feel exploited . . . [rather] I felt like I was contributing, and I liked that . . . Another [man] gave me notebooks . . . [he paid me in] notebooks, pencils, and a backpack. I don't remember what happened to that piglet. But for me, that was the beginning of my work life. I liked the idea of contributing.[42]

Hence, while their family was comparatively fortunate to have a real roof over their heads, most of its members, even the younger ones, labored in one capacity or another to guarantee their livelihood.

Full-time work was not far off for Andrea, Silvia, Ana, and Pamela either. In Ana's case, shortly after giving birth to Carlos, she went to work in the city of Chinandega. Leaving Carlos with her mother, she moved in with her aunt, who helped her find work to support herself and her son. She lived and worked there for two years, most of this time as a maid and nanny. As was also true for Andrea and Silvia, Ana found that working in people's homes had its challenges; she was frequently subjected to unwanted advances from the adult male of the household.[43] The situation unfolded like this in one case:

> My aunt found me a job with a teacher, there in the same neighborhood where [my aunt] lived in Chinandega . . . I went to her house [to work] every day, but her husband wanted to abuse me . . . I was only there two or three weeks, not long . . . the Señora went out . . . She had to attend a meeting somewhere else, and she had to spend the night there. She asked

if I could do her the favor of staying with her child . . . That night I stayed with [the child] and the [teacher's husband] came and wanted to abuse me during the night. I said [to myself], this can't be! . . . So I told him, "If you touch me, tomorrow I'll tell your wife." So he stopped [harassing me]. I said [to myself] . . . I'm not staying here. [The next day] I took my things and said to the Señora, I'm sorry, but I can't stay. I left the house . . . It happened to me twice [more] in other jobs later on in Chinandega.[44]

Here again, class and gender inequalities joined together to make life more complicated for Ana.[45] Because her livelihood depended on her job and because she was a woman in a society in which men held more power, her male employer assumed that the "normal" way of doing things—in which he would be able to extract sexual favors from her—would be operative here. Nonetheless, after each of these incidents, Ana immediately moved on to find another job. Eventually, she went to work at a restaurant, waiting tables and cooking chicken. It was exhausting work, though, and she ended up getting sick and returning to her mother's home to be nursed back to health.

When she was well again, another aunt invited Ana to join her in Managua, where she could find a job as a domestic worker. Once there, she worked about two years for a Nicaraguan family.[46] By then, the Sandinista revolution had been under way for some time and she moved on to work for a German couple who were employed by a NGO that carried out projects there. This would be a seminal experience for her:

I met . . . the Germans . . . And at that time they were looking for someone [to take care of] the twins, and they paid much better . . . So . . . I went to see about the job, and the Señora was happy with me, and I was happy with her and with the children. They were newborns. That's how I started to work with them. I stayed with them . . . almost three years . . . When they decided to return to Germany, they asked if I would go with them, because the children were so used to being with me. They said, "Come with us for a few months. You can help us during the transition period . . . If you want to go home after a few months, you can." And I said to myself, "Why not?" It was an opportunity to spend time in and get to know another country . . . So I went to Germany with them, and I kept staying on and on . . . I ended up being there a year and a half.[47]

Thus, Ana's work with this family introduced her both to what it was like to work for foreigners, who tended to pay higher wages among other things, and to the concept of working overseas.

Ana's son was about seven years old when she went to Germany with this family. He remained behind with her mother. He had been living with his grandmother since Ana first left to work shortly after he was born. However, this meant that her visits to see him—which had been every two weeks when she lived in Chinandega and once a month (for four days) when she lived in Managua—would not resume until she returned to Nicaragua. But in addition to seeing it as an opportunity for herself, the German couple also provided material incentives when she first went with them (including a TV for Carlos) and a significant increase in her salary. This enabled Ana to send money home to help support him and her mother.[48] As she noted, her stay in Germany ended up being a lot longer than she had expected. Moreover, communication with her family in Nicaragua was difficult as there were no phone lines to where they lived, and Carlos was too young to respond to her letters without encouragement, which he unfortunately did not receive. When Ana did go home to Nicaragua:

> the idea was to return to Germany again . . . [but this time] to take Carlos with me. [I went] to get his documents and return with Carlos. I started the documentation process at the [German] embassy. And . . . they turned down my own visa request, as well as that of Carlos . . . The Señora said she would send more documents to support our applications. But I said [to myself] that it wasn't worth it . . . I'd be better off staying in my own country.[49]

Undoubtedly, the path to her accepting this outcome was eased by the fact that even as Ana was awaiting a response from the consulate regarding her visa application, she started working for another family she was introduced to through her German employers. Hence, her transition back to life in Nicaragua was relatively smooth.

The mother and daughter in this next family were German,[50] and the mother's partner was British. When they departed on the completion of their work contracts, Ana's next job was with friends of this family, another foreign couple and their son.[51] Although in this case the father had become a

Nicaraguan national, he maintained his Italian citizenship and connections to his homeland. The mother was from the United States. That is to say, Ana's path into the world of being employed by those who had come to Nicaragua because of the Nicaraguan revolution was now firmly established.

When the time came for Andrea to look for full-time work, she, too, moved to the city of Chinandega. She went there at age fifteen:

> I needed to leave the house, I needed to work . . . My aunt worked there, my mother's sister . . . She talked with her boss and her boss needed a nanny . . . and . . . given that she was [working] there . . . She said she'd show me [how to do things] . . . I started to see how to be a nanny, but I [also] felt exploited there. Because I started out as the nanny, they had a small boy; and my aunt was the cook, and another employee did the washing and ironing. There were three of us. After a little while, my aunt left, and [since] she'd taught me how to do some things, they [soon] had me taking care of the boy and doing the washing and ironing . . . The other [woman] did the cooking. She spent hours and hours and hours cooking. There were a lot [of people in the household]. She spent almost all day cooking. After that, the cook left, and they didn't look for anyone [to replace her] and I [ended up] doing practically everything. But at that age, I didn't have much experience . . . above all, experience in the city . . . They [the family] had a watch business . . . It was a rich family . . . They sold and repaired watches . . . I lived there [with them]. I had permission to go home once a month. It was [all] arranged . . . They gave us Sundays off, so I spoke with them and asked if they would let me have my four days off [a month] together, so that I could go to see my mom . . . After . . . [about six months], I got sick with asthma and I went home. I stayed there.[52]

The family Andrea was working for seemed to believe that the hours and intensity of work that could be asked of her were unlimited. While they may have taken things to the extreme in holding this belief, it is not uncommon for domestic workers in many parts of the world—especially those with a live-in arrangement—to be subjected to working very long hours and taking on innumerable tasks (c.f. Hondagneu-Sotelo 2001; Bonizzoni 2013). In

Andrea's case, however, when exhaustion made her sick with asthma, she quit the job and went home to recover.

But while Andrea worked there, and going forward in the jobs that would come after this one, she sent money home to her parents to help support the family. As she commented:

Almost all [of my pay] went to [my parents'] house . . . On my first payday in Chinandega, I still remember it . . . I earned three hundred córdobas . . . This was . . . after the revolution, that is at the beginning of the '80s . . . my mom said to me, when they give you your first pay, buy yourself some clothes. So I bought myself some clothes, and of the three hundred córdobas, I sent 120. My father came to Chinandega to pick them up. And he stopped . . . halfway home [and] he drank them all up. He didn't even take [my mom] one córdoba, not even one.[53]

Over time, Andrea found other ways to get money to her mother. One of these was to send it with the bus driver who drove back and forth from Chinandega to their hamlet, and then she would alert her mother by telegram that it was on its way.

Once Andrea recovered from that bout of asthma, she returned to Chinandega to look for work again. The first family to hire her as a nanny would not permit her to study at night (to complete elementary school). So she quickly left that job. Finally, the third family she worked for during this period allowed her to live outside their home, enabling her to study. But, as Andrea said:

I had problems there, too . . . because, the Señor liked to . . . this Señor was strange. He liked to go out with the *domésticas*, right? It was strange for me because he gave me money . . . So then I'd go to the Señora and . . . I'd give her the money back. I didn't do it on purpose [to cause problems]. He didn't want to take it, and because he wouldn't take it back, I went and gave it to her [and] I said, "Have this, it's money that your husband gave me but he didn't explain what it was for, so I'm returning it." And that was my perdition, because then she started to be jealous . . . I didn't understand what he wanted. And then she wasn't the same with me. She was always serious . . . she would respond with an unkind tone. And the worst [thing] was that she didn't explain anything. Afterward, when I was older, I thought, well, if she had only explained things . . . But I didn't understand what her husband wanted, nor what she wanted . . . He did [finally] explain [what he wanted] later on, when I was just about to leave [the job]. I was there almost all of the fifth[/sixth] year [of school] . . . He would go by me and he would touch me [in passing] . . . And the Señora realized it. She was watching . . . He thought she wasn't there, but she was [always] around me, right? One time she told me that she didn't want me to pay attention to her husband. Her husband would never leave her. She didn't want me to have any illusions . . . I think [she said it] to protect me. And I said, I didn't [want to be with him]. I was [innocent as to his intent], in the sense that . . . I was naïve about all of this evilness . . . It went on like that for months, and months, and months . . . It was [all very] confusing for me . . . [Finally] I left because the [situation] was unbearable.[54]

Although her male employer in this case was subtler than Ana's employer had been in expressing his interest in having something more than a work relationship with her, it still made the situation untenable for Andrea. Nonetheless, as suggested by Andrea's observation about sexual harassment on the job that opens this chapter, it became such a common experience for Andrea that it was noteworthy when she worked for a family where it did not occur.[55]

Andrea's next job was in Managua. She went there on a lark with one of her older halfsisters to "start over." Neither one of them knew the city:

We caught the bus and we went to Managua. But, you know, there wasn't a direct bus. We [first] got to León, and then we caught another bus to Managua. We arrived in the terminal . . . We got there and looked at the [ad my sister had torn out of the newspaper for an employment agency in Managua] and the agency was . . . close by the entrance to the Oriental [Market]. We got together the little bit of money we still had left, because we didn't know how to get there, and we paid for a taxi, which took us there. But you know what the taxi driver did? He took us around and around, and he charged us everything we had on us, and besides that, we didn't understand where we had gone . . . We got there, the two of us completely lost, to look for work . . . We didn't have letters of recommendation from any workplace, or any other documents. Nothing, nothing. We were fresh off the bus. And [Doña] Juana [the owner of the agency] asked, "What do you know how to do?" I started to tell her, I've done this and I've done that, and I worked in the store, but I didn't have a letter of recommendation. [Doña Juana asked us,] "And do you have a place to go?" "No." We didn't have money to go anywhere to spend the night, nor to eat. We had ended up without a cent on us. She asked if we had any place to stay. "No." "Did you bring any money with you? Where are you from?" She looked at us from head to toe. I think she felt sorry for us. It wasn't as if we were dirty or anything. But we were very young. Camila was two years older than I, but she seemed even more lost than I did. She said, "Well, you can spend the night here," and the next day she had jobs for us. Then we were crying, because we would have to go our separate ways. It had been an adventure to just go off with our backpacks. We had Doña Juana as a way to communicate with each other [that is, we could leave messages for each other with her].[56]

Clearly, Andrea and Camila did not know what they were embarking on when they stepped onto the bus in Chinandega, and they did not go well prepared to apply for jobs. But Doña Juana took them under her wing and opened the way for them to support themselves in their new lives in Managua. That this was Doña Juana's business and that, therefore, she too benefited from assisting Andrea and Camila goes without saying. But given their age and lack of experience in the capital, the two young women were fortunate to have ended up at her door rather than at that of someone who might have been less sensitive to their plight and/or unscrupulous.

Andrea worked in various homes in Managua before she found one where she decided to stay awhile. It was as a housekeeper at the home of the foreign couple (the Italian/Nicaraguan man and North American woman) where Ana ended up more than a decade later. It took a long time and was not easy to get there and back each day, as public transportation in the mid-1980s was very unreliable (due to the parts shortages, gas rationing, and so forth associated with the country's economic crisis). But the job had some clear advantages: "I earned much more, [they] always paid me well, in comparison with what I could earn [working in a secretarial position, which I studied for, while holding the job]";[57] her employers regularly permitted her to use their ration card to purchase goods at subsidized prices for herself and her family;[58] they paid for her to take a variety of courses with the goal of helping her move into a more stimulating and remunerative line of work;[59] and, as Andrea noted, "When I arrived [there], I felt like it was the kind of job I was looking for . . . it was a place where one felt respected, in terms of the wages and as a person."[60] This job was Andrea's initiation into working for foreigners.

Andrea had her first child, Clara, within a year of starting to work for this couple. This stint of work with them lasted six years. It was followed by a job with a North American friend of the couple and her young daughter, who came to Nicaragua for a year. There Andrea and her sister, Silvia, shared the responsibility of taking care of the house and the little girl.

When that position ended in 1991, Andrea took a hiatus to give birth to and stay home with her second child, Daniel. By this time, the Sandinistas had been voted out of office and neoliberalism had gained a strong foothold in the country. It brought with it a retrenchment in state spending (c.f. Jonakin and Enríquez 1997; Enríquez 2010). Numerous projects were adopted by NGOs and the private sector to fill the void this created, including the promotion of microcredit. The idea behind microcredit, or very small-scale loans, was to assist small producers of all kinds in developing their businesses, when they would otherwise be excluded from the formal credit system. During her pause from the job market, Andrea came to be part of a microcredit group. The plan was that she would contribute to the household income even while she stayed home to care for Daniel. But it did not work out as she had envisioned. As Andrea recounted:

> I had also studied [to be a tailor] . . . because they only required sixth grade to study to be a tailor . . . I studied there one year. And then I worked . . . at the house . . . I had a [sewing] machine and I worked day and night . . . I had studied to be a tailor, but I worked making skirts . . . at that time [the demand] was for skirts [and] uniforms and I got involved in making skirts and that type of thing . . . and I got totally indebted because . . . you take your [pile of] skirts to the market, but they don't pay

you until they sell them . . . What did one do? You went to the bank [for a loan] . . . in order not to have problems with that [bank], you went to another [bank] . . . Finally, I had loans with three banks. And it wasn't just me. It was everyone in the community there . . . It was a group of women who took out the loan, and each one was responsible for someone else . . . there were sixteen of us. If one of us didn't pay, everyone else was required to pay [their part of the loan]. The problem was that there wasn't any solidarity [between us]. And aside from that, it wasn't just. . . . the loans weren't . . . very big . . . so you couldn't do much with what they lent you. It was a vicious circle. At the end of it, I was in[debted to] three banks. I didn't know how to get out of the three[debts]. One day, one [of the women] arrived and said to me, "We have to pay," and I didn't have any money. I said to her, "I don't have money now," and she said, "You have to pay," and I said, "But I don't have any [money.]" She said, "You have to pay." I picked up the [sewing] machine and I gave it to her and said, "Sell it, I don't want to see you all again." I haven't had another [sewing] machine since then. Because it made me sick . . . I [finally] got out of the debts after I'd been working with [the foreign couple again] about six months . . . I paid a little at a time, a little at a time . . . and bye-bye debts. I felt burned. It was a situation with no way out.[61]

Clearly, for Andrea, microcredit was no panacea.[62] Although she was precisely the kind of person such programs were supposed to assist, the small size of the loans, a payment schedule that was out of sync with the consignment nature of her income from the retailers of her goods, and the intense social pressure to recover the loan only got her further and further into debt.

After finding that sewing skirts would not help her and her family "get ahead," when Daniel was almost six years old Andrea went back to work for the foreign couple she had been employed by in the 1980s. This time she worked as a nanny, because the wife had just given birth to a son. Six months into the position, Andrea started traveling with the woman and her child. They were away for three days a week for several months, traveling to different parts of the country. This was a prelude to her spending four and a half months a year away with them in the United States, when her employer traveled there for work (to be discussed further in Chapter 4). When the woman and her son eventually moved to the United States so that he could start elementary school and she could continue in her job there, Andrea worked both for the husband and for a couple of other foreign employers in Nicaragua for periods of time.

Andrea's sister Silvia leapfrogged over the intermediate step of working in the city of Chinandega when she left their parents' home in rural Chinandega, instead moving directly to live with Andrea and her family in Managua. She took her first job at age fifteen. It was in Managua's infamous Mercado Oriental,[63] where she worked for a month selling plastic goods. She left that position when her boss would not let her have Mother's Day off so that she could go to see her mother. She then had several temporary or short-term positions as a maid, before taking yet another position as a maid that she left quickly when her boss's brother began to harass her sexually. After working with Andrea as a maid and nanny in the home of the North American visitor for a year (as mentioned earlier), she returned to work in the Mercado Oriental.

Silvia worked in two different stores there. As she recounted:

SILVIA: I worked in . . . a store that sold cosmetics and toys . . . the store was enormous . . . I was there five years.

INTERVIEWER: How was the work there?

SILVIA: Really hard. [It was hard] because of the hours we had to work, and the type of work . . . You had to lift boxes full of heavy things, creams, and all that kind of thing . . . [and] the [work] schedule was from six o'clock in the morning to seven o'clock at night, from Monday to Sunday.

INTERVIEWER: Monday to Sunday?

SILVIA: Yes.

INTERVIEWER: How did you stand it for five years?

SILVIA: I don't know. It was the only time in my life I've lost that much weight.[64]

The Mercado Oriental forms part of Managua's vast informal sector. The lack of government regulation of that sector meant that working conditions such as these were not kept in check.

Moreover, Silvia was the only female worker in both of these stores. That made for complications in these two jobs. In the first position, she recalled:

I started working for a Señor who had a store . . . his wife and sister-in-law had other stores that were separate from his . . . When I started the job there, I was the only woman working there . . . So his wife and sister-in-law started to say, why did he have me there . . . They said, why did he have a woman working there, women weren't good for anything . . . [Interviewer question: Were they jealous or worried?] . . . Jealous? I'm not sure in what sense they would have been jealous. I don't know. [Perhaps] worried because it was a hard job . . . you needed to lift heavy boxes . . . It was rather difficult for the men. Many men arrived and were only able to work one day . . . They said women were useless, that they were practically only a hindrance. I worked [in that specific job] two years.[65]

In the second job there, she was let go when she started dating a co-worker from one of the company's other locales, although her male dating partner was not. Silvia felt that the money she earned in the Mercado Oriental was reasonable. But clearly the work atmosphere was quite hostile for women employees, thereby reflecting the gender inequalities that were so prevalent in Nicaragua.

From there Silvia went to the Zona Franca, or maquiladora factory zone. The term *Zona Franca* refers to firms operating in a free trade area. These are by and large foreign companies that have set up manufacturing plants whose products, which are often clothing, are exported to consumers elsewhere. The imported goods used as inputs are not taxed, nor are the exported final products, which is why the physical area where the plants are located is called a free trade zone. The labor force in these zones is overwhelmingly female; women make up 90 percent of the 42 million people employed in this sector around the world.[66] The percentage of women in Nicaragua's Zona Franca labor force is roughly identical to that at the global level. The legal groundwork for Nicaragua's Zona Franca was prepared by the Chamorro government in 1991, as part of the country's neoliberal opening to the international market. This shift in economic orientation had also resulted in the closure of the previously existing state-owned garment industry, which left its sizable, trained labor force unemployed.[67] Foreign firms started to be established in these areas in short order and "by late 2001 there were forty-four assembly factories in operation," which employed almost forty thousand workers.[68] The wages received by these workers were not good, their conditions of employment—workplace setting, control over their work, and so forth—were arduous, and the vast majority of them were not unionized.

Silvia worked for a U.S. firm with a clothing plant there, taking loose threads off the newly sewn clothes.[69] She *only* had to work from seven a.m. to five p.m., Monday to Saturday. Given what she was paid for her piecework there, she did not make enough money to survive. Moreover, the maquila workers were under surveillance all the time. As Sylvia recounted:

> The environment [there] was hard, because they [the supervisors] were controlling us all the time . . . you couldn't put the scissors down for a moment, aside from the fact that they were cutting all the time . . . the work was continuous. You couldn't go [off] to the bathroom quickly, because if you did they'd come looking for you.[70]

As was true for workers in the Zona Franca more generally, Silvia was not in a union there. All of these disadvantages led her to leave this job after six months.

Then Silvia spent several months in the United States while filling in for Andrea as a nanny with the North American woman and her son. Following her return from the United States in late 2000, she worked in the homes of three foreign families as a maid and nanny, and in the office of an Italian NGO as a janitor. These families were known to each other and to the local coordinator of the NGO, and several of them had come to Nicaragua during the 1980s to work with the Sandinista government. Hence, Silvia's employment trajectory at this point was shaped by the transnational network of which these families formed a part.

Pamela was also employed in the office of that NGO, which had initiated work in the country in the late 1990s. This organization was of a leftist orientation and had projects in several Central American countries, along with Africa and the Middle East. Despite its relatively recent arrival in Central America, the organization had been active since the 1970s. Its history embodied a number of elements of the larger story of the Italian NGO sector.[71] The international NGO sector had its roots in the post–World War II reconstruction of Europe. Then, between the 1960s and the 1980s, it was an arena of activity for countries in the Global North to mount initiatives designed to gain influence in the Global South in the context of the Cold War and decolonization. In the case of Italy, it sought to foster social, economic, and political development through publicly funded projects that were implemented by its citizens in various former colonies. The philosophical origins of the Italian NGOs that carried out these projects can be traced to several distinct traditions: Christianity (especially the Catholic Church's liberation theology, with its "preferential option for the poor"), Marxist and socialist thought, and liberal and libertarian currents. A common assumption they shared was that these kinds of efforts, which were collectively termed "cooperation," would contribute to achieving and maintaining peace in countries that might otherwise be war-torn.

In carrying out their projects in the Global South, Italian NGOs coordinated their activities with local governments, NGOs, and other civil society groups. Moreover, they employed local citizens in a variety of capacities, some more technical and others in more of a support role (including administrative and custodial staff). The number of Italian NGOs working in Nicaragua expanded significantly in the 1980s and 1990s. That is how Silvia and Pamela came to be employed within one of them. But Pamela would eventually work at this particular NGO in a distinct position from Silvia. Given that Pamela had completed high school and also earned a technical degree in accounting, she had many more job prospects than Andrea, Ana, and Silvia.

On receipt of her technical and secondary degrees, Pamela initially did an internship with the Nicaraguan government. When that was completed, she was offered a regular position in the same government office. As she recounted:

I went looking for a job at the Palacio [the central administrative offices of the government] and immediately . . . they gave me a job and I worked there eight years . . . It was in the DGI [General Tax Office] . . . in Collections, where they collected the taxes . . . I started my job as a coder [in accounting], doing the codes on the accounts. But I was only there a little while, because [almost] immediately, they bumped me up to be the associate director . . . And then, in less than a year, my boss was about to leave and he said, "You will take charge of accounting, because I'm superfluous, you already know how to do everything." So I learned all kinds of tasks . . . My boss showed me everything. After that, even when I was no longer in Collections . . . when the administrator, who was our supervisor, wasn't there, I substituted for him.[72]

Pamela worked for the DGI, in one office or another, about eight years. Then she was hit by the downsizing of the state that formed part of the neoliberal structural adjustment imposed by the government of Violeta Barrios de Chamorro after 1990. Roughly a quarter of all state employees were laid off during the first few years of that economic reform (c.f. Evans 1995; Stahler-Sholk 1997). The contraction of the state would continue throughout the decade.

Most of those who were laid off during this period went on to search for a livelihood in the informal sector of the economy. This was the first path Pamela pursued as well. By the time she was let go from the DGI, Pamela was married and had four children. When her husband asked her for help in establishing a business, she gave him part of the severance pay she had received when she was laid off:

My ex-husband said, "Don't worry, we'll start a business. I'll set up a business in the Mercado [Oriental]." Okay, I thought, it's time to give him a chance . . . [so] I gave him part [of my severance pay]. Look . . . I have no idea what happened to that money. When I went to the Mercado to see [the business] . . . he had drunk it all up with a friend in parties and the like. There was nothing there . . . Look, I was left with nothing.[73]

Her husband next proposed to work in the Zona Franca. However, given that Pamela had to pay his bus fare to and from work and his meals while there, it cost her more money than he brought home. Whether or not she realized it, Pamela was repeating the pattern set by her parents. In that pattern, her mother worked steadily to support the family, including her father, who provided no real contribution to the family's income.

Meanwhile, again following in her mother's footsteps, Pamela worked selling tortillas and corn, along with assisting someone in his accounting business. These dynamics reflected Nicaragua's gender inequalities, which left mothers to figure out how to take care of their children whether or not the father provided them with the resources to do so.[74]

After several years of trying to make ends meet through these various means, Pamela found that if she was to succeed in supporting her family, she needed the stability that a salary provided, and she went to work at the Italian NGO. Although Pamela's husband was not providing for her and the family, he was very unhappy about her taking this position:

> He comes along and [constantly] made scenes . . . He waited for me in the park [across the street from the office]. I didn't know what to do. For him, all the Italians were my lovers. All of them. I said to him, "Do you believe that if they were my lovers I'd be living in these conditions? I'd find one who would support me. Why would I look for one like you, who wouldn't help me to resolve any of the problems in my life?" Look . . . it was a problem because, for him, I was always better than him, and that made him feel like a nothing. That's what made him feel bad . . . So I said, look, to get past this . . . Why don't you study a technical career or anything you'd like to? I'll support us, as I've always done . . . No . . . he didn't like that either. Look . . . to finish this [story] . . . He totally infuriated me once when he was waiting outside . . . I was leaving, and he was drunk . . . And I was totally embarrassed, because it's a street that everyone goes on . . . What didn't he say to me . . . "Just because you work for the Italians, you think you're equal to them, and that I'm nothing." . . . He said things to me that I think he wouldn't even say to a prostitute on the street. I didn't say anything in response . . . You know what made it even worse, when he said to me, "You prefer your kids over me." "Look," I said, "even the thought is stupid." . . . Then he said, "You'll see what I do to your kids. I'm going to pay a gang and you'll see. I'm going to get you where it will hurt most."[75]

Interestingly, Pamela did not mention her husband being disturbed by her working around Nicaraguan men in the government office all those years. However, with her employment at this NGO, she assumed a more prominent role in familial breadwinning than she had in the past and surpassed her husband in this regard. According to the prevailing gender ideology, men were to be the providers for the family. Independent of this ideology's weakened basis in reality, Pamela's husband may have felt his masculine identity being threatened by the modification of their positions within the household. There is a notable literature on the potential reactions of men who find themselves in this situation.[76] Among these reactions is their increasing engagement in domestic violence, including verbal and emotional abuse. This would seem to speak to the circumstances that Pamela found herself in on this occasion.

Regardless of her husband's behavior, Pamela stayed on at this job. Aside from the difficulty of obtaining a position in the downsized state sector, work with foreign NGOs typically paid better than what Pamela could have earned in the Nicaraguan private sector. So having once gained entrée to that world of work, she was not about to let go of it.

Pamela had started out there in the position that Silvia would eventually occupy, that of office janitor. But when the office receptionist left, Pamela's previous work experience allowed her to shift to that position. This job gave her a higher salary and status than the positions of nanny, maid, and retail clerk held by Andrea, Ana, and Silvia. Nonetheless, Pamela still had a very hard time getting by, given that she had five sons to support and her husband did not contribute much to the household's sustenance (to be discussed further in Chapter 4).

Their Health

The challenges that Ana, Silvia, Andrea, and Pamela faced as they went through school and sought work reflected the structural violence—derived especially from but not limited to their class position within Nicaraguan society—that has characterized their lives since they were born. The poverty that is one expression of that structural violence has impacted the well-being of these women in various ways, including vis-à-vis their health. Prior research has demonstrated that poverty puts children at risk for numerous health issues, and the effects can be long lasting.[77] This dynamic begins with the lack of access to medical care that their own mothers had when they were carrying them and the implications of that lack for this next generation. They go on to include the conditions of their homes and any effects that those conditions might have had on their daughters' health. Their daughters' own access to medical care and medicine, as well as the circumstances in which they work and live, also come into play. And their health is directly linked to their ability to reach their full potential as human beings.[78]

One of the many illnesses that have been linked with living in poverty is asthma.[79] Andrea and Silvia both have severe allergies and asthma. In

Andrea's case, allergies have been with her since she was an infant, and they are strongly linked to her asthma. But it was not until she was about forty years old that she started to understand that connection.

> The [link between my allergies and my asthma] was always there. I only started to get better when I realized what I had. And I'll tell you, many years passed before I realized it . . . many times I got to work after going to the hospital or many times when I left work I went to the hospital and I spent hours there . . . [When] I arrived, I practically wasn't breathing . . . They took me right to the emergency [room]. They nebulized me and gave me adrenaline, too, one in each arm, so that I'd react . . . And then I'd go home. But they never said, "Your asthma comes from your allergies." Never . . . they didn't say, ". . . if you take care of your allergies, you'll have fewer asthma attacks." . . . It was I who started to gather information about . . . how to control it.[80]

Although Andrea's access to healthcare was virtually nonexistent while she was a child (see the discussion of this that follows), limitations in the medical information she was given by those who provided her with that care as an adolescent and young adult meant that her well-being continued to be significantly impacted even once she was able to see a doctor and go to a hospital. Despite the commonness of doctors not sharing much medical information with their patients in many parts of the world, the class inequalities that likely colored her interactions with healthcare providers would have only contributed further to this dynamic. Had doctors shared with Andrea the connection between allergies and asthma, she could have modified her exposure to allergens, thereby potentially reducing their effects.

Andrea is allergic to many things, including dust and dust mites, mold, pollen, horse hair, milk products, and seafood. As mentioned earlier, she grew up in western Nicaragua, which is located in a dry tropical zone. That zone is characterized by a six-month rainy season, during which flora flourish, a tremendous amount of pollen is released, and mold develops quickly, and a six-month dry season, during which dust is everywhere, especially in the countryside. Hence, the very geography of Andrea's childhood was a problem for her health. She remembered having asthma crises about three times a month as a child, and was told that it was even worse when she was an infant. Yet because the public healthcare system was almost entirely absent in the countryside prior to 1979,[81] and because her parents had very limited economic resources, she was not seen by a doctor until she moved to Chinandega to work. Before that:

> They treated me, you know, with oils, with roots, with leaves, with tea . . . now, I can't stand to see a tisane, because [it makes me want to throw up] . . . The memories I have are traumatic, because everything they told my family to give me, they gave me . . . And little by little, [the asthma] would go away on its own. That is, with all this "medicine," it's not as if it cured me, right? . . . I couldn't lie down because I'd "drown" [or at least that's the way I felt] . . . Three days sitting up, with a family member fanning me with a hat. I slept little . . . Because aside from the fact that you feel bad, they'd cover your body with lard and oils. You're bad off from the illness, and you're bad off from what they're putting on you . . . They covered me up, because I had asthma, they'd completely cover me up. I'd be struggling to breathe, and it was made worse still, because you'd have to try to breathe while you were sweating from all the heat . . .
>
> If you ask me, what does hen oil, armadillo oil, iguana oil, or possum soup taste like? I can tell you . . . For me it was traumatic and I suffered, because they'd give me hot lard in a mug . . . The mug was already hot, and then that lard was as hot as could be, almost boiling so that you could get it down. In the middle of my efforts to breathe, I felt like throwing up, and I would throw up . . . then my father would hit me on my back with a strap . . . I'd go on drinking and then vomiting, and he'd hit me again. Finally, I'd drink it from fear . . . Sometimes, they'd do me the "favor" of mixing it with coffee and sugar . . . But I can guarantee you, it didn't help me.[82]

Andrea's parents were clearly concerned about her asthma attacks and sought to care for her as best they were able to with the advice they received from those around them. Unfortunately, though, the advice that would have really helped to address this health issue was beyond their reach.

Later on, when Andrea was working and studying in Chinandega and went on a field trip with her class to Corinto (Nicaragua's most important port city), she was given a shrimp and rice plate. Her allergic reaction to it was so strong that she had to be hospitalized and almost died. Fortunately, by then she lived where there were public hospitals and clinics so that she could be seen by a doctor. But as Andrea got older, her allergies became increasingly resistant to the sprays and other medication she was given and it became harder to keep them under control. Since her allergies triggered her asthma, when her allergies got out of control, she often had asthma attacks. She was hospitalized numerous times for her asthma.[83] It was not until her first trip overseas that she realized how environmentally related her health problems were. Recently, she has been able to obtain allergy shots, which have massively reduced her need for other medications and improved the quality of her daily life.[84]

Silvia's allergy-related asthma started later than her sister's and has been less severe. She is allergic to dust, smoke, pollen, cat and dog hair, and pesticides, among other things. Aside from the dust and pollen Silvia grew up and lived with in Nicaragua, she also worked in homes where there were household pets and where the house was sprayed periodically for pests.

> The problem is that, little by little, it has gotten worse, it has increased [in intensity]. It got to the point that I couldn't even laugh without having problems breathing . . . I still have it sometimes, but it's under control . . . In Nicaragua, [I controlled it] with antihistamine pills . . . I took them by instinct [in terms of when I needed them] and based on Andrea's experience. I took the pills [for allergies], and when the asthma attacks came, I'd take pills for the asthma. They were terrible, they gave me tachycardia. But when it wasn't too bad, it was the only thing that allowed me to breathe calmly . . . With the asthma [now], I'm still under treatment, it's a spray two times a day. I've been using it on an ongoing basis for some time.[85]

Hence, many of the environmentally related allergy triggers that had affected her sister also plagued Silvia. But aside from the larger context of Nicaragua's wet and dry seasons, with all of the issues they brought with them for Silvia, she was also not in a position to leave a job simply because the work environment might set off her allergies. So, to a large extent, the ability to control her exposure to them was not within her grasp.

Allergies and asthma were not the only health issues these women faced. As a child, Andrea also had an eating disorder:

I don't know when it started . . . I'd always vomited, as long as I can remember. From when I was old enough to remember, I always vomited . . .
I even vomited the water I drank. Nothing stayed in my stomach . . . I
didn't put a name to it. What was even worse was when they joked about
it. My brothers and sisters teased me relentlessly about it. My mom
said . . . "Now you're just like the chickens." Because chickens drink a lot
of water when they're thirsty, and afterward, blah, they vomit up a bit . . .
I was very, very skinny . . . When you don't know you have something . . .
who would have known? I ended up with tremendous anemia . . . It's
only been recently that I knew it was an illness . . . Many times I was left
hungry.[86]

This disorder receded with time.[87] Meanwhile, Andrea also remembered
having anemia throughout her childhood.[88] It drove her to eat dirt, for which
she got spanked. And it led to her becoming very weak and her skin sallow
in color.

Then, when Andrea was about fifteen years old, she was hospitalized because she was very sick with anemia and malaria, and she had a borderline
case of tuberculosis:

The first three days I had a fever, and a higher fever. After those three
days, I started to have a pain in my back and in my chest . . . and I started
to cough in a strange way that my father said he recognized. It was then
that they took me to the hospital . . . The place where they put me is where
they put all of the contagious patients. I believe that I had borderline
tuberculosis. I was in [the hospital in] Chinandega another week [after I
had been sick in bed at home for a week]. In the place they call "quaran-
tine" . . . they do a bunch of tests and everything. After those eight days,
they realized they had to send me to a sanatorium . . . There they had me
another week, and it hadn't become full-blown tuberculosis, but I was on
the way there . . . On the X-ray, aside from the lung, they could see air
in the lungs and there were little black spots where holes were starting to
develop . . . which showed where my lung was getting ruined . . . When I
went in, I had sixteen pills for breakfast, for lunch another bunch of pills,
and for dinner as well. At midnight they woke you up to give you shots,
and at four o'clock a.m. they gave you more shots. That's how it was for

a week. After a week they released me . . . When I got sick I weighed 165 pounds . . . and when I came out of the hospital, after three weeks from the start of my illness to when I left the hospital, I had dropped down to 110 pounds.[89]

When Andrea was released, she went back to convalesce at her parents' home. Public health officials visited regularly to see how she was doing, give her medications, and make sure that no one else in her family contracted the disease. By this time (roughly 1980), with the Sandinista government in power, a new emphasis was given to providing public health services in the countryside. Their visits reflected this. She was declared cured after one year. Nonetheless, the multiple maladies she had experienced until that time clearly affected her early development, and some of them have continued with her to the present day.

Although Pamela grew up in an urban area and, therefore, had at least somewhat better access to public healthcare, she has also had an ongoing health issue: neuralgia. It has affected her face and caused her tremendous pain. As she recounted:

> [In general,] well, I've been healthy . . . just when I had the problem of the tension I experienced living with my ex-husband, it unleashed the neuralgia . . . I [actually] think the problem came when I was little . . . it comes with anxiety and stress. My mom also suffered from this because of the stress with my dad and everything. I remember when I was [six months] pregnant with my youngest son . . . I had this pain . . . [and] the eighth nerve would get swollen . . . all of this would get swollen . . . my gums and my face. You should have seen it, my face was [totally swollen] from anxiety and stress. . . . I couldn't vent to anyone because I was [living] at my mom's house, and I was always trying to avoid having problems with everyone else [there]. So I went to the health center, and I said to the doctor, "You're going to take this tooth out."[90]

The dentist at the health center told her that he would not pull the tooth out because it was healthy. Eventually she badgered him into pulling it out. In what Pamela described as something like a scene from a movie, the dentist perched on the chair and worked and worked until he finally yanked out her tooth. Afterward he commented to her, "'You see? I told you so. It was a healthy tooth. Look. You ran the risk of having a miscarriage. You must, immediately, go to see a psychologist, a neurologist . . . because you are suffering from anxiety.' It was all pure stress."[91] The stress came from the tension between Pamela and her husband, which resulted from his not contributing to the household's income in any meaningful way and his extreme jealousy of her. When he finally left the family some time later, Pamela's neuralgia receded.[92]

Poverty and neuralgia may not be directly related. But given that stress can trigger the condition, an indirect connection is clearly possible. So the dire economic straits that Pamela found herself in on several occasions generated strains that most likely compromised her health.

The health issues each of these women faced were long-running—some of them dating back to their early childhoods—and complicated by their limited access to good medical care. But by the time, Andrea, Silvia, Ana, and Pamela were coming of age, countervailing forces were gaining strength in Nicaragua that contained the potential to ameliorate their circumstances, along with those of the poor more generally. The most strident of those forces was the armed struggle being waged against the Somoza dictatorship. We turn now to examine the ways in which the revolution that took hold in Nicaragua mitigated, or failed to mitigate, the effects of the structural violence that had characterized their lives until that time.

The Nicaraguan Revolution and Its Aftermath

When asked, Andrea, Silvia, Ana, and Pamela contended that the process of social transformation that was initiated once Somoza was overthrown in 1979 did not fundamentally alter their lives. But they did acknowledge that the routing of Somoza's National Guard (la Guardia) had led to people, especially youth, breathing easier when they were outside their homes. According to Ana, who was ten years old at the time of Somoza's ouster . . .

> People were afraid of the Guardia. The Guardia looked at you threateningly . . . always . . . That's why it was liberating when the Sandinistas [gained power]. The Guardia were people that caused fear, instilled fear in one. I remember that when, perhaps, I'd be waiting at the bus stop

and the Guardia would go by, two or three of them, and they looked at you like that. I couldn't look at them. Because if you [did] . . . , they'd say, "What are you looking at? Do you want to die?" I lowered my head. [They were] totally arrogant. I didn't want to die . . . Personally, when I realized that they had gone, along with Somoza, for me it was liberating. I was very, very happy.[93]

So not having to deal with the ever-present threat implied by the mere presence of the Guardia was "a radical change."[94]

Their families benefited from the revolution in a number of additional ways. These benefits took both material and other forms. Andrea's and Silvia's father gained access to land to work:

He joined an agricultural cooperative and he was there for a few years . . . it was in the Sandinista era . . . I know that my father formed part of [the group] that organized the cooperative because he was one of the first to be there, in the cooperative . . . he wasn't there long. About three or four years . . . [The area of the cooperative] was large . . . I think there were ten members at the beginning and it kept growing . . . the cooperative still exists . . . [Interviewer question: Why did your father leave the cooperative?] I think because he didn't like it . . . I'm not sure, but I think he didn't like living/working with the other . . . with the cooperative.[95]

This cooperative was established on land expropriated and redistributed through the agrarian reform initiated by the Sandinista government. Given the minuscule size of the plot their parents lived on, having access to more agricultural land to farm had the potential to make a major difference in the family's well-being. Later on, their mother joined another cooperative and was granted her own house on it, which had a significant impact on the gendered power relations within the family (see Chapter 3).

On a more modest but still important scale, both Andrea and Silvia were able to move forward in their studies when they took a newly offered combined-level course (fifth/sixth grade) through the public education system. Moreover, Andrea was able to place her infant daughter, from age seven months old until she started elementary school, in a public childcare center so that she could work.[96] The public childcare/preschool system experienced a massive expansion—alongside the rest of the public educational system—during the Sandinista government of the 1980s (Barndt 1985; Kampwirth 1993). This made it possible for women like Andrea to obtain access to subsidized care for their children in a center where education was part of the package.

Also on a material level, Ana's mother and stepfather gained access to land through a cooperative (as mentioned earlier). This provided their family with a place to live and a means to earn their livelihood. A decade later, Ana and her husband obtained a lot where they could construct their home.[97] That lot formed part of a larger piece of land that had been expropriated in the 1980s. Although they paid for the materials with which they built their home, the grant of the lot made it possible for them to leverage the resources they did have. With a home of her own, Ana could finally bring her eldest son to live with her when he was fourteen years old. She had had to leave Carlos in the care of her mother and stepfather since he was a little over a year old.

In addition, the Sandinista revolution brought about changes in people's consciousness about what they might aspire to. Andrea put it especially well:

> With the revolution, many doors were opened . . . in the sense of support for women that didn't exist before . . . That is, women didn't count for anything [before] . . . The [Sandinistas] taught us that we mattered and that we were worth as much as men. That, afterward, they showed us the opposite is another issue. It was wonderful to see and hear that women could also do all kinds of work that men did.[98]

She added, "For us women [the change was enormous in the sense of our] self-esteem, that, yes, we were important. It was crucial . . . in going from where one feels that they are worthless to people respecting you. It was something fantastic."[99]

That change in self-esteem was the product of years of women's organizing and promoting initiatives to improve their position. The growing discussion worldwide concerning women's oppression and the presence of large numbers of women in the effort to overthrow the Somoza regime opened the path to there being a conscious project of bettering the lives of women woven into the Sandinista revolution. This project produced multiple outcomes for women.

In addition to improved self-esteem, another outcome of this organizing was the growing presence of women in the leadership of the government, and in other organizations and endeavors in the 1980s. As Norma Stoltz Chinchilla (1990: 371) notes, by 1987 "31.4 percent of government leadership positions" were held by women. Women also participated heavily in the Literacy Crusade of 1980 and the multiple vaccination campaigns that were carried out by the Sandinista government. Moreover, women were members of the Sandinista Popular Militia, representing almost 45 percent of that force in 1984 (Stoltz Chinchilla 1990: 381). The women's organization that had formed during the war against Somoza was renamed AMNLAE (after a female guerrilla fighter who died in that armed struggle) and grew substantially after 1979. Efforts to increase the participation and visibility of women in all of these spheres was thought to be critical for both changing women's consciousness and facilitating their ongoing initiatives for improved material conditions.[100]

Other outcomes took several forms. These included the development of subsidized childcare facilities, such as the one that Andrea's daughter attended. Maxine Molyneux (1986: 290) comments that the number of facilities built remained relatively small—just forty-three by 1984, absorbing about four thousand children. But the fact of their existence and that they were established in both urban and rural areas was novel for Nicaragua. Given the long-standing pattern of women being responsible for the well-being of their families, women also benefited from the improved social welfare programs throughout the country, in terms of both education and healthcare. Maternal and child health initiatives were especially significant in this regard. Furthermore, the government promoted the formation of cooperatives of various types among women, so that they could work together in their small businesses. It was hoped that joining together would bring women greater economic benefits.

Just as important, new legislation was enacted that was significant in terms of redefining relations between men and women. The Ley de Patria Potestad, a feudalistic law that had given men virtual property rights over children, was abrogated in 1979. In the month following the overthrow of Somoza, the Statute of Rights and Guarantees was enacted by the executive branch of the new government, which reformed multiple elements of family law (Stephens 1989). The statute made more possible enforcement of the legal obligation to share parental responsibility for children—thereby paving the way for the collection of child support; it also made it legal to establish the paternity of a child, as well as for women to acquire custody rights for their children. Enabling legislation for this statute was contained in the Family Relations Act that was ratified in the legislature in 1981. While fathers did, at times, still find ways around assuming full parental responsibility for their children (see Chapters 3 and 4 for discussions of this topic), the fact that this legislation provided means to ensure their compliance in meeting their obligations to their children was remarkable. Two other areas of legislation that were designed to bring benefits to women were directed at their status as workers. Health and safety provisions for female workers improved, much as they did for male workers. Moreover, whereas in the past women agricultural workers' wages were subsumed into the "family wage" that the male head of household received, new laws entitled women to collect their own wages (Molyneux 1986).

While these legal changes were noteworthy, efforts to ratify further legislation that would benefit women were not successful. For example, a push in 1983 to broaden the Family Relations Act to include, among other things, a legal obligation for parents to share responsibility for domestic labor did not get ratified by the executive branch of the government. Two additional areas of law were similarly contentious and proved impossible to make substantial headway on: divorce law reform and that related to women's reproductive health (especially the right to abortion on demand[101]). Resistance from the Catholic Church—which held great sway over Nicaraguan society—as well as from some of the opposition political parties kept the Sandinista government from pursuing reform in these areas.[102]

The government's bowing to these political pressures came at a point in time when the Contra war was at its most intense and its rationale was that striving for national unity rather than division was important. The women's organization AMNLAE chose not to challenge this position.[103] However, much as had been true in most major social transformations worldwide until that time, the Sandinistas viewed change in the area of women's rights and well-being as part of the larger process of change.[104] It was assumed that the position of women would be automatically improved by that overall process. So although AMNLAE's mandate was to represent women's interests, its lack of true independence from the FSLN meant that a feminist agenda would not be permitted to threaten the overall revolutionary process. To the extent that projects that had a feminist agenda contributed to that process, they would be promoted; to the extent that they might take support away from that process, they would be held in abeyance. And since no substantial feminist movement existed outside the FSLN until after it was voted out of office in 1990,[105] there was no other group that might insist on prioritization of such an agenda.

Nonetheless, the war also had an impact on efforts to improve women's lives in another sense. It curtailed the availability of financial resources to continue expanding social welfare infrastructure. The possibility of building more childcare facilities was just one casualty of the increasing shortfall in financial resources.

Aside from pluralistic politics and a tolerance for religious diversity that made the Sandinista revolution stand out from many of its leftist counterparts, an additional element of its distinctive nature also limited what was possible in terms of transforming the situation for women: its mixed economy. The private sector continued to make up the better part of the economy throughout the 1980s. Given that the state did not have the capacity to enforce implementation of labor and other kinds of regulations in each and every private enterprise, their implementation depended to some extent on the willingness of private employers to go along with the law, and not all private employers were so inclined. But an even bigger issue was the fact that most women who worked outside the home were employed in the informal and domestic labor sectors. In both of these sectors, enforcement of labor laws was significantly less likely than in the formal sector.

Despite these limitations, the achievements resulting from the efforts of women who worked for the Sandinista government, and others who were organizers with AMNLAE, did bring about some change. As described earlier, the changes Andrea experienced were both concrete and in her way of thinking. Andrea had attended some events sponsored by AMNLAE, although she was not a member. Her consciousness about standing up for her rights as a woman had also been raised by participating in self-defense classes when she was living and studying in Chinandega.[106]

In sum, the families of Andrea, Silvia, and Ana had clearly benefited from the Sandinista revolution. Some of those benefits were material and others were of a different nature. Yet the advantages the revolution gave these women and their families did not come readily to their minds when I asked them how it had affected their lives.

At the same time, they were forthright about the ways in which their lives were made easier when the Sandinistas lost the elections of 1990 and Violeta Barrios de Chamorro's government came to power. The principal things they mentioned were that the military draft was brought to an end and that all kinds of goods became more available for purchase. Silvia and Andrea both mentioned what a relief it was when the Chamorro government eliminated the military draft.[107] Silvia commented:

> In the '90s it was easier because the Obligatory Military Service didn't exist [anymore]. The young men were freer. They could study and they could do what they wanted . . . When my brother was in the military service, I was always the one who went [to visit him] . . . I remember one time we went with Andrea . . . it was Easter Week, Holy Friday, we went to see him. We went there walking with my father, I think it was about thirty kilometers, more or less . . . But they didn't tell us . . . they had sent him to another military base [until] . . . we got there . . . I remember that Andrea couldn't walk for the following three days . . . Sometimes, I'd get to one of the bases and they'd tell me he wasn't there, that they'd sent him to another. I'd have to get [back] on the bus, with the [great] difficulty that bus travel [implied] then. Aside from the schedules, the [buses] were always full, always. That was the impact [the change in government] had in my life.[108]

Although Silvia related the draft to the difficulties it created for her personally, she had traveled to see her brother regularly because she cared about him deeply and was concerned about him being killed or injured in the war. Along with tens of thousands of other Nicaraguans, Silvia suffered greatly because a loved one had been called up for the draft.[109] It had been implemented in 1983 in response to the intensification in the Contra war at that time.

Silvia also mentioned that once the economic blockade was lifted, when Chamorro became president, more goods became accessible. The economic blockade put in place by the U.S. government in its efforts to oust the Sandinistas from power, and the economic crisis more generally, had created terrible shortages of all kinds of goods. However, Silvia noted, "the problem was that there was less money now . . . you could buy anything you wanted, but there was less money."[110] She was referring to the fact that because of the Chamorro government's economic policies, people had a reduced amount of disposable income with which to buy the newly available goods.

Much has been written about the increase in poverty and inequality that resulted from the Chamorro government's economic policies.[111] Nonetheless, when I asked Andrea, Silvia, Ana, and Pamela if the various economic changes that were initiated in 1990 had affected them, each said that the shift from the Sandinista to the Chamorro government had not impacted them. Ana commented that she "did not depend on [the government]."[112] Pamela responded that it is up to each person to determine where they end up in life.[113] That is to say, government policies do not define such things. Andrea, in discussing the debt that she got into in the 1990s when she decided to start her own sewing business, reflected that "I would have had economic difficulties regardless of which government [was in office]. Because it was a question of . . . I felt that the serious problems that I had were due to my lack of work experience in this sector."[114]

Yet Florence Babb (1996a) writes at length about the ways in which the neoliberal economic reform that was implemented by the Chamorro government starting in 1990 affected a sewing cooperative she studied over a period of years. Not only did cooperative members lose access to the lower-priced materials that the Sandinista government had made available to them, but the Chamorro government also put in place policies that favored larger textile firms, such as the maquiladoras associated with the free trade zone, and reduced tariffs on the importation of new and used clothing. These factors were compounded by the reduced purchasing power of the Nicaraguan population that was associated with the economic reform, thereby greatly weakening the prospects of the country's small-scale seamstresses. Andrea, however, remained unaware of these macroeconomic dynamics.

While giving voice to the vision of their lives held by Andrea, Silvia, Ana, and Pamela, it seems essential to pause and note how well their accounts of the economic circumstances in which they found themselves in the post-1990 period coincide with an analysis focused on the individual rather than the society and political economy in which they were immersed. This corresponds with what has been characterized as neoliberal subjectivity. As Rosalind Gill (2008, 436) observes, "the neoliberal subject is required to bear full responsibility for their life biography no matter how severe the constraints upon their action."[115] I am not suggesting that any of these four women would argue that they have, at each and every stage of their lives, determined their own destiny. Yet it has to be more than a coincidence that, having lived through many years of neoliberal structural adjustment that has had demonstrably negative effects on the poor in their country, they argue that the new political economy that became hegemonic at that time had no bearing on their lives.

CONCLUSION

Andrea, Silvia, Ana, and Pamela were raised in poverty, had limited access to education, started to work when they were still children, and had their own first child relatively young. The first three of these women also found their job opportunities largely restricted to the service sector, where they earned low wages and had little job security. Structural violence—most especially that stemming from class inequalities—is evident in these various aspects of their life histories. But in their employment trajectories and family dynamics, the ways in which those class inequalities intersected with gender inequalities to complicate that violence are also evident. The sexual harassment so commonly experienced in the domestic work positions Andrea, Silvia, and Ana held exemplified this. When sexual harassment occurred, each of these women felt compelled to leave the job where it was present. Their actions expressed a consciousness that they did not have to submit to the harassment and could become agents in protecting themselves from it. But shifting to another occupation to avoid it was not a viable option for them. This conjoining of inequalities was also apparent in the economic well-being of their households frequently depending on what they alone brought to it, as seen herein in Pamela's case, because their partners were unwilling to be responsible contributors to their family.

In many of these senses, their life stories could well describe—in broad brushstrokes—the lives of poor women of their generation throughout Latin America. Yet the prospects of the families of at least three of these women were expanded by the Nicaraguan revolution. Furthermore, it gave them a new consciousness about expressions of such inequalities that they need not tolerate, as well as role models who suggested what they might aspire to for themselves and their children. In addition, it brought these women in touch with the community of foreigners who had come to work in Nicaragua during that period of the country's history. Engagement with that network may also have exposed them to distinct agentic orientations, to use Emirbayer and Mische's (1998) terminology. In so doing, it may have opened up more possibilities for thinking creatively about how to resolve the challenges their lives presented.

Their ongoing efforts to resolve those challenges also shed light on the dynamic relationship between structure and agency. The "structurally transformative agency" (Hays 1994) that produced Nicaragua's revolution gave rise to the diverse changes just mentioned. In the end, the material benefits it brought were not sufficient to allow them to break out of the class-based structural violence they had been born into. But the alterations they experienced in their consciousness permitted them to think that despite their social origins, they—and/or their children—might do something else with their lives than what generations before them had done. This, in turn, impelled them to seize the opportunities that did open up to them over the years. Hence, even though these women had not been politically involved on an ongoing basis during the 1980s, the process of transformation that had taken place in their country then had a meaningful impact on the way they proceeded going forward. This was expressed, among other ways, in the agency they employed to push the boundaries of that structural violence in search of a more dignified existence for themselves and their children.

That search extended to finding a way out of another expression of gender inequality that three of these women experienced as children and adolescents: sexual violence. Moreover, this experience made them determined that their own children would not have to live through anything like what they had. It is to this violent expression of gender inequality that we now turn.

3 | VIOLENT EXPRESSIONS OF GENDER INEQUALITIES

> One wrong touch, even if it's for a brief time,
> can destroy a child's life forever.
>
> *M. V. Kasi,* Soulless

> In this climate of profoundly disrupted
> relationships the child faces a formidable
> developmental task . . . she must develop a
> capacity for intimacy out of an environment
> where all intimate relationships are corrupt.
>
> *J. L. Herman,* Trauma and Recovery: The Aftermath of
> Violence—From Domestic Abuse to Political Terror

SEXUAL AND PHYSICAL VIOLENCE colored the childhoods and adolescence of Andrea, Silvia, and Ana. Both are associated with relations of power and authority. Moreover, sexual violence also falls under the umbrella concept of structural violence, as it is inextricably interwoven with unequal, gendered relations of power and authority, although it has its own particular features as well.

Sexual and physical violence cut across classes and are relatively widespread in both the Global North and the Global South. Once these types of violence take place, they can have long-term implications. Several of the dynamics that came into play in the case of these women, however, may be specific to the places of their upbringing and to the class-based violence that surrounded them. And sexual violence in particular further complicated their difficult economic circumstances. Hence, there was a clear interaction between these distinct elements of structural violence.

The pages that follow describe this aspect of the lives of Andrea, Silvia, and Ana. We will also learn about the ways in which sexual and physical violence during childhood affected their transition to adulthood and their later relationships. In addition, their impact on the life course of each of these women will be addressed. The reader may find the accounts these women provided about this violence deeply disturbing, much as I did. Yet since it is not only part of their stories but also helped to shape their lives moving for-   · ward, their accounts are presented here. Prior to embarking on that discussion, though, it is important to begin with a broader review of what research has suggested about these phenomena.

THE LITERATURE ON SEXUAL AND PHYSICAL VIOLENCE

Although the academic literature on sexual and physical abuse of children has a number of shortcomings, starting with discrepancies in how these phenomena are defined, it does make several crucial points. These are that the phenomena are common; that they occur across sexes, ages, races, ethnicities, and classes; and that they can have long-term consequences for the affected child. I focus most of this brief discussion on these points.

Definitions of sexual violence have varied on the basis of what is considered an appropriate age of consent, whether that between siblings is included, and whether it should take account of phenomena that do not involve physical contact with the child. But as such definitions have increasingly converged to include abuse by siblings who are in a position of responsibility over a younger brother or sister, and voyeurism and exhibitionism, it has become clear that the number of children affected is significant. Drawing on data from twenty-one countries around the world, Naomí Pereda and colleagues (2009) find that sexual abuse affects an average of about 24 percent of females and 12 percent of males. Marije Stoltenborgh and colleagues (2011) examined 217 studies published between 1980 and 2008, noting that self-reported instances of sexual abuse occurred at a rate of 127/1000. Self-reports vastly outnumber official reports—which are considered to speak to the "tip of the iceberg" of the problem—for many reasons, including the fact that the child may not want to go to authorities to report the abuser, who is often a member or close friend of his or her family.

Both girls and boys are subjected to abuse, although girls may be twice as likely as boys to be victims (Collin-Vézina et al. 2013).[1] In some cases, abuse begins even before age six, but most abuse occurs while the child is of school age or in adolescence. A number of additional factors increase the risk of abuse for a child, including "the absence of one or both parents or the presence of a stepfather, parental conflicts, family adversity, substance abuse, and social isolation" (Collin-Vézina et al. 2013: 3; see also Finkelhor and Baron 1986). In addition, the literature points to an increased number of people living in the home, including children (Ramírez et al. 2011; Polanczyk et al. 2003), and an overall tendency toward disintegration of "traditional family structures"[2] as putting children at risk of being subjected to sexual abuse (Veenema et al. 2015). As to the relationship between socioeconomic position and sexual abuse, there are more reports of sexual abuse of children from lower socioeconomic groups (Putnam 2003). Yet although some researchers have suggested that children living in poverty are at greater risk (MacMillan et al. 2013; Hussey et al. 2006), there is no proven correlation between class and this phenomenon.

Instead, the kind of inequality that would appear to have the greatest explanatory value with regard to sexual violence, including the abuse of children, is that related to gender relations. That is, where patriarchy—defined as a social system in which men are the primary power holders—prevails, men's power often extends to control over the bodies of members of their society (Walby 1990; Connell 1987). Sexuality is one area where such control may be expressed, including over that of one's children, and most especially one's daughters. Understanding sexual violence as an extension of this larger pattern of exerting power is particularly useful for explaining the overwhelming role of men in perpetrating it and of women and girls as its victims (e.g., Herman and Hirschman 1977; Solomon 1992), as well as the strong coincidence between intimate partner violence and violence against children—in both cases as carried out by men (Namy et al. 2017).

Sexual abuse can have consequences for a child's physical and mental health. The more immediate physical effects include contracting a venereal disease, pregnancy, and physical injuries; other effects can emerge over time, such as eating disorders and obesity (Wonderlich et al. 2001; Gustafson and

Sarwer 2004). At the same time, much research has focused on the impact of sexual abuse on the psychological and emotional well-being of the victim. Post-traumatic stress disorder (PTSD) is often experienced by children who have been subjected to sexual abuse (Ackerman et al. 1998). Mood disorders are another common result, including depression (Sadowski et al. 2003) and low self-esteem (Mullen et al. 1996). Substance abuse and engagement in risky sexual behavior by the victims are also often associated with having experienced sexual abuse as children (Kilpatrick et al. 2000; Houck et al. 2010). These effects commonly continue into adulthood (MacMillan et al. 2001).

Much as is true for the literature on sexual abuse of children the world over, the literature on Latin America is still growing. A lack of consistency with regard to how the phenomenon is defined makes comparisons between countries within this region difficult as well. However, its incidence in Latin America *may* be in the neighborhood of or slightly higher than the patterns discussed earlier. For example, researchers in Mexico found that 18.7 percent of their survey sample of adolescents had experienced sexual abuse, with the rate for girls about 2 percentage points higher than boys (Pineda-Lucatero et al. 2008). Likewise, a study of women in El Salvador found that 17 percent had experienced sexual abuse as children (Barthauer and Leventhal 1999). In contrast, research on college students in Costa Rica found that 32 percent of women and 13 percent of men had experienced sexual abuse as children (Krugman et al. 1992: 158).[3] A study of pregnant women in Lima, Peru, had findings consistent with those from Costa Rica; 32.2 percent of the Peruvian sample had been subjected to such abuse (Barrios et al. 2015).

In Nicaragua, it appears that the incidence of sexual abuse of children is somewhat higher than the average worldwide. In a study carried out in the country's second largest city, León, Ann Olsson and colleagues (2000: 1583) found that 20 percent of men and 26 percent of women reported experiencing some form of sexual abuse. Yet a survey of families in three cities and one region of Nicaragua identified an even higher incidence of child sexual abuse, on the order of 25–32 percent depending on the specific study site (as cited in Valladares and Peña 2006: 13).[4] Olsson and colleagues (2000: 1583) observed that the median age for the first instance of abuse was ten years old. For girls, the majority had been abused by a male family member; for boys, the majority had been abused by a woman who was not a family member.

The age gap between the perpetrator and the child was greater for girls than boys. Abbie Fields (2002) and M. E. Quintana and R. Cajina (1992) point to several factors specific to Nicaragua that may increase the vulnerability of children there to sexual abuse: the high levels of extreme poverty that lead to overcrowding, children being left alone while their mothers work away from home, the frequent inclusion of stepfathers within the family structure, and children being sent out to work.

Since physical abuse was another element in the childhoods of Andrea, Silvia, and Ana, it behooves us to also briefly explore what the literature can tell us about the incidence and implications of this type of violence before returning to their stories.

As with sexual abuse, variations in definition have implications for the perceived incidence of physical abuse against children. Measurement of this phenomenon is also complicated by willingness to acknowledge it as a problem, which is at least partially influenced by cross-cultural differences. Nonetheless, concerned scholars are working toward common definitions and gathering statistics that describe this issue. Taking into account these difficulties, Rosana Norman and colleagues (2012) found that in high-income countries, the annual prevalence of physical abuse ranges from 4 to 16 percent. Yet in a review of studies on physical violence against children across the globe, Maryam Abbasi and colleagues (2015: 357) concluded that almost a quarter of those interviewed had been abused, while Susan Hillis and colleagues (2016) suggest that the figure is substantially higher—over half of all children globally experience physical abuse.

As with sexual abuse, there are short- and long-term consequences from physical violence. In the short term, physical injuries and, in extreme cases, death may result. The psychological and emotional effects are both short- and long-term and include many of those associated with sexual abuse: depression, anxiety disorders, eating disorders, and substance abuse, among others (c.f. Norman et al. 2012; Durrant and Ensom 2012). Overwhelmingly, it is the parents or guardians who inflict this violence.

Returning to Latin America, studies of the region point to the high level of incidence there. Of the pregnant women included in the survey from Lima mentioned earlier (Barrios et al. 2015), 37.3 percent had been subjected to physical abuse (and 24.3 percent reported experiencing both physical and

sexual violence). Research on Guatemala and El Salvador found that 35 percent of women and 46 percent of men in Guatemala reported being beaten
as punishment in childhood, while 42 percent of women and 62 percent of
men in El Salvador reported this (Speizer et al. 2008). Scott Krugman and
colleagues (1992: 158) observed that 80 percent of children in Costa Rica had
experienced spanking, while 46 percent had been hit on other parts of their
body (but not the head), and 30 percent had been whipped. In contrast to a
number of other studies—in which boys consistently experienced higher levels of physical abuse—they found no significant difference between the sexes
in terms of this phenomenon. A study completed in Nicaragua for the NGO
Save the Children found that most of those interviewed (80 percent) had
been subjected to corporal punishment as a child (Antillón 2012: 7). For 40
percent of the study participants, it had occurred one or two times a month;
for 18 percent, it occurred one or two times a week; and for 20 percent, it occurred every day or almost every day.

In sum, the problems of sexual and physical abuse are widespread around
the world. Moreover, incidence levels are quite high in Nicaragua. The consequences of these types of violence are both short and long term, and they can
affect the person subjected to one or both of them throughout their lifetime.

SEXUAL VIOLENCE IN THE LIVES OF ANDREA, SILVIA, AND ANA

As mentioned earlier, a number of factors put children at risk of sexual
abuse. Aside from Andrea, Silvia, and Ana all being female, their childhood
households had several characteristics that would have increased their risk
of abuse. Their family homes often incorporated members of their parents'
extended families and their parents' children by prior and simultaneous
relationships—both temporarily and permanently. And a stepfather was part
of the household in one of these cases. These circumstances stretched the
"traditional family structure" in ways that may have added risk to their home
environments.

Kristin Yarris (2017) notes, however, that when it comes to the traditional
family structure in Nicaragua, class matters. What she means is that it is typically only in the upper middle class and upper class that the nuclear family
of two parents and their children form the household. Moving down the
social hierarchy, multiple generations—often with their own partners and

children—cohabit in a household.[5] This situation stems largely from the economic limitations that make forming separate households difficult. It is also
not uncommon for the male partner in the intimate relationships that make
up households to be absent, as men's commitment toward their partner(s)
and children is often quite weak. In fact, Beth Stephens (1989: 139) cites a
study that found fathers absent in 34 percent of households nationwide and
60 percent of households in Managua.[6] Male "serial polygamy" (Molyneux
1986) joins this list of factors contributing to Nicaragua's high degree of family instability. Stephens (1989: 140) comments, though, that despite his absence, the father of the children in each household remains a strong figure
who makes many critical decisions in relation to the family. Hence, she observes that analysts have characterized the Nicaraguan family as "a blend of
the patriarchal model inherited from the Spanish colonizers and the matri-
archal model of the indigenous tribes" that they conquered following their
arrival in Mesoamerica.[7]

Moving beyond the immediate family, the larger, societal context of patriarchy[8] and the economic dependence of the mothers of Andrea, Silvia,
and Ana on their partners would have made them less able to confront those
who brought this hardship on their daughters. That context (which will be
discussed shortly) meant that women—including the mothers of these three
women—were ultimately responsible for ensuring the well-being of the family, at the same time as men had greater access to power and control within
the society and within their intimate relationships. In the pages that follow
we will examine the implications of all these factors for Andrea, Silvia, and
Ana, as well as their consequences.

As described in Chapter 2, the household in which Andrea and Silvia grew
up was large; it was distended even beyond the multigenerational household
that Yarris (2017) speaks of. In addition, in order to attend their first primary
school, they each spent periods of time living with the woman they called
their stepmother and the ten children she had with their father. Thus, both
households in which Andrea and Silvia lived when they were children were
large. And there were periods of time during which their father's two families
shared the same dwelling or lived close to each other on the same small farm.

Andrea and Silvia seemed to react differently from one another to this
situation. For Andrea:

This Señora appeared almost immediately . . . Ada . . . after I was born . . .
It's complicated. Now, the son of the other woman (Ada) is eight days
younger than my brother Pablo, who is two years younger than I am . . . I
remember when this woman arrived. I remember that she arrived there,
[about] a minute before her son was born . . . because [my father] installed
her in the house, she lived there [with us] . . . [My mom and Ada had]
different rooms. [Interviewer question: Did your father go to one room
or another depending on how he was feeling?] Um-hum. [Interviewer observation: Well, that happens in various countries of the world, right?] . . .
Yes, but in other places, where, let's say, it's seen as . . . they normally live
like that. [Interviewer observation: But perhaps that was the culture of the
countryside at that time?] . . . I don't know. The only thing I know is that it
stayed imprinted on my memory . . . that I saw her arrive and after that she
didn't leave . . . I think that when I was so young, to see my father suddenly
arrive with another woman must have been something tremen[dous] . . .
that it's still with me. Not only for [what it meant about] my father, but
[also] for my mother. I didn't see her put up resistance. It was me who
showed how I felt. My mother never showed how she felt . . . [Ada and my
mother] took care of each other. It was impressive . . . they got along . . .
Now, they [were] shar[ing] a man and the work and all the [little ones] . . .
I describe my father as a stallion, with his various mares. Because it wasn't
only [those two]. Afterward, I discovered another one. But at a certain
point, [Ada] went with her children to live on the other hacienda of the
Señor, of Don Guillermo, where my father was also the administrator.[9]

Andrea obviously resented her father's unabashed polygamy, in referring to
him as a "stallion with his . . . mares." And she took exception to the arrival
and ongoing presence within her family home of her father's other "wife"
and the numerous children she would bring into the world. While Andrea
was able to appreciate that Ada and her mother got along, she felt bad for her
mother and what this must mean to her. That combination of feelings stayed
with her well into adulthood.

In contrast, for Silvia:

It wasn't as traumatic as for [my sisters], Andrea, Camila, and María . . .
because I grew up with [Ada], I have memories of her from when I was

very young. She was present, part of the family. The only thing was . . . there were heavy moments . . . There was a time when my mom and dad lived on the cooperative and . . . I had to live with [Ada] during the week for school and there were things . . . I'll tell you an anecdote. [Ada] had a nephew who was my classmate and with whom I got along well. We joked and things like that. Once when we were walking home from school, this boy [her nephew] was there—we were small, I don't even remember how old we were, maybe ten. This boy hit me with a ruler. We were absolutely forbidden to say bad words, like "son of a . . ." When that boy hit me with the ruler, playing around, I responded with "son of a . . . ," playing around. One of [Ada's] sons was with us (that is, one of my half brothers) . . . [Ada] threatened me, saying that her nephew's mother had said that the first time my father arrived . . . she was going to tell him and I knew that if she told him he was going to hit me. So she had me under threat . . . From the first moment she told me this, I was sure it wasn't her nephew that had told his mom, but rather my half brother who had told [Ada]. . . . it was [Ada] who threatened me—to bother me. But in general I got along well with her aside from some episodes like that . . . [Later on] she always said that I was the only one who visited her [when I went home] . . . even her children didn't stop by to ask how she was. She said that I was always watching out for her.

[Interviewer question: Did the situation with Ada bother your mom?] Yes, because there were episodes . . . at least one episode when my father hit my mom. He beat her up because of Ada. Ada had said that my mom had a relationship with someone else. [Interviewer question: Was Ada trying to provoke a fight between them?] Yes. Sometimes she did it to save herself . . . she provoked my father so that he'd go after my mother to save herself.

[Interviewer question: Was it common for men to have so many children and various families?] Yes, only their situation wasn't normal . . . to live like a family . . . to live together in one house.[10]

In Silvia's case, given that she had not known a time before Ada was around, her "stepmother" seemed like part of the family. Although by the time she was an adult she did not consider the situation a "normal" one, because at times their father's two families lived under the same roof, she had not felt that it was out of the ordinary while she was growing up and clearly felt a continuing bond with Ada.

Aside from the many children in their father's two families,[11] extended family members often came and spent time in the home where Andrea and Silvia lived with both of their parents. In particular, an aunt and uncle on their father's side stayed with them for periods of time. From Andrea's recollections, that is where the abuse started. Their father had four siblings who would visit them (see the family tree of Andrea and Silvia), and Andrea would be sent to visit them. She noted that only one of them did not try to abuse her or her siblings.[12]

The first to abuse her was Roberto. Andrea was cognizant of it happening from when she was about four years old:

> The first abuse that I remember experiencing . . . I can't tell you when it actually started . . . with him, was once when my grandparents were dancing and I was in a hammock nearby. He got into the hammock with me—the [rationale] was that there was my uncle rocking me [in the hammock]; he was taking care of his niece. But in reality . . . I remember him touching me. I'm not saying that he penetrated me, because he didn't. [But he touched me] with his fingers.
>
> This time in particular . . . it's the first thing I remember that wasn't normal. [He touched me] with his mouth—in the room with my mother and father dancing nearby . . . There was no electricity then, things were lit up with candles. That's my first recollection, because it did not seem normal . . . I know I was four years old [at the time].[13]

This occasion stuck out for Andrea, because it was somehow "different." That is, she now supposes that the abuse started earlier, in the form of touching, and that the principal reason that she became aware that something not quite right was happening at this point was that at the dance he used his mouth to touch her.

Andrea went on to say:

> Then there was my uncle Juan. It was with his hand . . . in my underwear. For me, it seemed normal . . . in the sense that it had been going on for some time. You know that if someone grabs you all of a sudden, it will

not seem normal. But if they're doing something to you from when you're very small, it will seem normal.

It was the same with my aunt . . . Julia . . . With my aunt, it was in bed [when we were supposed to be sleeping] . . . My aunt touched me with her fingers, and she did put her fingers inside me. I don't know when it started, because from the time of my earliest memories, she [did it]. And that's when she started with, "don't say anything to your *mamá* . . ." She brought me many gifts . . . But at night she'd do that to me . . . My little half sister was also abused by her. I don't know about the others. I think she was abusing the two of us in the same period. So for us, it seemed normal . . . Right now, I'm telling you about this [calmly], but it's been very hard at times [crying].

Then the last one . . . until then I had been passive . . . That is, I didn't do anything. [But] when my father wanted to do it to me, then I [really] understood . . . It was as if I had had blinders over my eyes . . . That's the way I see it now . . . [But] when my father wanted to do it to me, it's as if those dark blinders that had covered my eyes came off. And I started to rebel . . . He'd spent the night drinking. The next day . . . my mom was at the well . . . about ten meters from the house . . . She was preparing to make him soup so that he would feel better [from his hangover]. She asked me to get some eggs. Our house was very small, and the hens' nests were under their bed . . . She said, "Go get some eggs from the nest, I'm going to make egg soup for your father."

When I went in, he was lying down [in bed], he got up a bit . . . his eyes were red and shiny. They weren't like his eyes usually were . . . I was furious [with him] . . . Aside from the fact that he hit us when- ever he liked, I resented him, because he'd been drinking and when he drank he was very violent . . . When I went in, he called me. He always liked to give orders, and we'd have to obey. At that moment, he grabbed my hand, actually it was my arm. He said, "Come over here." I went. The moment I was closer, he grabbed me tightly by the hand. He had never grabbed me like that before . . . I was caught there . . . he was pulling me toward the bed. So, I struggled with him. I got free . . . [I was] probably twelve or thirteen . . . I don't remember anything hap- pening before that. He didn't [succeed in] do[ing] anything to me, but [for me] it was as if he had . . . I went running outside. My mother asked, "And the eggs, didn't you bring them?" I said, "No. I'll get the water . . ." I didn't tell her [then]. I don't know if my mom knew . . . I don't know if I had bruises on my arm. I just remember that I was very upset. Not just because I was afraid. I was furious. Since then, I haven't tolerated anything like that. Since then, I have to make a great effort to not tell him off, even though he deserves it. . . . With my dad, I never succeeded in getting past this . . . I don't think people [who have been abused] ever get past it, but you learn how to live with it so that it doesn't destroy you . . .

But the emotional damage for me was massive. . . . Especially after my father [tried to abuse me]. It was as if I lost my identity . . . of the family, and with regard to him . . . With my aunt and uncles, it was a little further away . . . But when it's right there in your own home, it's tremendous . . . You lose . . . well, I lost all my tranquility. Because at night . . . it wasn't as if I went away . . . I was still living there. When my father moved around [at night], I listened. I wondered, "And if he comes over here?" [I was filled with] both fear and rage.[14]

Hence, because the sexual abuse by her father's brothers and sister had started when Andrea was a very young child, except for particular instances it seemed *almost* natural to her. But when her father tried to abuse her, Andrea finally reacted by resisting his efforts. The experience shook her to the core, as it called into question her very sense of what her family represented to her. Moreover, the family home was supposed to be a safe space. But with her father's actions, she had lost that feeling of safety within her family.

In reflecting back on the period, Andrea was aware that abuse had taken place all around her as a child.[15] There was her younger half sister, who was also abused by their aunt Julia. And when Andrea was about seven, her older half sister, María (one of the daughters her mother brought to the partnership with Andrea's father), went to live with their uncle Roberto.

They were a couple [he wasn't her uncle by blood]. But she had a reason . . . they say that when she lived with us [my mother and father], my father went to her bed at night. My uncle realized it was happening and said to her . . . why don't you escape with me? So she did, she went with him. They lived close by . . . on the other side of the river. . . . That was the reason that she left the house. They say that she told my mother, and my mother didn't believe her. Isn't that classic? They said that she was telling lies, they punished her and everything. "You're lying." She didn't feel supported, so this was the solution. The [end] result was that she had her first child when she was thirteen years old . . . with [Roberto].[16]

Ironically, Roberto was the first of her father's siblings to abuse Andrea. And yet he offered himself as a savior to Andrea's half sister, María, when the latter was being abused by Andrea's father. After receiving no support from their mother in bringing an end to that abuse,[17] María sought a way out of the household. So, despite being barely into adolescence, María found "protection" in a conjugal relationship.

Then, when Andrea was about eleven years old, she was made to witness her cousin being abused.[18] She had gone to visit her cousin, who was helping out their paternal grandfather after their grandmother died. When he forced her cousin—who was about fifteen at the time—to have sex with him, Andrea was alongside them in the same bed the three were sharing.[19] Because this was before the "blinders" had come off Andrea's eyes, with her father's attempt to rape her, this experience with her grandfather may have just been of a piece with the rest of the abuse she had experienced but had not fully understood at the time it occurred.

Although Silvia, Andrea's younger sister, was also subjected to sexual abuse as a child, she was not conscious of it being all around her during that period of her life. Her father's siblings did not bother her. Given the age gap of six and a half years between Silvia and Andrea, it is possible that the lives of their aunt and uncles had moved on and they no longer spent as much time in the sisters' household when Silvia might otherwise have been of interest to them.

However, she did not escape the eye of their father. When I asked her why she moved to Managua to live with Andrea, and how old she was at the time, she recounted:

SILVIA: [I was] fourteen [years old]. Why did I come to Managua? Well, because at that time . . . when we were living on the second hacienda, which was called El Jicaro . . . In that period, my father started to bother me[20] . . .

He touched me and he touched me, that's why. And Andrea knew . . . about that kind of thing . . . one time, he was forcing me to kiss him. And Andrea knew this and she . . . made as if she needed someone to help her in the house in Managua and she invited me to go [to be] with her. That's why I went.

INTERVIEWER: Can I ask, where did he touch you?

SILVIA: Everywhere.

INTERVIEWER: Did he do more than that?

SILVIA: Once.

INTERVIEWER: Where was your mom?

SILVIA: There, with us. [The house] was one room.

INTERVIEWER: You were all together?

SILVIA: Yes.

INTERVIEWER: Was she in bed at the time?

SILVIA: Yes.

INTERVIEWER: Did you tell Andrea?

SILVIA: No. No. Andrea doesn't know this, exactly. Andrea knows about the rest.

INTERVIEWER: So, how did she find out about the rest?

SILVIA: Because . . . because I believe that my mother told her, or it was [simply] evident . . . the truth is that I don't remember. The other thing . . . when my father . . . got into my bed and all that, I think my mother realized it . . . it would have been impossible for her not to . . . my bed was here, and their bed was [close by].

INTERVIEWER: . . . unless your mom sleeps like a rock. Does your mom sleep like a rock?

SILVIA: No. Not that I remember.

INTERVIEWER: Were you conscious before this that your father had a history in this sense?

SILVIA: No.

INTERVIEWER: Today, are you aware of him molesting anyone else?

SILVIA: Yes.

INTERVIEWER: Who?

SILVIA: As far as I know, María, and Andrea as well, [and] Ada's daughters— at least two or three [of them].

INTERVIEWER: Do you think he just tried with them, or that he was successful?

SILVIA: With one of them, I think he succeeded, with one of Ada's [daughters].

INTERVIEWER: Did any of them have children by him?

SILVIA: No.

INTERVIEWER: How did you feel when this happened?

SILVIA: At the beginning, I felt that it was my fault.

INTERVIEWER: What made you think that?

SILVIA: It's what [people] say. What he said. He didn't say it was my fault . . . But he said that . . .

INTERVIEWER: . . . you provoked him?

SILVIA: Yes . . .

INTERVIEWER: . . . something like that?

SILVIA: Yes, yes. And . . . I knew that it was something that shouldn't happen, that I had to say something about it. But I didn't have the courage to do so. I didn't have the valor to confront something like that . . . In part, it was because I was afraid, I was really afraid of him.

INTERVIEWER: Were you afraid that he would hit you?

SILVIA: Yes . . . Because, when he touched me, he said things, he said not to tell anyone—because my mother would be mad at me and would hit me. And he [said he] did it because he loved me.

The truth is that I've never told absolutely anyone. This is the first time I'm talking about it . . .

INTERVIEWER: Did Andrea take you away right after that?

SILVIA: Some time passed. That was when I was eleven. Andrea took me [away] when I was fourteen years old.

INTERVIEWER: He didn't rape you again?

SILVIA: No. But he always . . . even when I didn't live with them anymore . . . I remember one time . . . I went to visit them . . . and he said . . . Remember, Ada lived close by the house. He was drinking, like almost always, and he said, "Do you want to see me hit Ada?" I said, "Why? Why do you have to hit Ada, she's working." I remember that they were taking water from the well, the two of them, she and my mother. And he said to me . . . "Just because! Just because! Do you want to see me mess with her." [I said,] "No, they're working, they're not doing anything." At that moment . . . I remember that I was making tortillas . . . I turned around to take the tortillas off the fire . . . and I saw that he was . . . that he was going to hit me with, you know, reins, that they use on horses . . . So I grabbed his hand and I said, "No. That's enough! Never again! Never again will you dare to raise your hand against me. Because I won't let you put your hand on me again!"

Afterward he said, "Why do you do that to me? Why do you act like that? After everything I've done for you? [After] how I've been with you?" I think he was referring to all the times he'd touched me, the times he bothered me, as if . . .

INTERVIEWER: . . . as if it were a compliment?

SILVIA: . . . from what I understand, yes. It was as if he had done something lovely to me, he had done something loving, something . . .[21]

As his daughters grew old enough to leave the family home, Andrea and Silvia's father moved on to abuse their younger sisters. And Silvia was another one of those he abused. He tried to present that abuse as a compliment to her but also threatened her to keep her silent. Given his history of physical abuse, which will be discussed shortly, those threats carried real weight. Although Silvia believed that her mother knew about the abuse,[22] she was too afraid to talk about it with her. Instead, when Andrea orchestrated Silvia's departure by requesting her help in Managua, she left home to remove herself from his orbit of control. In so doing, she was following in the footsteps of María and Andrea. But both Andrea and Silvia were able to leave through the assistance of an older female relative[23] rather than that of an older man who wanted to have a partnership with them.

Andrea and Silvia remained close to their mother until she died in 2014, despite the latter's apparent unwillingness to confront her own partner with his abuse of their daughters. Yet their relationship with their father continues to be impacted by his abuse of them as children. That abuse reflected, in an extreme form, the larger societal context in which men were the predominant power holders. As such, they controlled much of what went on, both outside and within the household. And within the household, their wives and children were heavily subjected to those power relations.

Extreme patriarchal power relations were also at play in the family life of their friend Ana when she was a child. She grew up with her five siblings, four of whom were the children of her stepfather. However as mentioned in the previous chapter, several of his approximately ten children from a previous relationship came to live with them for periods of time. Her stepfather, Don Raúl, and several of these stepsiblings would abuse her over the next decade or so.

Ana was three or four years old when Don Raúl moved in with her mother, Ana, and Ana's younger sister.[24] The trouble started shortly thereafter. Given that Don Raúl did not sleep in the same bed as Ana's mother—sleeping, instead, in a hammock—he was free to roam the house during the night. And roam he did. In those early years, he simply touched her. She would wake up during the night and feel his hairy hands on her.[25] When she screamed, her mother would call out for Don Raúl to put a light on. By the time the light was on, his hands were off Ana. Ana became terrified of nighttime and of the dark. As she commented: "When the lights were turned off, the torture began."[26] Ana was so frightened that she wet her bed until her first child was born (when she was thirteen years old). Clearly the ongoing abuse was quite traumatic for her. Yet Ana did not say anything to her mother because she did not think her mother would believe her.

When Don Raúl's son, Pablo, came to stay with them for an extended period of time, he also abused Ana. He also touched her all over, including inside her vagina.[27] She calculated that he would have been fourteen or fifteen at the time, and she would have been five or six years old.

Then another of Don Raúl's sons—Bayardo—came for a visit when Ana was seven or eight years old. And he started to take advantage of her.[28] One day her mother sent Ana to see her aunt, with Bayardo as her guardian for the walk there. As they were going through a canyon, he started to grab her. At first she thought it was a game and kept running away from him. But she finally understood that it was not, when he grabbed her and, in tearing her clothes off, even tore her underwear. Although she fought with him, he succeeded in raping her.

> And well, after that time, I remember, I arrived at my aunt's house . . . I was very sad . . . I had to go to my aunt's after everything that had happened to me. My hair was all tousled, because I hadn't been able to brush it . . . without underwear, because I didn't have them anymore. He had torn them apart. I couldn't tell my aunt what had happened because . . .

she wouldn't have believed me . . . I was always afraid, because my mom punished me for everything. That is, she never believed me when I went to talk with her, to tell her things. She said that I lied, that I invented things. She always believed her husband . . . She loved him . . .

And I tried. Sometimes, I tried to talk with her. I'd say, "Mamá, I want to talk with you about something." [Her response was,] "What lies are you going to tell me? You're a liar. You invent things." She said, "I'm not going to believe anything." And sometimes she said to her husband, "Look, hit her." Always. She said, "Punish her." [She had him hit me] for everything and nothing.

And he would beat me badly. [It hurt so much] that I couldn't even sleep. So I was afraid. Where would I get the courage to talk?[29]

As with Silvia, fear kept Ana from talking with her mother or aunt about what was happening to her. Given that there was a history of physical abuse, that fear was well founded. Moreover, Ana did try to talk with her mother about it, but it seems that her mother was not prepared to hear what Ana had to say.

Bayardo returned to Honduras shortly thereafter. But that wasn't the end of her tribulations. Like son, like father:

And then it started . . . [Don Raúl] too started to [rape] me . . . It was as if, now that [his son] had done that to me . . . why not? . . . I remember the first time. I was seven, eight years [old]. He started to [rape] me. He hit my legs so that I'd let him, he squeezed me, he pinched me, he did everything to me so I wouldn't shout and so that I wouldn't say anything to my mother . . . And one day I said, "I'm going to tell my *mamá*, today's the day I'll tell her . . ." He said to me, "If you tell her, I'll beat you up badly." Where would I get the courage to tell my mom?[30]

So, like Silvia's father, Ana's stepfather used threats of physical violence to silence her into submission. In so doing, his control over her body—which was part and parcel of the patriarchal relations that were predominant in Nicaragua—was expressed in both his sexual abuse and the history of battering he used to keep her from talking about it.

For Ana, the cost of the abuse was tremendous. As she recounted: "I felt dirty, tortured, like I wasn't worth anything . . . it shouldn't exist . . . I . . .

shouldn't [have] to live this life. [crying]"[31] Yet because she did not feel safe talking with any of the adults who were around her and because none of those adults were attentive to or willing to face it, she was trapped in this harrowing situation.

And then Bayardo, Ana's stepbrother, returned to live with them. This time he stayed for a year or two, and thus her abusers multiplied.

> And so it went . . . over all those years, from when I was three or four years old, when things started, until Carlos[, my son,] was born. It was pure torture . . . abuse after abuse, by both the son and the father.[32]

What finally brought the sexual abuse to an end was the birth of her son. Ana was thirteen years old when she became pregnant by her stepfather. She was six months along in her pregnancy when her godmother insisted that her mother take her to the doctor because she thought Ana was probably pregnant. Ana had a number of clear symptoms of pregnancy, but her mother had failed to notice them.

Much as seemed to be true for Andrea and Silvia's mother, logic suggests that Ana's mother looked the other direction rather than acknowledge what her senses must have been telling her was occurring within her household:

> The worst thing is, look . . . I slept here, and my mom's bed was right here . . . It wasn't as if we were in [two different] room[s] . . . Our beds were close by one another. And she never . . . how can a mother . . . [Interviewer question: Was she a sound sleeper?] I'm not sure. Either she slept like a rock or he gave her something to make her sleep . . . Later on, no; when she was older . . . she was always awake . . . When I was a child, she was always quiet. It's like she was also intimidated . . . The truth is that I don't understand . . . because . . . sleeping right by one another, and she couldn't hear anything? It's not as if he came [into my bed] and I was quiet. I was just a child. You know how it is when a child doesn't want something. I tried to get away from him. [I'd say something like] "Leave me in peace." And he'd hit me. I cried . . . because he'd hurt me. And she'd never hear anything . . . she'd never say anything.[33]

So an additional element of the trauma for Ana was the feeling of being profoundly betrayed by her mother's willingness to let her partner violate her own daughter.

When Ana got pregnant, though, it became impossible to pretend that all was as it should be. But rather than get to the heart of the matter, Ana recounts:

[My mother] wanted to know, but it wasn't even her . . . She had her husband ask me who the father was. And what was I going to say? He already knew who the father was. Of course, I didn't say . . . [Then] she'd say: "Tell me who the father is." [And I'd reply,] "No. I don't have to tell you who the father is. Period."[34]

That is to say, despite the evidence of the abuse that was right in front of her, her mother kept up the charade of not knowing who the father of her daughter's child might have been.

Not surprisingly, Ana was resentful toward the baby she was expecting. As she recalled:

I didn't want my child at the beginning.[35] I was hoping that Carlos would die. I'll be honest . . . But once he was born, I loved him so much . . . I adore Carlos. It's not his fault . . . I don't want my son to feel rejected . . . If I were to treat my son like my mother treated me, that would be to repeat the history that I lived [through]. I have never rejected him . . . I love him just like I love my other two [children]. They're my children; they came out of me. It's not his fault that he was the product of that . . .[36]

Ana's initial reaction was a common one among women who become pregnant through rape (c.f. Coleman 2015; Thomson Salo 2010). Typically, anything associated with the rape and/or the rapist has negative connotations for the victim. Being able to overcome those associations and love her son was a very positive outcome in the midst of such suffering.

Unfortunately, though, that was not the end of Ana's troubles:

One day when Carlos was about nine months old, [Don Raúl] tried to abuse me again. He dared to try to touch me, to abuse me. I stopped him . . . I grabbed a knife. He thought that we were going to repeat that history, that he'd give me another child . . . that I would stay quiet, and that we were going to go on as before . . . I grabbed the knife, and I told him that if he touched me I'd stab him . . . "You can't touch me anymore, my mother can't say anything, and the day you put your hand on me, that you try to hit me, or do something else to me, that's the day I'll stab you. You're not going to touch me again, or even put a hair on me." He was frightened and didn't do anything. But he went to tell my mom that I had to leave the house, because I was spoiled, that I didn't obey [him], and that since I'd had my child I thought I could do what I wanted . . . And what did my mom do? She threw me out . . . All of these things hurt me . . . At fourteen years of age. She threw me out of the house, with my nine-month-old child. I didn't know where to go . . . [So] I went to my aunt's and I asked her if I could stay with her.[37]

Somehow, going through the pregnancy and having a child of her own had given Ana the strength to defend herself from her stepfather. But these changes did not appear to have modified the behavior of Ana's mother in any way. Instead, her reaction to Ana's failure to "obey" her stepfather was to side with him and put her young daughter and grandchild on the street. Not surprisingly, aside from her hatred of Don Raúl, Ana developed quite bitter feelings toward her mother. Those feelings remained intense even after both her mother and stepfather had passed.

And when Ana eventually left for her first stint abroad, she worried about whether Don Raúl would start to abuse her sisters. She was especially concerned about Carmen, who was not his daughter by birth. But such are the taboos around this topic that Ana has never discussed what happened to her with them.

PHYSICAL VIOLENCE

As the preceding interview quotes indicate, all three women were also subjected to, and frightened by, physical violence they experienced at the hand of the elders in their households. Andrea, Silvia, and Ana all referred to beatings they received from their father (in the first two cases) or stepfather (in the last case), as well as the threats of them.[38] The only suggestion that Andrea and Silvia's mother might have also participated in this punishment was that their father threatened Silvia with a beating from their mother if she reported his abuse. And Ana's mother seemed to have taken part in the physical violence indirectly, by encouraging her partner to engage in it.

In Andrea and Silvia's family, their father's physical violence was often associated with his drinking. The threat of violence was ever present, as Silvia acknowledged in response to the following questions:

INTERVIEWER: Did he hit you?

SILVIA: Yes, yes, many times . . .

INTERVIEWER: Did he hit you for anything and everything?

SILVIA: Yes.

INTERVIEWER: And was it the same with your siblings?

SILVIA: Yes. And even for my mom.

INTERVIEWER: And Ada?

SILVIA: Yes.[39]

Andrea commented that their male siblings received even worse treatment from their father than their female siblings.[40] He typically hit all of them with a belt. In addition, sometimes he fired a weapon around their mother or used his fists on her. Once Andrea had moved away from home, she tried to support her mother in the face of her father's physical violence. She sent her mother messages over the airwaves through a radio station in Chinandega (the "19 de julio" station), suggesting that she keep a bat handy to use to defend herself, something apparently her mother did on at least one occasion.[41] However, through her messages broadcast on the radio, Andrea was also announcing to the world that her father was a wife batterer.

In contrast, Ana did not talk about drinking being a precipitating factor with her stepfather. Another difference was that although it was her stepfather who engaged in this violence, her mother often seemed to instigate the violence that was directed at Ana. This can be seen in the following exchange:

INTERVIEWER: Did they beat you? . . .

ANA: More him, my stepfather; my mother almost never hit me . . . He hit me with a whip . . . it left lashes on my body . . . it hurt [a lot], so that I couldn't sleep. Sometimes he hit me so hard, so hard, that I had marks all over my ribs. . . . She told him to do it. [So] in part, it was *her* punishing me . . . it felt like it was her punishing me. But it was he who did it. My mom did all the talking. She said, "You lie." And then, "Hit her, because she did this and this and this . . . Hit her . . ." They beat me, they always beat me, for everything and nothing . . .

INTERVIEWER: Did he hit your mother as well?

ANA: No, I never saw him hit her . . . It was only me that he hit; not even the others, it was only me; not even my sisters . . .

INTERVIEWER: Did he hit his sons?"

ANA: "No, none of them. . . . not even Carlos, except occasionally, when he did something wrong. But not just for any old reason . . ."[42]

Hence, Ana lived with her stepfather's physical violence day in and day out. Here again, her mother was not a source of protection for her. Rather, her mother encouraged his physical violence against her. And Ana seems to have been the focus of her stepfather's and mother's aggression. The fact that Ana was the only one of her mother's daughters who was not his— through either adoption or biology—may well have played a contributing if not determinative role in this dynamic. A substantial amount of research documents the "stepfather effect," which is associated with the physical abuse of children borne from a wife's former partnership (c.f. Hilton et al. 2015; Daly and Wilson 1999). This pattern may stem, at least in part, from the fact that for the stepfather his stepchild represents continuing evidence of his wife's former relationship. This constant reminder would work against his sense of ownership of his wife and children, a "right" he was accorded within patriarchy.

In reflecting on the situations of Andrea, Silvia, and Ana, it is essential to highlight that for all three of these women, the principal perpetrator of this physical violence was also the principal perpetrator of the sexual violence. Physical violence was typically the threat employed by their violators in forcing their acquiescence to being sexually abused. To wit, these two types of violence were interwoven with one another in the lives of the three women. Their experience coincides with patterns from around the world, which show that those who are subjected to one of these types of violence are more likely to be subjected to the other as well (c.f. Mullen et al. 1996). Aside from this reality making things doubly hard for their victims, it also complicates sorting out the effects of each.

THE CONSEQUENCES OF SEXUAL AND PHYSICAL VIOLENCE

The consequences of the sexual and physical violence experienced by each of these women have been numerous and long-lasting. These consequences range from the effects that the violence had on their physical health, to caring for a child resulting from the sexual abuse, to the low level of self-esteem each felt at least at times, to the implications of the life decisions that stemmed from the violence. These effects have interacted with one another, which will become clear even as we examine each effect on its own.

Physical Effects

The physical and sexual violence to which Ana, Andrea, and Silvia were subjected affected their health in both short- and long-term ways. As Ana described in one of the preceding quotes, the beatings she received at the hands of her stepfather left her with at least superficial injuries on more than one occasion. Meanwhile, research suggests that physical injuries often result from forced sexual relations with children (Forjuoh and Zwi 1998). We will never know whether these women suffered such injuries because if they underwent a medical examination for them when they were children, which is unlikely, the results of those exams were never shared with them.

Other effects of the sexual violence experienced by these women were, however, manifest. For Ana, this took the form of contracting a venereal disease as a child. As she recounted:

> When we lived at my grandfather's house . . . [after] the first [period of] abuse I suffered . . . I had an infection in my [private] parts. The infection caused blisters . . . It was herpes. I would have been seven or eight [then] or maybe even six, I was just a child . . . I remember crying when I had to go to the bathroom. . . . [My mother] didn't say anything . . . It's possible that the doctor said something to her. [But] she only gave me the medicine that she had bought and applied it until the infection was gone. Once it was gone, the abuse went on.[43]

Ana's mother had taken her to the doctor to see what was wrong. The medicine that the doctor prescribed was evidently appropriate for herpes, given that it cleared up the infection. Yet the medical visit did nothing more than resolve that precise aspect of the problem. If this doctor mentioned to Ana's mother what the source of her infection was, she chose to ignore the information and remain complicit in her partner's behavior. Hence, once the problem was resolved, life went back to "normal" for Ana's household.

While the herpes that Ana contracted was seen to by a doctor, a long-running medical problem that Andrea experienced was treated within her family as if it were her own idiosyncrasy even though it may well have been related to the sexual violence she regularly experienced. As described in Chapter 2, Andrea experienced an eating disorder for many years, starting from when she was as young as she could remember.[44] Coincidentally, the sexual abuse to which she was subjected also started when she was a very young child. As noted earlier, research has shown that eating disorders are often associated with having been subjected to sexual violence (Wonderlich et al. 2001). Andrea never received a diagnosis pointing to the sexual violence as being at the root of her eating disorder, nor was the latter ever diagnosed. Yet research such as this suggests that there is a reasonable probability that they were related to one another. With time that malady has receded.

Resulting Life Changes

Andrea, Silvia, and Ana all experienced major life changes as a consequence of the sexual abuse to which they had been subjected. Perhaps the birth of Ana's son Carlos was the most dramatic of these changes. His arrival in her life brought an end to this period of Ana's schooling, forcing her to leave her studies after only a few years of secondary school.[45] Whether she would have found work in another sector of the economy, with higher pay, had she been able to complete high school is uncertain. However, Ana's failure to complete high school, much less pursue college, and her need to take care of a child starting when she was only a child herself would have clearly set limits on her job prospects for the future.

Moreover, all three of these women left home very young to curtail the abuse to which they had been subjected. As mentioned earlier, Ana was thrown out of her house when she resisted the reinitiation of her stepfather's advances after her son was born. She was then forced to find full-time work as a maid to support herself and her son. Andrea also sought full-time work in Chinandega at about age fifteen, to escape the clutches of her father. It took her quite a long time and several jobs before she was able to find one where the employers would allow her to live outside their home so that she could study at night. Nonetheless, working full time would have affected her ability to focus on her studies. Silvia left home at age fourteen with Andrea's help. She went to live with Andrea and her family in Managua, where she completed primary school. But then she began to work full time to contribute to her new household. Hence, in each of their cases, their childhood was first cut short by the abuse, and then by the need to work to support themselves away from home.[46]

High-Risk Behavior

As discussed earlier, both sexual and physical abuse can have long-lasting emotional and psychological effects. Among the potential outcomes of these effects is engagement in substance abuse and other high-risk behaviors. During Andrea's adolescence she went through a period that she described as one of "rebellion."[47] She attributed this period to the fact that she had become stymied in her efforts to continue her studies. It is understandable that she would have been terribly frustrated and depressed about this situation. But it is also possible that the way that Andrea acted out her frustration was influenced by the physical and sexual abuse to which she had been subjected as a child.

In Andrea's words:

> I was disillusioned in the sense that I could see that I wouldn't be able to keep studying. A sadness came over me. I didn't want to go back home [to my parents' house], I didn't want to work, I didn't want to do anything. [So] I spent several months just hanging out. [Interviewer question: How did you support yourself?] . . . I helped out my cousins. I'd take care of their kids. I'd do things around the house. And they gave me [room and board] . . . I was about fifteen years old . . .
>
> When I started studying, I was clear on what I wanted to do . . . Then when I didn't have [the possibility of continuing], I was left up in the air. So the desire to [do things] left me. And I started to just hang out, on the street, or at [the volcanic lagoon of] Xiloa. I'd go to the beach with friends, and we'd stay there, and sleep there. I drank a lot, went dancing . . . I was totally lost . . . Sometimes I'd leave on Friday and wouldn't reappear until Monday . . .
>
> [My cousins] didn't know anything. My family didn't know anything. My cousins started to get worried. But then they started to see me as a hopeless case . . . in the sense that they'd tell me to go here [and there], and I wouldn't pay attention to them. Well, then they started to get upset

with me. And they were right to, given that I didn't have a job, I didn't do anything, I didn't contribute, and I didn't help them out. It got to the point where I wasn't [even] helping them out. I'd get there and throw myself on a cot. I'd lie down and I couldn't get myself up, sometimes for a couple of days. I [just] had no desire to get up . . . It was as if I didn't have the energy to get up. Time passed like that and they . . . were entitled to get angry with me . . .

Then, with time, I turned sixteen, and I ran into the Señor [from my last job] again and he asked me out.[48] We started to go out. He'd take me out to eat . . . For me, it was just hanging out, without any restrictions—with no one controlling me, not myself, nor my family . . . I agreed to go out with him and I let him support me [while I lived with my cousins] . . . It's not as if he paid me for each date, but rather he just always supported me. He gave me lots of money . . . He'd come by for me, and take me out. We'd go places. We'd go to the seashore . . . It's not as if it bothered me to see him. He was young, and very handsome . . . and very interesting . . .

So it ended up being me supporting [my cousins], right? I brought [home] the money, I bought food, and then everything was fine [with them]. Then one day . . . my mind had been, like, foggy . . . like all this time it was foggy with smoke . . . One day, it was as if I woke up, right? I woke up from everything that I was doing that wasn't normal or good for me.[49]

Eventually, Andrea came to see this period of engaging in lots of drinking, hanging out, and being in a relationship and being supported economically by a married man as less than positive for her well-being. In fact, an argument could certainly be made that she was engaging in what analysts commonly term "high-risk behavior." Moreover, in Andrea's case, her high-risk behavior was colored by the structural violence that characterized her life: class and gender inequalities enabled this well-off man to spend time with a very beautiful young woman, and this young woman accepted his company because the time spent with him was enjoyable, but it also put food on the table. Ultimately, she decided to move on from her "rebellion," and she did so before there were lasting consequences like an unplanned pregnancy[50] or something else that might have constrained her options for the future even more than they were already. Here again, Andrea's resilience as a person enabled her to simply leave this situation and see what else the world had to offer her.

Troubled Relationships

Low self-esteem is pointed to in the literature as a common outcome of physical and sexual abuse of children, as mentioned earlier. At the same time, having low self-esteem can contribute to a person being in an intimate relationship with someone who may not have the highest regard for them.[51] That lack of high regard can then translate into the relationship being troubled. However, the larger context of patriarchy that prevailed in Nicaragua during the youth and young adulthood of Andrea, Silvia, and Ana would have complicated dynamics like these even further. Patriarchy devalues women, which would only have intensified the potential consequences of the low self-esteem that may result from having been subjected to sexual and physical violence. In the following discussion we will see how these forces played out in the lives of Andrea, Silvia, and Ana.

One might describe Andrea's relationship with the married man in Chinandega as problematic. Yet once in Managua she would form a partnership that would become equally, albeit distinctly, problematic from the point of view of her emotional well-being. When Andrea "escaped" with her half sister Camila to Managua, she began the next period of her life. As described in Chapter 2, she and Camila both found jobs quickly, and those jobs came with places to live. Shortly thereafter, Juan came into Andrea's life. Juan would become her partner and the father of her two children.

Andrea was seventeen years old when she met Juan. As she related:

> He lived across the street [from where I was a live-in maid], with a family. He rented a room. At that time, both of us were doing military training [for the Sandinista Popular Militia[52]]. So we started to go out and everything . . . We started out as friends. [But] after I moved [from the neighborhood for another job], something changed for him . . . I didn't go to live with him. I would go to stay with him, and then go to work during the week, and then I'd come back [on the weekends]. It was only later that [we lived together] on an ongoing basis.[53]

Juan was twenty-one years old when they met.

> He worked for a long time for a kind of . . . employment agency . . . it was
> a kind of association; they were all members . . . [The members of the
> agency] did guard and custodial work, and driving, I believe. But most of
> it was guard and custodial work . . . in various places . . . And when I met
> him, Juan was [working as a guard] at a computer business.[54]

Ultimately, Andrea moved in with him when the owners of the next home
she worked in were not happy about his coming there to visit with her during the week:

> I said to him, "Okay. While I'm looking for work, can you support me?"
> And [he responded,] "Yes, yes, I'll support you." So I went. We had a
> room. In a short while . . . the idea of being without work was [clearly] not
> sustainable . . . This was aside from [the fact that] he didn't have a huge
> salary to support me . . . Above all, because I had a big responsibility . . . I
> needed to [be able to] send money to my mom.[55]

So Andrea went back to work. But the relationship with Juan continued and
before long they had a baby daughter, Clara, and later on a son, Daniel.

However, before Andrea undertook her first extended period of work
abroad, which was in 1997, she made a decision that she had been contemplating a long while. She announced to Juan, her partner of fourteen years,[56]
that she did not plan to return to their relationship once this sojourn in the
United States was over.

> I separated from him when I left, fortunately . . . I wanted to leave him
> a lot . . . practically always, but I didn't have the courage to do so [until
> then] . . . I felt that I wasn't part of his life . . . That is . . . he came from a
> family with a lot . . . His father had a whole lot of land, he had 100 *man-
> zanas* of land,[57] and a lot . . . of animals [cattle, etc.] and everything. And
> my family had practically nothing.
>   . . . He looked at us as if we weren't worth anything. He looked at us
> as if he were a millionaire and we were slaves . . . [And] it wasn't as if he
> had anything either . . . But he had this idea . . . he [would] say, we have so
> much, we have so much [speaking of his birth family].

He lived with illusions in his head . . . of grandeur . . . you saw that he was very white[-skinned] . . . For him, that was a big deal, to be white . . .[58] So I always felt out of place. Even though his family always treated me better than he treated me. His family never made me feel different.[59]

Hence, although Juan had embarked on the relationship as readily as Andrea had, he made evident his sense of superiority stemming from their relative class and racial differences. As Andrea noted, he did not have anything either and worked as a laborer to support himself. This meant that he, too, was affected by Nicaragua's class inequalities in many of the same ways she was once he left his family's home. But although his birth family was not wealthy, since they were better off than Andrea's, he considered himself to be above her in status. And the fact that his skin color was notably lighter than hers seemed to have contributed to his feelings of greater worth.[60]

Juan's attitude toward Andrea took a toll on the relationship, though. As she commented:

And after so long of that, I began to be less respectful of him as well . . . to have stayed all those years . . . my excuse was the children . . . [Interviewer question: Weren't you dependent on him economically for periods of time?] . . . Never, never! I worked day and night sewing, making things. I supported myself and the children . . . He . . . always gave the same amount . . . it never [changed], even when he got pay raises . . .

I never pushed him much on that, because he didn't want the children . . . He would have preferred not to have children.

Even when we separated . . . He quit his job because they told him . . . that if I wanted to go to the Social Welfare agency, part of his salary would go to his children. So he quit . . . If I went to Social Welfare, he would be obligated to give a third of what he earned to his children. That was the normal thing . . . When he heard this, he opted to quit his job . . .

When we separated, he separated definitively from the children. And this is what I hadn't wanted [to happen.][61]

Thus, in addition to Juan acting as if he were the superior one in the partnership with Andrea, he also was not willing to assume his full share of the responsibility for supporting his children. Even though he contributed something to the household while he still lived there, the amount he contributed was stagnant even as his wages rose. And once Juan moved out of the household, rather than have his wages garnered by the Social Welfare Ministry for Child Support, he left his job in the formal sector and provided nothing further for his children. Juan's move into the informal sector of the economy effectively put his earnings out of the reach of the state. Here was a perfect example of the limitations of the legislative reforms of the early 1980s, discussed in Chapter 2, that had mandated shared responsibility between parents for their children. Juan's lack of willingness to take responsibility for his children reflected the gender inequalities that have prevailed in Nicaragua, which leave the mother to ensure that the needs of a couple's children are met and the father free to use his income as he pleases.[62] Although Andrea had clearly resented all of this over many years of their partnership, her first priority had been keeping their father in the lives of Clara and Daniel. Nonetheless, her patience finally ran out and she advised Juan that he would have to find another place to live.

But there was even more going on in the relationship than these problematic economic dynamics and Juan's disrespectful treatment of Andrea. For years Juan had spent very little time at home, ostensibly working extremely long hours on the job. Eventually it became clear that he had another family:

> It was during the second time [that I went to the United States], I believe, that he took [our children] to the woman's house . . . when I came back, he was still working [at Willard[63]] . . . and with his longtime companion. Because he had a permanent companion; for the whole time he was with me he had someone else . . . I didn't know it . . . It seems that he met her after meeting me . . . he raised a son that she had [from before].
>
> And this woman told the children . . . my children [about their relationship] . . .
>
> There were times that people would say to me, "but Juan was with you . . ." He would go to parties, to gatherings at work . . . to everything, everything, everything, everything with her . . . as the official wife. And she passed as me . . . she used my name . . . So he led a double life . . . I didn't realize it until afterward . . . in '98, when he took the children to live with him at her house.[64]

Hence, the context of patriarchy that allowed Juan to shirk responsibility for his children also facilitated his engagement in the polygamy that Molyneux (1986) spoke of. Despite not having children with his second "wife," he did help her raise her child. And Juan moved back and forth between the two households with a sense of ownership/membership in each. Fortunately for Andrea, by the time this became entirely evident, her own life had largely moved on from Juan except in terms of his being the father of her children.

Andrea's sister Silvia also became involved in and stayed in several relationships characterized by her commitment to the other person and their lack of commitment to her. Silvia's first serious relationship was with a man she knew from the Mercado Oriental named Pedro. She lived with him from the time she was twenty-one years old until she was twenty-three. She described their time together in the following way:

> We lived with his mother and sister. Later on his sister had two children, and we all lived together. It was an enormous family and we were all together in a little room . . .
>
> Whenever I had a problem with him . . . they took my side, never his. They always defended me. In fact, his mother always said, "If someday you separate, he would have to leave the house and you would stay with me."
>
> And that's what happened at one point . . . Yes, for a while . . . Because, well, he was married. But when he was with me, he was separated from his wife. Later on, he went back with his wife and went to live with her [again]. I stayed there at his mom's house.
>
> One day I decided to go, but the decision wasn't actually mine . . . [Andrea] came to take me away from the house . . . Andrea said, "You can't keep living there" . . . Because I was very much in love with him . . . And she was right . . . I had decided to [leave], but I was also very connected with him, and with his family. . . .
>
> When I left, his mom always came looking for me . . . and she always said to me that I should stop by to see them when I left work. I did that for a while . . .[65]

Thus Silvia found herself unable to definitively leave the situation, which returning to her sister's home would have symbolized, although her former companion had moved on from the relationship. This effectively meant that she remained "available" to him, should he decide he wanted to resume the relationship, rather than taking care of herself and finding a way to achieve closure. Silvia ended up living with her companion's family when her next relationship broke up as well, except that in that case, her ex-companion slept in one room and she in another.[66] That relationship also lasted about two years.

Then Silvia started seeing Samuel, a married man with a wife and child in Cuba, where he had studied. She was in this relationship for four years. As she recounted:

> He came to stay with me on the weekends. He lived in Granada [a city to the southeast of the capital] and I lived in Managua, so [we only saw each other] on the weekends . . .
>
> . . . The story was that he had come back to Nicaragua with the idea of having [his wife] come with their daughter, because he had a daughter with her. But they could never get it organized; they never had all the documents that were needed, were required, so that the family could leave—that is, so that his wife and daughter could come to Nicaragua. They never did it. Now they aren't thinking about living together any longer . . .
>
> [Interviewer question: But he wasn't able to separate himself from her completely during the whole time you were together?] Yes, [that's right]. [Interviewer question: Perhaps when there is a child in the middle, things get more complicated?] I don't think that had anything to do with it . . . It should be that way. But with Samuel, I don't know; he was different . . . He should have left what he was doing in Nicaragua for a moment and gone to Cuba with all of his papers [documents] to get them out. So no, it wasn't for that. I don't know how it was. I was with him for four years and I never got to know him well . . . [that is,] to understand him . . .
>
> . . . With him . . . everything was up in the air . . . With him, I felt like a tramp. . . . I didn't feel committed,[67] but I [also] wasn't free to do what I wanted . . . He was never clear [about the relationship] . . . when I'm with someone, I feel like I have a commitment to them . . . He wanted a commitment. He didn't want to commit himself, but he wanted a commitment

from me . . . That's why . . . when we separated it was very sad; but at the same time, it was like being liberated.[68]

Hence, Silvia was willing to give of herself in each of these relationships. And she was also more than happy to "marry" the whole family when she became involved with each of these men. But they were not men who were willing to commit to her. In this sense, her relationships embodied the gender inequalities that colored most heterosexual partnerships in Nicaragua. Each of these men wanted her to make a clear statement of her commitment to them—by moving in with them and their families of origin or simply by agreeing not to see others. But the men either were unwilling to make the same commitment or felt no compelling reason to make the relationship permanent. The first of these, Pedro, had evidently remained in contact with his official wife even as he was living with Silvia or he would not have found it so easy to move back in with her, thereby ending his two-year partnership with Silvia. And with Samuel, despite his "inability" to find a means to bring his official wife and daughter to Nicaragua, that "project" ostensibly kept him from being able to make any promises to Silvia. The lack of definition that characterized their relationship ultimately made Silvia feel like a "tramp" because, as she confirmed, she accepted behavior that left her feeling disrespected. It would be some years later, and in another country, before she found someone who reciprocated her willingness to be in a committed relationship.

Meanwhile, Ana also had a long-lasting, troubled relationship. She had met Rafael, who would eventually become her husband, before she went abroad with the German couple (as described in Chapter 2). At that point, he was quite young and was not attractive to her. However, when she returned from that sojourn in Europe, she became reacquainted with him at a friend's house. Ana was about twenty-one years old at the time and Rafael was about nineteen.[69] They became friends and he visited her every day after work. After a while they agreed to become partners and got married in 1991.

Rafael was working as a security guard with a Finnish aid organization when they got married. Sometimes he was asked to guard the organization's office, and other times he was sent to guard the homes of the volunteers who worked there. He was relatively well paid for a laborer in Nicaragua. Between Ana's salary and his, they were able to build their home on the plot of land they received after it had been expropriated (see Chapter 2). Thus they were doing relatively well, economically speaking, especially bearing in mind that they had both come from families of quite limited resources.

Yet Rafael started having affairs with other women early on in their marriage. The ones that hurt the most, though, were with Ana's sisters:

> From what I know . . . it started when I went to have [my son] Pedro[70] . . . I had brought my sister Sandra to live with me. I was pregnant with Pedro when I brought her to live with me. She was working and needed a place to stay at night. She went to work every day and I told her, "Come live in my house, there is space, and it won't be a problem . . ." [Then] it was time for me to give birth to Pedro and she stayed in the house with Rafael. I—innocently, calmly, [I] never thought anything like that would happen—left . . . I went to my mom's house [on the farm in the Department of Chinandega] . . . I was there almost a month. In that period of waiting, she stayed in the house, and in that period what happened with her, happened . . . It happened and I never realized it [at the time] . . . It seemed like it was . . . just a few times . . . He told me about it [years later], otherwise I never would have realized it.[71]

When Ana returned from Chinandega with their new baby, she brought her sister Carmen with her. Carmen, too, caught Rafael's eye.

> Now, about the episode with . . . Carmen, it was more intense . . . [I brought Carmen] with me to help with the kids, and so that she could study, because I wanted her to study, to prepare herself, to do a course . . . and to help my mom as well. At least if I had her with me, my mom wouldn't have to be thinking about her. I took responsibility for her. That was the arrangement . . . Let's say that it was good for everyone . . . because I also needed to work . . . and with her here I could work freely, I wouldn't need to be worried because someone was at home taking care of things . . . She lived with me a number of years . . . I don't know if it was right from the beginning that they were attracted to each other . . .
>
> When I brought her with me to Managua, I didn't think about it [for a minute]. Many times, Rafael said to me, "I'm going out, I'm going to go with your sister, I want to take her to a concert in Managua" . . . He

would say, "It won't bother you if Carmen comes with me? I'm going to take her here . . . I'm going to take her there." And I would say, "No." You know, I thought, they're brother and sister . . . she's my sister, so they're like brother and sister. So there's no problem, they can go out. I always thought like that. It never crossed my mind that something else could be going on . . .

Many years went by like that—I don't know how much time . . . Until I started discovering it. Because I felt a lot of tension in the house. I would get home and I would feel it . . . they were always going out everywhere . . . And it got to the point that she would be upset if he didn't take her with him. I wondered why she would get upset . . .

Sometimes, he would come . . . maybe I was in the bathroom having a shower, and the next thing I knew Rafael would be in the bathroom with me. When I left the bathroom, Carmen would be upset . . . Sometimes at home, we wouldn't want to get up in the morning . . . it would be on the weekend, and we'd stay in our room, we'd be laughing, playing with the kids, they'd jump in bed with us . . . and she'd be . . . she'd get [upset]. I think that all that time things were going on between them . . .

[On occasion,] I'd have to race home [from church[72]] to change [Monica, when she was a baby[73]]. I would find [Rafael] in bed, and [Carmen] sitting on the side of it or . . . they'd be in the bedroom with the door closed. But I couldn't say anything, because how could I think that of my husband and my sister . . . and that tension . . . Sometimes I'd come home from work when nobody expected me and they'd be shut in the bedroom . . . many times . . . I didn't catch them doing anything. Because I'd go in . . .

Until that sister from the church came and said to me . . . "Sister Ana, open your eyes, things are happening in your house that aren't agreeable in the eyes of God . . ." She just had a vision, because they say that God reveals things to [those who are] . . . very involved with God . . . things that are hidden, that no one can see . . . with human eyes. I was seeing with human eyes, but I didn't want to see it . . .

I went to her house and we started to talk and she said, "Sister Ana, I see your husband and your sister together." And I said, "What?" It was as if I fell down, boom! . . . I said, "That can't be." I still didn't believe it. For me, my husband was something sacred, and my sister was something sacred. I couldn't believe these things . . . I started to pray and to fast . . . because at that time I was very involved with the church and always went . . . I didn't talk with Rafael . . . I was just waiting for God to talk to my heart . . . Or that something would change, be different, that it wouldn't be true. But no, it was as if God came, and opened everything up. Then I was able to see things as they were . . .[74]

Yet Ana, was still unable to confront Rafael about his infidelity, until:

One day, after being intimate with him, I went to the doctor to have a Pap smear . . . and it turned out that I had an infection. They gave me medicine, medicine, and medicine . . . and the infection hung on, it wouldn't go away . . . [It was chlamydia.] . . . [Finally,] they said . . . "The problem isn't you, it's your husband. Tell him to come in." They start[ed] to do tests on him and everything, and it turned out that the infection came from him. They gave him very strong antibiotics . . . It was then that I started to talk with him.[75]

After first denying that he had slept with anyone else, he mentioned that he had a young lover, who was a virgin when they started seeing each other. But eventually, he shocked Ana by acknowledging that he had also been with her sister Carmen, it had been going on for a while, and Carmen had become pregnant by him and he had made her have an abortion. At this point, Ana asked him if he had been with any of her other sisters and he admitted that he had been with Sandra.

It would be a bit more time before Rafael would leave of his own volition—when he emigrated to the United States ostensibly to be able to continue to provide for the family.[76] In the meantime, Ana sent Carmen home to their mother, and several of Ana's friends took her to talk with a counselor. Ana then succeeded in convincing Rafael to go to the counselor with her after she had been to a few sessions on her own. But ultimately the counselor expressed doubts about the prospects for the marriage and concern that Rafael might be capable of doing something to their daughter.[77] So Ana supported his decision to leave for the United States as the best way out of this very difficult situation.

Thus Ana's partner of many years, and the father of two of her children, also did not hesitate to become intimately involved with other women while he was married to her. He did not even have qualms about including her sisters among those with whom he embarked on sexual relationships. Yet, although sensing that something was wrong for quite some time, Ana awaited confirmation from elsewhere (from her church sister, from God, and finally from Rafael) before she talked with him about the situation. Moreover, it took Rafael's infecting her with a sexually transmitted disease to force his infidelities out into the open. Until then, Ana was unable to confront her husband about her suspicions. In hesitating to speak, Ana was keeping her marriage intact. Given gender inequalities within Nicaraguan society, men being unfaithful to their wives was considered relatively "normal" and mostly to be tolerated (c.f. Yarris 2017).

The troubled intimate relationships of Ana, Andrea, and Silvia caused each of them a lot of pain, though. Moreover, these relationships greatly undercut the women's self-esteem. Silvia went so far as to say it made her feel like "a tramp." Andrea pointed to her lack of strength in lamenting that she had stayed with a partner whom she had wanted to leave "practically always." At the same time, tolerance of behavior by their partners that reflected a lack of respect for them points to the women feeling, on some level, that they did not deserve better treatment than what they were receiving. As discussed earlier, low self-esteem is a common outcome of being subjected to physical and sexual violence. Such violence, and especially sexual violence, is in strong measure a product of patriarchy. Within this system of unequal gender relations, women and children are subordinate to men. The devaluing of women in general within patriarchy is only accentuated for girls who experience sexual abuse as children. Hence, the willingness of these women to be part of such problematic relationships was not surprising. But these relationships would have only deepened their preexisting sense of worthlessness.

Perhaps what was most notable about the painful relationship history of Andrea, Silvia, and Ana was their decision to finally separate from each of the men who had been so important in their lives. In so doing, they stepped out of the gendered role of forbearance they were supposed to assume as women subjected to the foibles of their male partners. Herein lies another expression of the fortitude in the midst of adversity that has served them well throughout their lives.

THE ROLE OF THEIR MOTHERS IN THE ABUSE ANA, ANDREA, AND SILVIA EXPERIENCED

When Ana sent her sister home in the aftermath of discovering her relationship with Ana's husband, their mother reacted quite strongly. Her reaction was telling with regard to her feelings about Ana; about the behavior of Carmen and her son-in-law, Rafael; and about her view of gender relations. When I asked Ana where Carmen went when she sent her away, her response was:

> To my mom's farm. And my mom was really upset with me about it. When I sent Carmen to the farm, my mom called and she said to me: "You're unfair . . . [and] ungrateful. Your sisters have given their lives to raise your children and then you just throw them out of the house like that." [Carmen] hadn't told her [what had happened]. I responded: "Look, Señora, don't say anything to me. I'll wait for you here. When you have time, come and we'll talk." That's how it was. When she came, I told her [what had happened]. But even then, my mom [acted like] it was normal; when I told her what my sister had done with my husband she said, "And you made such a big deal just for that?" It left me cold. I said, how could my mom say something like that? Instead of . . . grabbing my sister, and . . . calling her attention by saying that he was my husband and she needed to respect that . . . No, she told me that I had made a big deal out of it. As if to say that it was normal that something like that would go on. For that . . . these things that happen[ed], I didn't understand my mom, why she treated me that way.[78]

Evidently, Ana's mother was willing to accept behavior that Ana considered problematic. The attitude of Ana's mother also appeared to have reflected what she felt could be expected from the men in their lives more generally. That is, men were not to be held accountable for anything they wanted to do, and did do, with the women around them.

This same line of thinking might well explain the silence of Andrea's and Silvia's mother vis-à-vis the sexual and other abuse that they experienced at the hands of their father and other adult relatives. Given what Ana, Andrea, and Silvia had to say about the circumstances in which the abuse they suffered occurred, it was highly improbable that their mothers were not aware of it. And yet their mothers still failed to protect them from it.

It would seem that at a minimum, several issues were at play in the posture their mothers assumed vis-à-vis the sexual abuse their daughters experienced. These issues would have also colored the attitude of Ana's mother about the disregard Rafael showed for expectations concerning marital fidelity, especially in terms of considering one's sisters-in-law as untouchable. As suggested earlier, one issue was the larger context of patriarchy in which all of these women were raised and had to live their lives. Patriarchy affects dynamics within families in much of the world (Walby 1990; Connell 1987; Ollenburger and Moore 1992). Because it is men who have had, and continue to have, the better part of the power within most societies, they have historically also been granted control over women and children.[79] This may extend to control over their bodies.

Nonetheless, unequal gender relations have had somewhat distinct manifestations in different contexts. In the Nicaraguan context, patriarchy has fostered and been sustained by a culture in which it is assumed that "men will be men" and that they are either unable or unwilling to restrict the acting out of their sexual appetites to one partnership (c.f. Yarris 2017).[80] Moreover, their status as men rises when they are perceived to have more than one sexual partner, the latter of which is put in evidence when they have children with multiple women.[81] Women raised in this kind of cultural context may not approve of men's behavior but may find it, to some extent, unavoidable. In this effort to understand women's apparent acquiescence to these circumstances, the concept of *marianismo* may be helpful. Stemming from the Catholic faith's reverence for the Mother Mary, it refers to the semidivine status women attain when they demonstrate forbearance and abnegation in the face of the difficulties and indignities they suffer as a consequence of the close relations they have with men (as partners in particular).[82] *Marianismo* does not necessarily bring with it an acceptance of sexual abuse of children.[83] But it may facilitate a sense that abuse is not that extraordinary.

However, I would argue that another issue—the economic, social, and psychological dependence of each of these mothers on their partners—played an even stronger role in their choice to ignore the abuse being suffered by their daughters. Each of these mothers came into their relationship with the man in question (Andrea and Silvia's father and Ana's stepfather) as single mothers who were trying to support their children on their own. Within this context of patriarchy, particularly when their mothers were raising Andrea, Silvia, and Ana, men could choose whether to provide financial support for any children they might have helped to conceive. Hence, to the extent that Andrea and Silvia's father and Ana's stepfather provided their mothers with some economic support, it was more than they had before then. Moreover, as their mothers conceived and raised children with these partners, they were ever more dependent on them economically. Having a partner also gave them more social legitimacy than they had had as single mothers. So holding on to that partner became important in the face of the alternative of returning to being single mothers, now with more mouths to feed.

The economic dependence of the mothers of Ana, Andrea, and Silvia sheds light on yet another expression of the ways in which gender and class inequalities can intersect. Neither of these mothers came from economically privileged backgrounds, which, if they had, might have given them some independence from their abusive partners. Instead, they were poor *and* relatively powerless vis-à-vis the men in their lives. This conjoining of inequalities had the overarching result of submitting them and their daughters to structural violence.

In addition, Andrea and Silvia's mother, in all likelihood, would have been afraid of the physical abuse their father heaped on her. That is, even if the girls' father stopped short of leaving their mother on her own with many children to support, he did not hesitate to be physically violent toward her. It was not until their mother left their father and he sought to rekindle their relationship and live with her again (in the house her older children had paved the way for her to receive) that she was able to stop his physical abuse of her and their children. As Silvia recounted, in response to the question "Did your mother suffer a lot because of your father?":

At the beginning, yes. At the beginning [she suffered a lot] . . . until the time that she left him and went to live in the cooperative where [her older children had] bought her a house[84] . . . until that time, she suffered a lot and was very frightened of my father because my father was very, very violent . . . [But] as of the time that she left his house, that she left to live [on the cooperative], something changed. There was a moment when he wanted to retake the reins over my mother's life again, but she wouldn't let him anymore.

[Interviewer: Where did your mother get the courage (to make that change)?] . . . I think that . . . it was how he was treating my younger brothers and sisters. He punished them, he hit them violently. He had also done it with the older ones, but at that time my mother didn't have the courage [to stop him] and didn't have anywhere to go. Because he [always said], "This is my house, and [here] what I say goes." So from the moment when my mother had the chance to have her own house, she had the courage to confront him and say that there, he couldn't do just what he wanted . . .

This once he [tried to] kick her out and she said, "No, I'm not leaving here! This is my house and if someone has to leave, it will be you." So she changed completely. She didn't do what he told her to do . . . my mother put him in his place.[85]

Thus, Andrea and Silvia's mother had to tolerate her husband's abuse until she had "a place of her own" where she could define the rules. Attaining that home was made possible by at least some of her children being able to provide that measure of independence for her, which her own limited resources had kept beyond her reach.

In sum, it was probably a mixture of factors that led these mothers to endure mistreatment by their partners and the abuse of their daughters by those same partners, as well as to accept the problematic behavior of their daughters' partners. These mothers had learned to put up with emotional and physical abuse from their partners, and their silence conveyed that resignation, as well as conveying to their daughters that was just the way of the world they inhabited.

CONCLUSION

Despite their mothers' tolerance of the various types of abuse they and Andrea, Silvia, and Ana suffered at the hands of their partners—which largely stemmed from unequal gender relations within their families—this older generation of women did not succeed in socializing their daughters to assume the same degree of forbearance. Their daughters all sought means of escape as soon as they were able to by leaving their parents' home.

Although they did escape during their adolescence, the physical and sexual violence to which these three women were subjected as children had multiple consequences, such as their suffering from various illnesses, having the responsibility of raising a child that was a product of that abuse, having to start working full time at a very young age and thereby bringing their education to an end, and abiding long-term partnerships that were characterized by further emotional abuse and pointed to/reinforced their low levels of self-esteem. These consequences intersected with, and were further complicated by, the class inequalities that characterized the lives of Andrea, Silvia, and Ana. Hence, when Andrea had to leave home at age fifteen, she went with few advantages to enter the job market, as her formal education had been limited to two years of schooling at that point; when Ana was kicked out of her mother's home at age fourteen, she had not yet completed high school and was forced to become a maid in order to support herself and her baby; and Silvia also had attended school for only a few years when Andrea's home in Managua became a refuge for her. Thus the gender inequalities that had given rise to the sexual abuse they suffered were combined with class inequalities that offered them no alternative except to work to survive once they left home. This combination of inequalities stymied their possibilities for realizing their full potential as human beings in an extraordinarily clear illustration of the significance of structural violence.

Yet they each showed a strength not seen in their mothers by leaving their abusive home life. And as described in Chapter 5, they were determined that their own daughters would not suffer in the same ways that they had as children. Nonetheless, the troubled relationships that they had been part of and additional elements of the structural violence that they were subjected to ultimately forced them to leave home once again—this time to go overseas in search of a better livelihood for themselves and their children. It is to their emigration that we now turn.

4 | EMIGRATING FOR THEIR CHILDREN TO GET AHEAD

> On the planes, we leaned our heads back
> against the tall headrests, closed our eyes to
> what we had known, and imagined futures for
> our children—not for ourselves, because we
> knew that we were too old to start anew and
> filled with too much sorrow, too many regrets.
>
> *Kao Kalia Yang,* The Song Poet:
> A Memoir of My Father

> If you go anywhere, even paradise, you will
> miss your home.
>
> *Malala Yousafzai*

ANDREA AND ANA MADE their first major move from their small rural communities when they went to work in the departmental capital of Chinandega. After living in this city of approximately 48,000 for several years, their next big step was to migrate to Managua, which had a population of approximately 615,000 in 1980.[1] There Silvia joined her sister Andrea, and all three of them became part of the city's work force alongside Pamela. Then, between the late 1980s and the 2000s, Andrea, Ana, and Silvia each took another huge step in traveling abroad for work, and Pamela left her hometown—Managua—to do the same. Andrea and Silvia both began their time overseas with a short stint in the United States. In contrast, Ana and Pamela initiated their sojourns abroad in Europe—Ana in Germany and Pamela in Italy. But with time, they have all found Italy to be the most hospitable of these alternatives and have lived there for an extended period of time.

What made Andrea, Silvia, Ana, and Pamela leave Nicaragua in the first place? How did they orchestrate their moves abroad? How has the family back home fared in their absence, and what responsibility have each of these women borne toward them? How were they received in the host country? Where do they envision living in the future, when they are no longer able to work? All of these questions are addressed in the following pages. Some of the answers overlap with what migrants from any other Latin American country might respond about pursuit of a similar trajectory of emigration. In this regard, it becomes clear how structural violence—particularly with reference to inequalities stemming from class distinctions but also as these intersect with gender and racial/ethnic distinctions—contributed to the decision to pursue the trajectory of emigration. However, some of their answers are specific to the country they emigrated from and the period of history, which included a revolution, that they lived through in Nicaragua. Hence, the ways in which structured agency, of both the society as a whole and of these women, shaped their paths are put in evidence. In sharing their answers, the chapter presents in rich detail how these dynamics played out for the four women, as well as how their experiences aligned with what the literature would lead us to expect and how it differed.

THE DECISION OF ANDREA, SILVIA, ANA, AND PAMELA TO EMIGRATE

By 2008 Andrea, Silvia, Ana, and Pamela had all spent at least some time working in Europe. Given that most of the Nicaraguans who have emigrated have gone to work either elsewhere in Central America or the United States, these women stand out as forming part of a minority who have ended up in Europe. Since 2012, all four women have been settled in Italy for the medium to long term.[2] Nonetheless, the graduated way in which they engaged in this migration—three of them went for short periods of time before finally deciding to stay on for the long haul—suggests that it was not easy for them to come to terms with being so far from their families and homeland. So why did they decide to leave Nicaragua in the first place?

Ana was the first of these women to go abroad for work. As described in Chapter 2, in the late 1980s she had accompanied a family she was working for back to Germany when they returned there with their two small children. At that point Ana was still in her teens, and she looked upon this stint as an adventure and an opportunity to see another country. Although she already had a child of her own by then, she did not plan to stay abroad more than a few months, and the work in Germany allowed her to send more money home to her mother to provide support for her son. When she returned to Nicaragua after eighteen months, though, she was comfortable enough with her life in Germany that she hoped to be able to return there shortly with her son. However, the visas they needed to do so did not come through. So, she settled into the job in Managua that she had started on a temporary basis, became involved with the man she would marry, and resumed her life in Nicaragua.

The topic of working overseas did not arise again for Ana until her husband, Rafael, was considering emigrating to the United States in 2000 when he was laid off from his job with a Finnish NGO. Aside from the fact that he no longer had work and a regular income, their marital troubles also made his departure opportune. But it became clear relatively quickly that little in the way of support would be forthcoming from Rafael, although providing for the family was his rationale for going to the United States. As Ana recounted:

> He never returned to Nicaragua . . . And what he gave the kids was too little . . . almost like alms . . . and only because I asked him for it. I fought with him for it, so that he would give something, send something to his children. It's not as if on his own he said, I'm going to set up a monthly quota for the children; it was never like that.
>
> And still today, it goes on the same way. He thinks that the kids don't need [support anymore] . . . but they still need [it] . . . Now, they need it more than ever. Because when they were small, one had to buy them shoes, and to pay for school, and to eat . . .
>
> But the [children] will need [support] until they say, "I've got my diploma and I have a job," in their field . . . But he doesn't understand that.[3]

Even though Rafael was the father of two of Ana's children, he evidently did not feel obligated to provide for them once he emigrated to the United States.[4] Rather, as discussed in Chapter 3, the gender inequalities characteristic of Nicaragua meant that whether or not Rafael assisted her in this effort, Ana bore responsibility for her children's welfare.

Ana made do with her Nicaraguan salary while her three children were in primary and secondary school. But when her eldest, Carlos, was approaching college, she did not know how she was going to pay for his tuition, books, and other materials. And so she began to contemplate working overseas again. Ana and Andrea had been working together in Nicaragua and had become close friends in the process. In 2001 Andrea received a job offer from Italy. The offer came to her through an Italian woman who had worked for a NGO in Nicaragua for several periods of time starting in the 1980s.[5] The woman's family back home in Italy was looking for someone to help with domestic work and childcare. When Andrea was disinclined to accept the position, Ana proposed to her that she go in Andrea's stead. Ana commented:

> I was thinking of the two of us at the same time . . . There, they would pay me a little more. Since Andrea would be left without work, she could work here in my job. There wouldn't be a problem with that . . . I thought, "Why don't I go?" . . . I said, in six months I'll solve the problem of paying Carlos's university tuition, which had me a little worried . . . I'll save a little money, and that will help to sustain us for some months afterward. [But I] never thought to go back [to Italy] again.[6]

In a later interview Ana went on to say that another part of her motivation for going to Italy this first time was to get Rafael out of her mind.[7] These two factors—"escap[ing] a failed marriage [and] provid[ing] for children without male help"—are common reasons for women to seek work overseas (c.f. Ehrenreich and Hochschild 2003: 10). Even though Ana's husband had already "escaped" the marriage with his own departure, she had yet to let go of it and now hoped to do so.

Hence, Ana undertook a six-month stint in Bergamo, in northern Italy, working for the Rossi family.[8] Over time, this family would be the gateway to work in Italy for Silvia (in about 2002) and Pamela (in 2008) as well. Friends of this family would eventually hire Andrea (in 2002), bringing about her first move to Italy.

After Ana's first six-month sojourn in Italy, she returned to Nicaragua and went back to work for the foreign family that had employed her before she left. She had no intention of returning to Europe at that point. But after nine months Ana received a job offer from friends of the Rossi family, a couple who had moved to Portugal and were expecting a child and requested her help.[9] They were to pay her $600 US a month, in contrast with her salary of $150 US a month in Nicaragua. She decided to work for them for a six-month period. There, she was a live-in housekeeper and nanny and even took care of the yard and dogs. Several years passed, with her spending half a year working for the Italian family in Portugal and half a year working in Nicaragua. Then, after going for a year on her own to work in Portugal, it became possible to bring her two younger children there to live with her. Carlos, Ana's eldest child, was well into his studies at the university in Nicaragua. It did not make sense to move him because it was unclear how much credit the Portuguese universities would give him for those studies and he did not know Portuguese.[10] So Ana left for Portugal to stay in 2007 with just Pedro and Monica.

Things were fine for Ana with the family in Portugal until she brought her two children to live with her (in her employers' home). Then, when they asked her to travel with them to care for their children, and they expected her to leave her own children behind, she put her foot down.[11] Over time they came to an understanding that she would not be able to go with them when they left their home in Portugal.

Later on, when Pedro was approaching the end of high school and getting ready to start college in Portugal, history repeated itself for Ana. Her salary had not gone up since her first period of work with this family in 2002. Thus, paying for his university studies away from home was going to be a challenge. Somehow, she muddled through during his first year in college. But then it was time for Monica to join Pedro at the university, and Ana's salary simply was not going to be enough to cover both of her children's and her own expenses:

My kids were going to start college . . . that was far from where we lived. We lived in the south, and they would have to go to Lisbon, the capital, because there wasn't a university where we were. So I spoke with my boss. I said, well, I need to earn a little more money because my kids are going to go to college. I'm their only source of support . . . and I need to help them. Their response was . . . "Ah, no, we can't give you a raise. Your salary is set, and you're not going to earn more than that." . . . If they had appreciated me . . .

They regretted it afterward, because I did everything [for them]: I was always there at night [when they went out]; I always took care of their children, sometimes they went away for weeks leaving me with their children; and the neighbors' children even came over to sleep at the house. I took care of them all. When I left, they couldn't find anyone [to work for them] . . .

Others might have said, we'll give you a hand with your kids if you'll stay on. Your salary will stay the same, but we'll help you out with your kids. [But no], they shut the door on [that option] and said my salary was set, and there was no reason to give me more than that.[12]

So Ana emigrated again to make it possible for her children to get ahead, returning to work in Italy in 2012. There she could earn double what she earned in Portugal. Although Ana gave a month's notice, her bosses in Portugal never gave her the severance pay (about five thousand euros) that it was her right to receive. She chose not to fight with them about it, though, since Pedro and Monica were supplementing what she gave them for college with wages from working in that family's restaurant during vacations. That is to say, even with her new, higher wages, Ana still felt a dependence on this family, which opened the way for the latter to disregard an entitlement that Portugal's labor laws clearly spelled out. This situation reflected the class inequalities and immigration status distinctions that underlay her relationship with them. Hence, while Ana had left behind a specific constellation of inequalities that composed the structural violence that had characterized her life in Nicaragua, that violence remained a constant in her life. The combination of inequalities that made it up had simply been modified somewhat by her move to Europe.

Meanwhile, Ana's new place of employment in Italy was with a wealthy woman who was a daughter of the woman Andrea was working for by that time. Ana's boss was sixty-eight years old and lived on her own in Milan.[13] She had been diagnosed with brain cancer. Thus, hiring Ana—who was to live with her—gave her a measure of security that as her condition deteriorated, she would have the assistance she needed.

The downsides of this new arrangement for Ana were that she had to leave Pedro and Monica on their own in Portugal to pursue their studies at the university. And as her boss's cancer worsened and she was put on more and more medications, it affected her emotional stability. So she was verbally abusive to Ana at times.[14] In recognition of how much her employer appreciated Ana's companionship and work, however, she left her an inheritance when she passed at the end of 2016. She also left written instructions asking her son to employ Ana after her death, thereby ensuring that Ana would have continued employment in Italy.[15]

Andrea was the next of these women to leave Nicaragua. As mentioned in Chapter 2, she accepted the offer of her North American employer to go and work in the United States for four and a half months in 1997. Juan, her soon-to-be-former partner, was very stingy with support for their children.[16] So working overseas for several months was a means of generating more income for the family. And going with her employer was a way to keep her job, as she continued working for the family upon their return to Nicaragua at the end of that period. The whole experience was unexpected for Andrea:

> The first time . . . let me tell you . . . in all of my thinking and fantasies . . . I never thought about traveling, about leaving the country . . . I think what changed everything was the fact that I was traveling with [them]. That is, I wasn't going alone, and I knew I'd be back in four months.[17]

As in Nicaragua, Andrea worked as the nanny for her employer's small child while they were in the United States.[18] She earned approximately $1,200 US per month, in contrast to her $200 US per month salary in Nicaragua.[19] And she attended adult school at night to study English. At the school she was able to make a social world for herself.

In the course of three years, Andrea went with the woman and her son to the United States for two several-month periods and one ten-month period.[20] Then her U.S. visa was revoked, following a misunderstanding about exactly how long she was entitled to stay in the United States on her last trip there. After that, traveling to the United States ceased to be an option for her. So Andrea settled back into her life in Nicaragua. But by the early 2000s her financial situation was becoming problematic. As Rafael had done with Ana, when Andrea and Juan separated in 1997, Juan ceased to provide her with support for their children. In fact, when Andrea asked him for help with expenses for their children in late 2000, he simply disappeared:

When I lost my [U.S.] visa, I ran into him . . . and I told him . . . "They took away my visa, and I can't go [to the United States]" . . . I said . . . that I had never asked him for help. But . . . this year I needed his help because Clara was graduating [from high school] and I had many expenses. I was totally up in the air [jobwise] and . . . I didn't know what I was going to do . . . He didn't say anything, neither "yes" nor "no . . ." He was going to pick up the children on the thirty-first of December . . . I think I spoke with him around the twenty-seventh, because Christmas had already passed . . . The children were left with their backpacks ready to go, waiting for him on the thirty-first, and they didn't see him again . . . He didn't show any signs of life until . . . a year and half later. It was a little before I came [to Italy] . . . We realized . . . in about April 2002 when a letter arrived for each of us saying that he was in Costa Rica, that he had been gone since then, that he had been in Costa Rica for more than a year . . .

The truth is that he never gave anything, rather he came to ask the kids for money . . . Almost as soon as we separated [he began to ask for money].[21]

Juan clearly felt under no obligation to assume any responsibility for his children, much as the prevailing gender inequalities allowed of him. Meanwhile, the savings that Andrea had been able to accumulate while working in the United States had been consumed in supporting herself and their children and in helping out her parents economically in the four years since she had made her first trip there.

In the fall of 2001, Andrea was employed as a maid in the home of a Swiss woman who was working in Nicaragua. Her job situation there was not bad, and the woman's house was close to her own home. Andrea was even able to walk there if there were bus strikes. But, as she recounted:

The truth is, [my sister] Silvia [who was working in Italy at that time[22]] told me that [some friends of her employers] were looking for someone [to work for them] . . . I said . . . "See if you can find me a job, and I'll go." . . . Because where [I was working with the Swiss woman] I didn't have a great salary. Besides, she had this system that I didn't like . . . she basically paid you [in kind] . . . The things [she gave you] were useful, but money was more useful because with it I could feed the children, pay their school fees, and everything . . .

[So] I said [to Silvia], "Well then, I'll go for six months." I spoke with my children and said it would be for six months. They said, "Fine, yes, yes, there's no problem." My children never, either one of them, said, "Mamá, don't go." Never.[23]

Hence, when the second offer of a job in Italy came through for Andrea, at $500 US a month, she did not decline it. Given that by this time it had become clear it would be up to her to resolve her and her family's economic difficulties, she took this opportunity to earn a higher salary by working abroad.

After finishing her first six-month stint in Italy, Andrea did return to Nicaragua for a month to see her family. But aside from her holidays at home, she ended up staying and working for three and a half years as a maid and, later, a nanny for the couple that had brought her to Italy.[24] Andrea lived at her employers' home, which was located in a town on Lake Como. She returned to Nicaragua "for good," at the beginning of 2006, to get her son—Daniel—back on track in school and otherwise (to be discussed shortly). She went back to work for the Italian-Nicaraguan man in the couple that she had worked for off and on since 1984.[25] However, Daniel eventually ended up living with his maternal grandparents and going to school in their community in Chinandega, rather than in Managua. Meanwhile, Andrea found that her allergies and asthma worsened dramatically the more time she spent in Nicaragua. With no day-to-day responsibilities for Daniel, and Clara in college, Andrea was free to accept the standing job offer about which her employers in Italy continued to remind her.

Thus, in August 2007 she returned to Italy. By this time the couple she was working for there had two children, and Andrea was taking care of the house and the two kids. But not all was well within the couple and after two years of being in the midst of a very tense situation, Andrea resigned. Within a week, she had three offers for jobs as a live-in maid in Milan. She was hoping to not have another live-in position, though, as they typically entailed being available from early in the morning until well into the evening. In fact, in the position she had just left, she worked from 6:00 a.m. to 9:00 p.m. from

Monday through Sunday.[26] Ultimately, she accepted another live-in position with a neighbor of the couple in the town on Lake Como. Initially, this new position entailed helping an elderly woman take care of her adult daughter who has multiple sclerosis and uses a wheelchair.[27] Although her salary was to be 900 euros a month, the family quickly raised it to 1,200 euros a month. Within six months it had become clear that the elderly woman was not in condition to care for her daughter, even with Andrea's assistance, and Andrea ended up simply being the mother's aide. When the elderly woman turned ninety-seven in 2017, Andrea was still there assisting her as she aged at home.

Silvia began her work abroad when she followed in her sister's footsteps to the United States after Andrea had her visa revoked in 2000. There she lived with the North American woman and her son, taking care of him in the afternoons and doing some work around the house and in the garden. Likewise, she attended adult school to learn English and babysat other children on an ad hoc basis. She was willing to go

> out of curiosity. The advantages were enormous, because . . . in Nicaragua I wasn't doing anything then; at that time, I wasn't working. There were no disadvantages. And the possibility of getting to know other places legally . . . I would have never gone illegally. I'm a coward in that sense. [But] I had the possibility of going and of going legally, tranquilly.[28]

When the woman, her son, and Silvia returned to Nicaragua after four and a half months, Silvia stepped into Ana's shoes in the woman's home in Managua, as it was about this time that Ana left for her first job in Italy.

However, when Ana returned from her six-month stint in Italy, Silvia was left without a job. So once again, she stepped into Ana's shoes.[29] This time it was for the position Ana had held with the Rossi family in Bergamo, Italy. That first stay started in 2001. It was supposed to be for six months but lasted for almost a year and a half.[30] Like Ana, she was the Rossi family's live-in maid and nanny, with all that implied:

> [I had to be] available twenty-four hours a day, practically speaking, because I lived with them. Well, I didn't actually live with them—they lived on the second floor [of the building], their mom lived on the first floor,

> and I lived in the basement . . . They are people who like to go out at night
> a lot, so when they went out, I had to stay with the children. And when
> they went away on weekends—to the mountains or to the sea, I had to
> go with them to take care of the kids. I had a day off every two weeks, on
> Sunday . . . that is, if they didn't plan to go anywhere. Because if they had
> plans, I had to be available for them, either to stay with the kids or to go
> with them wherever they were going.[31]

Hence, live-in domestic work is rife with the potential for exploitation. This
is true wherever it exists, but immigrant workers may be even more vulnerable because of their limited ability to leave a problematic situation that provides them with both employment and a place to live while they are abroad.[32]
These types of arrangements clearly accentuate the structural violence generated through the conjoining of the inequalities of class and immigration
status (and, one could argue, of gender as well).

When that stint in Italy ended, Silvia went home to Nicaragua to see her
family. Although the agreement was that she would return to Italy after a
month, she was initially blocked from doing so.[33] The Rossi family had not
completed all the paperwork necessary for her to have a work visa to return
with; they had also failed to buy her a round-trip plane ticket from Nicaragua to Italy, which she needed to be able to enter Italy as a tourist. Then they
delayed in deciding to buy the return part of her ticket. By the time they said
they were willing to do so, Silvia already had a job in Nicaragua and concluded she would rather be there than back in Italy.

Although an additional motivation for her first stay in Italy was a desire
to get to know another country, it had not been an easy transition for Silvia
to live there. The trouble started with a misunderstanding in the airport in
Madrid, where she had to make a connection between her flight from Central America and her flight to Italy.[34] Given a discrepancy between what she
knew about who she would be working for in Italy, and what her letter of
invitation from her future employer said, Spain's immigration authorities
stopped her entry. After being held for several hours and missing her connection, she was allowed to continue on to Italy. Nonetheless:

> I wasn't very happy. Not because of the work itself. It was everything . . .
> everything changed . . . the language . . . the culture; the people were very

different . . . I never succeeded in meeting any Latin Americans, even though in Bergamo there are many of them.

For me, the first time I came to Italy was terrible . . . I never went out anywhere . . . even though I had the center of Bergamo [right] there . . . If I went out, it was with [my boss] . . . I wasn't motivated to . . . The first time [there] I didn't succeed in adapting. That's why, when I had the problem with the plane ticket to return [after my trip to Nicaragua], I was happy![35]

The challenges of adjusting to life in Italy, added to the heavy work schedule she had in the Rossi household, had made the experience one she was not enthusiastic about returning to right away.

It would be another almost eight years before she went back to work in Italy. By then, the pull to Italy was both the potential of earning a higher salary and the presence of Andrea, who was working there:

INTERVIEWER: Why did you decide to go back?

SILVIA: Because economically [it was advantageous]. It was to be able to help my mom . . . Because of my mom's illness . . . I had to help with [the purchase of] her medicines, the tests she needed to do.

INTERVIEWER: Andrea was here [in Italy] then as well, right?

SILVIA: Yes.

INTERVIEWER: Did this make it more attractive for you?

SILVIA: Yes . . . But also, I knew the language, I knew the people I was going to [work] with, I knew the place well . . . It was very different . . . it wasn't something new.[36]

When Silvia returned to Italy to work for the Rossi family in 2011, they were living in a small community outside Bergamo. She moved in with them there and worked full time as their housekeeper and nanny for the next two and a half years. Her monthly pay was 750 euros, which allowed her to set aside much more for her mother's medical expenses than her monthly salary of $200 US in Nicaragua had.[37]

However, several things changed after that point in time. The Rossi family moved back to Bergamo but did not have room for Silvia to live with them there. Were she to remain living in the Rossi family home in the small town outside Bergamo, which was an alternative they offered her, the daily commute by public transportation would have been quite long. Her other option was to find her own place to live, where she would have an easier commute. Silvia had started to go out with an Italian man shortly after she returned to work in Italy. By the time the Rossi family moved back to Bergamo, Silvia and Mauro had a committed relationship. So with the Rossi family's move, she went to live with Mauro in a different small town outside Bergamo (which was better-connected with the city).

Shortly after the Rossi family's move, though, it became clear that Silvia could no longer be expected to work the long hours she had earlier. So they decided that they only needed her to work part time, and they dropped her salary to 450 euros a month.[38] This salary was below the minimum wage for part-time work (700 euros a month), but her employers gave her one excuse after another to not raise it. They also did not help her find a second job to complement her work with them, as they had promised to do. Silvia stayed on, first because of some issues with her legal status as an immigrant worker (to be discussed shortly), and then because she was working on getting her driver's license so that she would have more options in terms of finding additional part-time work. However, by the time both of these issues were resolved, unemployment levels in the area had made it very difficult to find another position. Hence, she continued to receive a salary that meant she was far from being an equal partner with Mauro—who worked as a heavy equipment operator—in covering the couple's expenses.[39]

Pamela also went to Italy to work with the Rossi family. Because she and Silvia had worked together briefly at the Italian NGO in Managua, Silvia agreed to recommend her to the Rossi family.[40] They then offered to bring her to Italy to work for them in 2008.

Pamela had decided to go because she was in the difficult position of having to support her five sons on her own:

> Look, when I left my sons the first time, I didn't have any other option . . . practically speaking, I was obligated to emigrate, independent of the country it would be that I would go to, given the situation I was in . . . I couldn't [support us any longer]. I was alone, with all the problems. I came

here [to Italy] with the hope of giving [my sons] a better life. At least, if I have to be far away, they won't be in need of anything essential.[41]

Pamela's husband had left her and their children about five years earlier. But he had never actually been an equal partner in providing for the family.[42] Instead, even when they lived together, Pamela had to take responsibility for the family's sustenance, in the same pattern of gender inequality that we saw with regard to Ana's husband and Andrea's partner. Reflecting on her former husband, Pamela spoke of the period after she was forced out of her job in the government tax office by the economic reforms of the 1990s:

> I couldn't find work anywhere. What did I do? I went out to sell tortillas in the street, to sell cooked baby corn, to sell anything . . . I always carried [things to sell] because of the responsibility [I had]. They said my husband was "another ornament in the house." I couldn't wait to divorce him. Thank God I'm [now] divorced. In fact, the lawyer said that [my ex-husband] owed me [money] for so many things. [Interviewer question: And has he paid you?] I don't even know if he's working. Why would I waste time [trying to collect from him] . . . The divorce was finalized three years ago.
>
> . . . We were married about fourteen years. Of those fourteen years, he was in Guatemala five years . . . He emigrated there looking for work. We never heard from him. He never did anything. He came back just the way he'd gone—without anything . . . What can one do? Nothing . . . In conclusion, I said, I'm better off alone. That way I can organize things. In the house, I'm both the husband and the wife.[43]

And, in fact, Pamela had succeeded in being included in a housing program for single mothers that was financed by the European Community (EC) at the end of the 1990s.[44] She had to pay for the house in installments. Yet this program—which she had learned about in the newspaper—allowed her to put a roof over her and her sons' heads.

As her sons got older, though, she found it harder and harder to make ends meet. By this time, she was working as a receptionist at the office of the Italian NGO, earning about $250 US a month. But with six mouths to feed, and college to think about for the eldest of her sons,[45] Italy seemed like the only reasonable option.

Pamela's starting salary with the Rossi family was 500 euros a month to be their full-time housekeeper and the nanny for their children.[46] However, she found the circumstances there very problematic:

> What I didn't like [was that] I arrived in June or July, [and] in August . . . they left me with their newborn [baby] and went away on vacation. [The baby] wasn't even two months old—and I didn't even know how to speak Italian, I didn't understand it [at all] . . . Cristina[47] said, if he gets sick, here's the address of where you should take him. The baby cried day and night . . . [he] never slept—I was like a zombie . . . And they were gone . . . about two weeks on vacation—all of them. I was left alone with the baby.
>
> And then they said to me . . . you have to work on weekends. I asked how much I'd be paid. They said that because I didn't have any documents,[48] they would only pay me 25 euros a weekend. That same day I went . . . looking for another job.[49]

This would not be the only occasion on which the Rossi family held Pamela's immigration status against her, despite its depending on them—as her employers—to request permission for her to stay and work in Italy. In this case we can see how the intersecting inequalities of class and immigration status played out in the Rossi family's plan to pay Pamela a low wage for weekend work because of her lack of legal documentation. Moreover, although Pamela had earned a high school diploma and held a number of higher-status jobs than those of Ana, Silvia, and Andrea in Nicaragua, when she emigrated to Italy she found herself relegated to domestic and care work alongside the other women because of those same two intersecting inequalities.

Pamela worked for the Rossi family for about five months, then left after a disagreement with them. She moved to Milan and stayed in the apartment of some Nicaraguan friends, from where she looked for work. After several false starts, Pamela found a job as a part-time nanny in a suburb of Milan. They paid her 450 euros a month.[50] There were two problems with this job: They expected Pamela to go away on vacation with them for two months each year, during which they would pay her 550 euros a month for working as a full-time live-in nanny; and her salary simply wasn't enough to live on, after Pamela paid her rent and sent money home for her sons. Moreover, given the hours she worked (2:00 to 7:00 p.m.) and the two-month "vacations" she had to accompany them on, it was impossible to find another job to complement her income from this one. She quit that job after three and a half years.

Then Pamela had a very difficult period during which she was unemployed two or three months. The landlady where she rented a *posto letto* (a shared unit where the only private space is one's bed) wanted to evict her because she was not paying the rent.[51] She was so short of money that she could not even pay the bus fare to go for job interviews. Pamela finally found a place she could stay free of charge with an Ecuadoran woman, who also helped her find another job. In her new position, Pamela initially worked taking care of an older woman with dementia and her daughter, who was mentally ill. However, after two years of caring for both women, with the mother's dementia progressing, it had become an untenable situation. The family of the two women finally understood that it was also taking a toll on the mental health of the younger of the two women. So they put the elderly woman in an assisted living facility, and then Pamela was only responsible for the younger woman's care. Her salary was 1,300 euros a month for the eighteen hours that she was with the younger woman each day. She had worked for this family six and a half years at the time of our last interview.

In concluding this section, it is important to underline that all of these women came to Italy primarily for economic reasons. They were on their own, economically speaking. For three of the four, their children were approaching college, when expenses related to their education would increase substantially. Moreover, their parents were getting on in years and not in good health, and consequently they needed more financial assistance. Yet the women had come up against a wall in terms of being able to earn more than they had until then in Nicaragua. Ultimately, diverse elements of structural violence—including class and gender inequalities—had produced a situation in which they felt that there was no viable alternative to emigrating. In these senses, their stories are not very different from many, if not most, other female immigrants from Latin America.

Nonetheless, their path to Italy was quite different. All of them went there to work with the Rossi family or with friends of theirs. And they had come to be in contact with the Rossi family through their connections with a network of friends in Nicaragua. That network was composed of foreigners who had gone to work there, in various capacities, because of their sympathies with the Sandinista government of the 1980s. Hence, this network was of a distinct nature from those typically discussed in the literature on immigration, the latter of which points to the importance of family, neighbors, or friends as a conduit for emigration.[52] Over time, three out of the four women had moved on from the Rossi family and their friends to find other employers. But this family had been their initial point of entrée into Italy.

A VISA AND A JOB

The situation of Andrea, Silvia, Ana, and Pamela was also quite distinct from the norm of Latin American immigration to the north in the sense that they had a job waiting for them. Moreover, they did not have to cross any borders illegally to get to that job.[53] Although not all of their employers ultimately proved to be generous or considerate people, they did provide these women with a means of entering Italy, which would give them the possibility of dramatically increasing their earning power. And they did not have to put their lives at risk to get there.

Each of these four women received the visa they entered Italy with based upon the presentation of a letter of invitation from her future employer. A letter of invitation arrived for each of them once they had agreed to work for either the Rossi family or their friends. The future employer also sent them a plane ticket and met them at the airport when they arrived in Italy.

The initial visa Andrea, Silvia, Ana, and Pamela received, however, did not allow them to stay and work indefinitely. Rather, it was incumbent upon their employers to file certain paperwork to transform this initial, temporary visa, into a renewable Permesso di Soggiorno[54] (Permit to Stay), which would allow them to work for a specified period of time (typically two years). Although this process need not be complicated, for several of these women it was less than completely smooth.

For Pamela, whose first arrival was most recent, the experience was very worrisome. Since her tenure with the Rossi family was short-lived, they had not undertaken the bureaucratic process to make an extended stay legal for her. After one last disagreement with them, the man in the couple actually threatened her regarding her immigration status:

> That day, I didn't make the train [from Milan to Bergamo]. I called Cristina [to let her know], but she didn't answer. The next day, I went early in the morning . . . I got the first train and I arrived there. [Cristina] said, "Look, you were supposed to have come back here last night, because it's your duty to come here to sleep and to wake me up in the morning . . . So your punishment is that you can't go out today. Stay in your room. You're not working. Don't do anything. You're going to stay there," she said . . . I immediately went downstairs . . . I had ten euros that [my friend] Carla had given me . . . I grabbed all my things; I put them in a small suitcase. Cristina's mother-in-law came down and said, "Pamela, Cristina mistreated you, right . . . ? [Here,] take your ten euros," and I left. I had been there five [or] six months, I think.
>
> Afterwards, Ricardo [Cristina's husband] called me, and he said, "Pamela . . ." (they hadn't paid me for the last two weeks) . . . "I wanted to talk with you, because, look, we owe you money and everything." I said "Okay." "Let's meet at the [train] station in Bergamo." "Okay," I said. "We [also] want to see if you'd come back [to work] with us because we don't have anyone to leave the baby with, to take care of him." So I went [to meet him]. He said, "Will you stay?" "Yes, yes," [I said]. "I'll pay you the two weeks that we hadn't yet paid you." And he gave me [the money] . . . [Then he said,] "But remember, if you don't come, I can report you, because you're undocumented. I can report you." "Okay. Yes, yes. I'll come." [However, I thought to myself,] "He's now paid me" . . . I said, "Don't worry," and [then] I changed the number on my phone.[55]

In effect, Ricardo attempted to use Pamela's immigration status to extract labor from her, pointing again to the ways in which inequalities derived from class and immigration status can intersect. This instance is a precise embodiment of the concept of "legal violence" set forth by Cecilia Menjívar and Leisy Abrego (2012), which originates in laws that distinguish the rights of immigrants from those of citizens and which often works in sync with other types of violence—such as structural violence.

Herein I am including the distinctions associated with immigration status directly under the umbrella of structural violence, as they, too, can contribute to limiting the full realization of immigrants' potential. This can be seen in the fact that not having legal documents complicated Pamela's search for another job, when she chose to not go back to work for the Rossi family after the incident just described. And as noted in Chapter 2, when her neuralgia returned during this period of unemployment and the local first-aid office was unable to help her, she could not go to a hospital emergency room because the country's immigration authorities were detaining undocumented immigrants at hospitals where they sought care. Pamela's legal status was eventually resolved once she finally obtained the part-time job as a nanny in a suburb of Milan. Her employers there applied for her Permesso di Soggiorno and it was approved.[56] Despite the pay and conditions of this job being far from ideal, as mentioned earlier, Pamela held on to it for several years until she obtained her Permesso. After she left the Rossi family, it had become clear that she did not have the luxury of expecting the "ideal job," even in the domestic and care sector, as an undocumented immigrant.

The Rossi family also did not move quickly on fulfilling their promises vis-à-vis Silvia's immigration paperwork when she returned to work for them in 2011. As she recounted:

> The idea from the beginning was that as soon as I arrived here, we would figure out how to get my Permesso di Soggiorno . . . It was a condition [for my return] . . . We had talked about this, that I would be with them a year . . . and then, if I decided I wanted to change jobs, I was free to do so . . . without any problem. Clearly, if I wanted to continue with them, I could. But I could also go. The problem with the Permesso was, first . . . as soon as I arrived, there was a *flusso*.[57] This is when . . . you make a petition to bring someone from overseas, to work, or to live and work with you, and when immigration gives you the Permesso, then you bring the person [here] . . . [But] I had applied for this when I was already here [on a tourist visa]. Well, there was nothing to do about it . . .
>
> . . . A year and a half later, there was a *sanatoria* [amnesty]. This is for people who are already in Italy to become legal and to get work legally.

They did a petition for that [for me] as well . . . We waited more than a year for the response to that [application] . . .

During that time I met Mauro and we decided to get married . . . [the application process] still wasn't [finished] . . . they had approved me. But I [still] had to send . . . in a whole lot of documents that they requested . . . So one of [the advisors] . . . at an organization that helps immigrants get work and/or deal with legal issues . . . said that if I was thinking about getting married, I could [simply] not respond to [their request for more documents] and apply again once I was married—requesting the Permesso "for Marriage" [instead of "for employment"]. And we decided to do that . . . The problem was they had to start everything all over again in the office of the Immigration Police . . . they had to do all the verifications again . . . And it took them more than a year to . . . [complete this new process].[58]

So rather than pursuing the *flusso* option, which would have legalized Silvia's status there even before she arrived, the Rossi family had opted to bring her to Italy as rapidly as possible. The implications of this situation for Silvia were that it took more than four years for her legal status to get straightened out, and until she switched gears and applied for the Permesso "for Marriage" (almost three years into the process), she remained tied to the job with the Rossi family because the application was being processed on their behalf (that is, for their employee).[59] The disadvantaged position that Silvia found herself in during this period embodied the intersecting inequalities derived from her immigration status and class distinctions. That is, it was her employers who determined the method they would use to bring her to Italy so that it would suit their immediate needs, but it was Silvia who had to live with the uncertain immigration status that resulted from that decision.[60]

The organization that gave Silvia the advice to wait to apply for her legal documents until after she was married was affiliated with the Catholic Church, which has an office specifically to address the needs of immigrants. In addition, immigrants look to Italy's labor unions for assistance with their immigration status.[61] Given that a large number of immigrants work in the homes of Italian families, they likewise turn to unions for assistance in defending their rights as workers.[62] As mentioned in Chapter 1, domestic workers in Italy—whether or not they are immigrants—have legal rights as *workers*. And the four women at the center of this book have also used the services provided by the unions to protect their interests vis-à-vis their employers.

Meanwhile, the pathways of Ana and Andrea for becoming legally documented were much smoother than those of Pamela and Silvia. Ana's employers in Portugal processed her application for her, and eventually those of her two younger children.[63] When she moved back to Italy in 2012, she was under the impression that her Portuguese residency permit would be valid there as well. Instead, she had to apply anew for a Permesso. However, her employer was able to get her application included in a *sanatoria* that occurred the year of her return, and after some delay her permit was approved.[64]

The process of applying for a Permesso was the easiest for Andrea. In fact, it happened before she even realized that an application was submitted on her behalf:

[The first time] I came for six months . . . as far as I was concerned. I arrived on June eighth and right at that time they were legally accepting everyone who entered [the country] before June tenth. Everyone who entered before June tenth had a right to a work permit. And so, given that I worked for a lawyer, he said to me, "Why don't you go home in December and then come back?" . . . "Why don't we [do the paperwork to] get your documents." I didn't want to and I didn't want to, and things went on that way until a few days before I was to leave, when I said "Okay, let's do the documents." But I spoke with my children first.[65] And when I said "Okay, send in the [application] letter . . ." (I didn't think it was as difficult a process as it is), he said, "We've already [got your permit.] I'm a lawyer, and I couldn't risk having an undocumented person [working for me] . . . because I know the law. You are already legal."[66]

So Andrea's boss seized the occasion to apply for a Permesso for her even before she decided that she was willing to keep working in Italy, because he was concerned about having someone in his employ who was undocumented. Although he followed this path to ensure that he would not have any difficulties with his legal practice, it also made the process painless for Andrea.

When Andrea went home to Nicaragua "to stay" in 2006, she lost her first Permesso. But when she returned to Italy eighteen months later, a *fluzzo* enabled her to get another work permit.[67] The only thing was that it took a year and a half for it to be approved, during which she could not go home to visit her family. And, as discussed earlier, the situation with the family she was working for in Italy was quite distinct from what it was when she left in 2006 because of problematic dynamics within the couple. Given that she had understood she needed to stay in their employ until the processing of her application was completed, she remained in that difficult position longer than she would have otherwise.[68]

Despite any tribulations Andrea, Silvia, Ana, and Pamela might have had in the process of obtaining their Permessi di Soggiorno, they all succeeded in gaining documentation to be in Italy. Others have highlighted that obtaining such documentation was a much more likely prospect in Italy than in most other northern countries.[69] And, as noted in Chapter 1, Italy's recognized need for domestic and care workers led to the status of those who were destined for these types of jobs being especially prioritized for legalization by the country's immigration authorities.[70] Moreover, the fact that they went with jobs had put them in a privileged position vis-à-vis immigrants who arrive in the north having to start the process of looking for employment. But having legal documents put them at an additional advantage, because they could then seek out more favorable places of employment. Abundant research has shown that immigrants who are not documented tend to earn substantially less than those who are.[71] Hence, although the jobs they held were situated in the lower rungs of the employment ladder in Italy, they found those positions with relative ease and they entered the country legally to do so.

SUPPORTING THEIR LOVED ONES BACK HOME

Andrea, Silvia, Ana, and Pamela all left Nicaragua, in large part, to be able to provide more financial resources for their families than they were able to do while working in their country of origin. As their own and their families' expectations of what was possible grew—for example, that the next generation might attend college—so, too, did the expenses these women had to bear. Has their move abroad enabled them to meet these expenses, thereby allowing their children to have the opportunities they sought for them? Have they also had to assume increasing responsibility for other members of their extended family, given that they are earning more than their relatives in Nicaragua? It is to these questions that we now turn.

As discussed earlier, Ana was the first of these women to leave Nicaragua, when she accompanied the German family "home" and stayed with them there for eighteen months. While in Germany, she earned about $300 US a month, as opposed to her "good" salary of $70 US a month in Nicaragua.[72] She sent money home to her mother once a month for Carlos's care[73] and saved part of her earnings to take back with her. When Ana went to work in Italy for six months in 2001, she earned $300 US a month, about half of which she sent home every month.[74] Carlos, who was eighteen years old at the time, was responsible for managing the household's finances in her absence.[75] Ana's mother and her younger sister were living with Ana's children by then, so the funds she sent had to feed five people.[76] Her employer gave her an additional $300 US when she returned to Nicaragua at the end of that stay.

Ana's economic situation improved when she went to work in Portugal. There she earned $600 US a month. Despite sending money home every month, she stated:

> I didn't have a specific quota. [Rather,] it depended on their expenses . . . If [they had] a lot of expenses, I sent more . . . [For example,] if they got sick [for any medicine they might need] . . . Sometimes I sent up to $300, $400 US . . . The minimum I sent was maybe $250 US.[77]

As noted earlier, Ana's salary in Portugal remained the same, even after her two children joined her there. So the amount she remitted stagnated as well.

With Ana's move to Italy in 2012, she was able to send substantially more money to her children. She had continued to help Carlos financially in Nicaragua until his younger siblings were about to start college in Portugal, at which time he said that she should stop.[78] By then, having completed college, Carlos was working and able to support himself. The timing was fortuitous because it was at that point that Ana had to begin to send Pedro and Monica money for rent, food, books, and so forth:

At the beginning, when I arrived in Italy, I sent everything I earned. I was left with practically nothing, because neither one of them were working . . . I sent . . . about eight hundred [euros] at [the beginning of the month], because one couldn't send more than that . . . there was an upper limit to what one could send . . . So I couldn't send them everything at once . . . maybe a week or two later, I'd send more. [In fact,] they needed more than I earned. [So] I'd always have to ask for advances. I'd say to the Señora, "Can you advance me two hundred [euros], can you advance me one hundred fifty [euros]." . . .

Now, I send five hundred [euros], three hundred fifty [euros] a month maximum [to Pedro and Monica]. But I can't fail [to send it] because that's what the house [they rent] costs . . . Imagine, before I had to send five hundred [euros] for the house, then there were the water, electricity, telephone bills, and their food . . . I paid all of it . . . So I sent more than twelve hundred [euros] a month. The first year was really difficult. Andrea knows that history . . . because sometimes I'd go to her and say, "Andrea, do you have money you can lend me, because the kids . . . tell me their food is running out . . ." And that's how it was, month after month after month.[79]

Hence, the cost of sustaining her two children in Portugal while they went to college took all of her income once she was back in Italy. With time they started working and their dependence on her lessened, which allowed her to begin to save some of what she was earning. By 2017, Pedro had also graduated from college and was working full time. Presumably, what Ana needed to send to her children in Portugal then diminished still further. This was fortunate as, with the passing of her employer in 2016, Ana ceased being a live-in domestic worker and her own living expenses increased.

Andrea started sending money home to support her family during her initial stints of work in California. The first year she was away for four and a half months (1997), she left a reserve of money when she departed to support the household in her absence and only sent funds once. Then she brought back her savings at the end of her trip. This was providential, given that her now-former partner, Juan, essentially took what she provided for the family for his own use:

When I went the first time, Juan remained in the house . . . All the money I sent, [well,] he put the children on a diet. All the money I sent, he used for himself . . . He ran up huge debts at the [local] store. At that time, he was responsible for the household, and Claudia, our neighbor, was the housekeeper/nanny. She accompanied [the children] and helped them with their homework and everything. There were many times when she didn't have money to feed them. So she would go to the store to buy things on credit . . .

[Juan] said she could only give [the children] meat once a week, so they had chicken once a week . . .

[He was] never there. He'd leave . . . and come home once in a while. The children were sleeping alone [in the house]. So Claudia practically moved into the house . . . and her children followed her.[80]

It was not enough that Juan had never previously carried his weight in terms of sharing the household expenses. He went on to abscond with the money that Andrea provided to support their children in her absence even though he was also working at the time. This meant that she had to use some of her precious savings from her work abroad to pay off the debts that resulted from his effective theft of her remittances. At the same time, he failed to assume any parental role for his children in Andrea's absence.

So when Andrea went back to the United States in 1998, she left Silvia in charge of the household and of her remittances. Andrea sent money by Western Union every month for her children, for Silvia, and for their mother.[81] Supposedly, Juan was going to move back into the house with their children in her absence. Ultimately, he asked to be able to have the children stay with him where he was living. Only after Clara and Daniel had gone to live with him did they realize he was living with another woman and her son and that at least part of his agenda had been to extract resources from Andrea for the expenses of this other household.[82] His actions underlined the need for Silvia to be in charge of the remittances she sent.

When she started working in Italy, Andrea continued to send money for the support of both of her children. About this time, Clara was gearing up for college and was not working, and Daniel was early on in secondary school. Her daughter's godparents had committed to paying her fees for college, but

Andrea was still responsible for Clara and Daniel's living expenses.[83] Then, during Clara's first year of college, she had a baby. Although her partner had moved into their home by that time and was working, he wasn't able to pay for all of the expenses related to the new member of the family. Eventually, Clara began teaching in the private high school/college where she was studying computer engineering. However, Andrea was not able to discontinue her ongoing support until around 2014. In 2015, Clara became pregnant again, and the process was rough going. Once the child was born, it became clear that Clara had a serious health problem—and she was eventually diagnosed with antiphospholipid syndrome, an autoimmune disorder that can cause blood clots.[84] The news that Clara has this syndrome, which will be a lifelong illness, has been worrisome for all concerned. Fortunately, she has health insurance through her workplace. Nonetheless, she has had many health-related expenditures that the insurance has not covered and that have been paid for with further remittances from Andrea.[85]

Winding down her ongoing support for Daniel has been easier for Andrea. Shortly after he completed the technical high school he attended, he found a job. Once Daniel was well established in his position with the solar panel company that hired him (to be discussed in Chapter 5), he told Andrea that he no longer needed her financial support. Since then she has only sent him funds occasionally.

Yet, in continuing a tradition that began with her first job in Chinandega, Andrea has also helped to support her parents from afar. In fact, Andrea's parents relied heavily on her remittances from Italy until well into her second stay there. As her mother's health declined and several of Andrea's siblings in her family's household in Chinandega were without employment, she felt more and more responsible for supporting them:

> [It got to the point that] I was sending $400 a month to them . . . I sent so much . . . When I went back [to Italy] (in 2007) . . . everything started there . . . I went back in part for my health, and because I couldn't help [my parents when I was working in Nicaragua] . . . After I was already here [in Italy], they sent me a message saying that my younger siblings wanted to go to work in Guatemala . . . They were the ones taking care of my mom . . . [It turned out that] my dad had a debt . . . I think I

paid . . . more than $3,000 US toward my dad's debts, so that my siblings wouldn't leave my mom. That took me almost to bankruptcy . . . When I got paid, I sent my children exactly what they needed for school, food, and the person who cared for them, and the rest went toward [paying] those debts . . . I think it took me about eight months to pay the debt.[86]

After that Andrea drastically cut back what she was sending them, because she was left with almost nothing at the end of each month. Now she shares the obligation of supporting her father with her two sisters in Italy, with each sending funds once every three months.[87] Andrea still provides lower levels of assistance to several nieces and nephews for their studies. As she said, "When I see someone with a desire to study, [I cannot help but support them]."[88]

Silvia's support for their family began in earnest when she made her first trip to the United States in 2000. She brought her savings back for their mother when she returned to Nicaragua at the end of that stint. Then, as mentioned earlier, a major reason for Silvia's return to Italy in 2011 was to assist Andrea in supporting their mother, whose health-related expenditures and general support represented an ongoing outlay of funds. Before their mother's passing, Silvia, too, sent $150 US to her on a monthly basis.[89] Now, as noted, she alternates months with her two sisters in Italy in remitting funds to their father. Silvia also sends $75 US a month to one of their younger sisters, Carla, and had sent her an additional $75 US a month when Carla was in college.

Pamela sends money home to Nicaragua each month, too, for her sons' support. When she first arrived and was working for the Rossi family, she sent 300–400 euros a month to her sons.[90] Then, when Pamela was only working part time, she sent 200 euros a month. Over the past several years, two of Pamela's sons have emigrated from Nicaragua to Panama. There, they work in the construction industry and have good salaries. They also send money home to their brothers in Nicaragua. So, despite working full time and earning a substantially higher salary, Pamela now sends 200 euros at the beginning of each month, and more as needed.

These women have assumed major economic responsibilities for their families back home and overseas. Over the years, those responsibilities have changed, as their children obtained jobs and started to support themselves or as their parents' health declined or they passed. Their assistance has greatly eased the situation for their family members, even though it has meant that Andrea, Silvia, Ana, and Pamela have not been able to save much for themselves.

The willingness of these women to provide so much support to their parents and other extended family, in addition to what they remit to their children, reflects a larger, more cooperative emphasis within Latin American families. Scholars whose lens is more cultural in nature describe the population from that region as being strongly identified with their families (including the extended part of it) and as being inclined to engage in behaviors that benefit family members, at times at a cost to themselves (e.g., Carlo et al. 2007; Fonseca 1991). Mothers, in sync with predominant gender relations, are seen as exemplifying this pattern. Other scholars focus on the critical role of the family in fulfilling a social welfare function that the society and state has not fulfilled (e.g., Sunkel 2006; ECLAC 2000). This latter dynamic is particularly relevant in terms of support for the elderly, given the underdeveloped nature of social security systems in the region. Both of these explanations are helpful for understanding these women's commitment to ensuring the well-being of their extended (to say nothing of nuclear) families.

But some of their extended family, and friends of family members, have besieged Andrea, Silvia, Ana, and Pamela with so many requests for aid that, ultimately, their willingness to remit funds has lessened over time. Just a few examples should suffice to illustrate this dynamic. As described earlier, Andrea felt compelled to cut back her support for her parents when she found her own bank account in Italy empty:[91]

> Now when they call me and say, "Ah, I have problems," I say back, "I do, too." And that's where it ends . . . Little by little, even when my mom was still alive, I was cutting back [on what I sent]. When she was [still] alive, I said to my siblings, because it was true, I am having real troubles . . . It got to the point where I had . . . three euros in my account. I said, "I can't go on like this." Above all because my mom was receiving money from my nephews . . . María's sons, she has four of them in the United States . . .

[One] time I was talking to my mom, and I said to her, "I sent only a little money, $150, because I don't have any more." She told me, "Don't worry, that's not a problem, Alfredo[92] also sent me a little . . ." And so I asked, "How much did he send," so that I could relax about it. "He sent a little," she replied. "How much was that little," I asked. "$150." I was totally furious . . . and I said "'A little,' Mamá, do you know that Clara may earn that much, but maybe she doesn't even earn that much working a whole month, and you say 'a little.'"

I said to her and everyone else that they didn't have consideration for [those of us] who were working . . . that they only talked about dollars . . . that they had no idea what it took to be able to send [them money] . . . that they just bought food and whoever arrived they'd offer lunch to, [and] that everyone who arrived [at their house] arrived there to eat . . . Then, I said, it was time for them to start thinking of me . . . rather than thinking about the people who arrived there . . . who had their own homes. If I sent them everything I sent them, it was so that they wouldn't suffer hunger, not because I had so much [money].[93]

At that point in time, Andrea's parents had remittances arriving from several relatives working abroad. While their expenses had gone up as her mother's health declined, it seemed that they were also spending those funds on things other than their basic living expenses and her mother's medical expenses. Meanwhile, Andrea had been keeping her remittances to her children to a basic level of support, and her own savings had disappeared.

In Ana's case, when her mother died in 2013, she and her sisters inherited the land that had first belonged to their grandfather and then had become their mother's. As Ana related:

This last time I went [home, my sister] Isabel was saying that she wants to go to the farm, that she wants help to build a house there. She wants to go there with her husband to work the land . . . and they want me to help them . . . I can't do that . . . since I brought my children to Portugal, I need to support them. I can't support my sisters [as well]. Each one of them has made her own life . . . I said to [Isabel], I can help you get started, but don't expect me to continue helping you . . . I didn't understand the whole story . . . they want to go to Mom's farm, to take care of it, but they [expect] me to send them a monthly payment for . . . cultivating it. I said to her . . . there is no reason for me to pay someone to go to the farm. I don't want to sell it, because it's our mother's patrimony, we grew up there, and there it will stay . . . But I don't need someone to go and live on the farm, to plant it . . . I'm in Italy; I'm working.[94]

Isabel seemed to be under the impression that Ana was in a position to help her finance this project and also to send her a monthly "stipend." Yet the better part of Ana's earnings was going to support her own children.

Pamela had an even more disturbing request for remittances:

The last [thing] that happened to me . . . and stupid me, I get taken in . . . There is a friend of my sons, someone they met in the neighborhood . . . She starts to write to me about a month ago, or more than a month ago . . . she writes, "I have cancer" . . . And I felt sorry for her . . . She said, "Look, I don't have [money] for the medicine." [So] I wrote to my friend who lives in Los Angeles, who knows her . . . I wanted to check to see if it was true. But my friend [didn't respond]. [Since] she said she needed money for medicine, I sent her [some] . . . and the next day my friend responded. She said, "Pamela, it's all a lie. She goes out [all the time], she's at parties all the time, her husband doesn't work, and she goes around asking all her friends for money . . ." I sent [my sons' friend] a message . . . I told her that she was shameless, that she has no idea what it took to earn money here [in Italy].[95]

Silvia received multiple messages from the ex-husband of a friend asking for economic help.[96] When she wrote back saying that she was unable to send him any money, she did not hear from him again. That is to say, the circle of friends and acquaintances who appealed to them for "help" was large and it was not always possible to know how genuine the need was.

Clearly, some of their friends and family in Nicaragua cannot imagine how hard these women work for what they earn. And they think that because Andrea, Silvia, Ana, and Pamela earn their wages in euros, they have a lot of money. This has left them in the uncomfortable position of having to say no to some of these requests. Given that they already have significant obligations in terms of providing family support, the constant requests have also meant that they have not been able to make much headway in saving money for their own future. This is just one of the downsides of working abroad.

BEING FAR FROM ONE'S FAMILY

Probably the most difficult part of emigrating, particularly without one's children and/or partner, is being separated from them. There is the day-to-day missing them, the angst of not being there for them in crisis moments, and the sadness of not being able to watch one's children grow up. Moreover, a mother's or partner's absence can also have lasting effects. It is to these implications of emigrating that we now turn.

Andrea, Ana, and Pamela all left their children behind at least one of the times that they went abroad, and Silvia left behind the sisters and niece and nephew (Andrea's children) with whom she had been living for many years before her departure. Hondagneu-Sotelo and Avila (1997) characterize the situation the first three women found themselves in as "transnational mothering," meaning that these women continue to be a mother to their children despite being in another country.[97] This transformation in family relations was very hard for all of them. But it played out and expressed itself in different ways depending on the case.

When Pamela left for Italy in 2008, she left her five sons on their own. The eldest, who was twenty-three at the time, was in charge of the household. Because she quit her job with the Rossi family midway through her first year in Italy and it was not until she was well established in the part-time nanny job that she had her Italian immigration status resolved and had enough money to buy a plane ticket, she was unable to return home for more than two years. Of that first period of time she commented:

> One misses one's children so much when one is far away . . . I'll tell you, you can have everything. But if you don't have your children, it's not worth anything. Christmas here [in Italy] . . . doesn't exist [for me]. Nothing exists, absolutely nothing . . . In fact, when they tell me that I have to work [on Christmas], I say that's fine, because where would I go anyway? There is no happiness here. For me, it's as if one were dead.
>
> One of my sons . . . the one who applies himself most . . . the best of them all, he said to me about three years ago . . . he called and he was

crying and he said, "Mamá, have you abandoned us, do you not plan to come back?" I hadn't yet been [back] . . . He's a very special person . . . I said, "Son, wait, I'll come back, let me see what I can do. We'll resolve things there. Give me a little [more time]."[98]

Aside from the pain Pamela clearly felt, she understood that her son was deeply anguished. He and perhaps his brothers as well were worried that she had abandoned them and might not ever return to see them. Given that their father was no longer in their lives, the idea that their mother might not come home again must have generated great fear and anxiety for them.

Pamela went on to say:

Now when I went back [last month], all of them were crying when they met me [at the airport] . . . I barely recognized my sons . . .[99]

I explained to them that I have to be here because what would I do there [in Nicaragua]; there is nothing there [for me to do]. How would we eat? How would I give them [things]?

[So] the easiest thing to do was to bring the two youngest ones[100] here, through what is called Family Reunification (*ricongiungimento familiare*). I started the process, turned in the [required] documents, and the [Italian government] authorized the reunification for the two youngest [ones]. [They gave me] the paperwork . . . and I bought the plane tickets. The tickets cost me more than $2,000 US. I asked for a month of vacation time to be with them. . . . [Well], my other sons, who were used to them being all together, above all the eldest, got depressed . . . He said, "Mamá, now that the two of them are going . . . you won't come back, [will you]? And what about us?"

Just as I'm thanking God for everything . . . when they were at the airport, they had checked in and everything . . . They didn't let them leave, because the younger one's passport was missing a stamp . . . When they had done all the paperwork, no one had said anything about this . . . They had everything, and it had all been checked . . . and was fine . . . They called me from the airport . . . and said, "Mamá, look, they won't let Carlos leave, because . . ." But since they had individual tickets, [my] other son said . . . The other one was Héctor . . . the one I told you was so special . . . He said, "What should I do? I'll do what you say I should." But I could tell that he was nervous . . . [So I was worried] what might happen to him . . . I said, "If one of you can't come, the other one shouldn't come." That's how I am.[101]

This was a huge blow for Pamela. After deciding to bring two of her sons to live with her in Italy, taking the steps to make that possible, to be within a day of having them there with her and to see it all disappear before her eyes must have been excruciating for her. The loss of the cost of the tickets, which represented a substantial amount of money for her, would have only rubbed salt in her wound.

Pamela told her sons that she would see what she could do about saving the money for another set of tickets. As the expiration date for her sons' visas was approaching, she asked them what they thought about coming to Italy. They said they had decided to stay in Nicaragua. Pamela was actually relieved, because her other sons were depressed about their brothers' departure and she was worried about what might become of the younger ones in Italy. The incidence of terrorist attacks in Europe was increasing, which had her very concerned.[102] And given the high youth unemployment rate in Italy, she did not want them to leave Nicaragua only to go and work taking care of the elderly there.[103]

Nonetheless, the fact that Pamela was able to obtain Family Reunification visas for her two youngest sons in a relatively straightforward process was significant. In the United States, the northern country to which Nicaraguans primarily emigrate, such an effort would have been less likely to be successful and would have entailed much more in the way of expenses (e.g., for attorney's fees). In fact, only Italy has granted *the right* to family reunification for migrant domestic workers (Parreñas 2015).

Ana also eventually availed herself of the right to bring two of her three children to join her in Europe. Until then, she had found that leaving her family was quite painful. But each departure got a little easier. When she went to Germany, both she and Carlos cried.[104] Then:

The first time I came to Italy was also difficult, because it was the first time I was leaving . . . the other two . . . but it was somewhat more difficult because I was leaving Carlos in charge of the other two, he had to be their mother and their father . . . My mom and one of my sisters lived with them, to accompany them . . .

The kids suffered a lot, they cried a lot . . . I know they really missed me, because they were used to me coming home every afternoon after work. Monica said that she would sit down to wait for me at five o'clock . . . Monica was always the first to see me when I'd come home from work . . . she'd come running out to greet me and tump! glom on to my legs, like this! Of course, when I didn't arrive [because I wasn't in Nicaragua], she said she'd wait all evening sitting on the sofa looking out the door wondering when I'd arrive . . .

After that first time, they would say to me, "Mamá, you won't leave again, will you?" They were always asking me. [And I'd respond], "No, I won't go." Then [along] came the opportunity to go to Portugal for six months . . . [But] each time it got easier for them and for me as well.

Pedro even marked the calendar [every day to keep track of] how long it would be before Mamá would arrive [back].

[Coming here to Italy in 2012] was another shock . . . It was different [leaving them] in Nicaragua, because [there] they were at home . . . I suffered [then too], but I knew that they were at home . . . they had their grandmother and other relatives nearby and their brother was taking care of them. But when I came here [to Italy] from Portugal, I was leaving them on their own. They were young.[105] And I imagined everything they'd get into. I couldn't stop thinking about it, day and night.[106]

With time, Ana has adjusted to the distance. She has been able to see Monica and Pedro at least twice a year, given the inexpensive airfares within Europe. She was also able to return to Nicaragua for Carlos's graduation from college and his wedding.[107] Meanwhile, Monica and Pedro each have a partner, as well as each other, in Portugal. Carlos has his own family in Nicaragua. So although this is not how Ana would ideally like to live her life, she has become accustomed to having her family spread out among several different countries.

The emotional cost of separation is not always readily apparent, however, as Andrea has learned over the years. As noted earlier, the first time Andrea went abroad, the father of her children was mostly absent. Her son Daniel was six years old at the time. His older sister Clara and the neighbor (along with her children), with whom they were very close, were there with him. But this was the beginning of being left without either parent at hand. Over the years of his father being gone—he was absent from his children's lives for ten years while he was in Costa Rica—and his mother working overseas for periods of time, Daniel felt more and more alone.

It all came to a head in 2005, by which time Andrea had spent about three years working in Italy. Then, for the second time, he dropped out of school partway through the academic year.[108] Andrea recounted:

> [In addition], he was involved with gangs and drugs. Once he had to go to the hospital because he overdosed on a cocktail of drugs . . . He did all kinds [of drugs], but he didn't inject himself . . . He smoked, and I think he took pills as well. That time, they'd given him a mixture [of things] . . . and he was trembling and saying to Clara, "I'm going to die, I'm going to die. Call the hospital, call the hospital." Clara took him to Manolo Morales [Hospital], and by the time they got there, the [bad] reactions had passed.
>
> At that point I told him to come [to Italy]; I wanted to bring him [over here]. [But] he didn't want to [come] . . . He didn't go to school. He didn't talk to the family. He fought with everyone. He shouted at everyone . . . I wanted him to study languages . . . To take up a sport, given that he wasn't studying. He didn't want to do anything. And it reminded me of when I, too, didn't want to do anything[109] and I realized that it was time for me to go back and be with my children. More than anything, at that moment, he needed my presence more than my money . . .
>
> And he was stealing things with the gang. He stole a pair of shoes from [his aunt] Silvia. Actually not a pair, just one. I think it was some kind of initiation [thing] . . . He felt completely alone. When someone would say something to him, he said, "The only person who can tell me anything is my *mamá*." And I was [over] here, [so] what could I say? I did say things to him . . . At that time, I was calling him almost every day. But that was different from being there. So, I went back.[110]

Andrea gave up her job in Italy and returned to Nicaragua to pull Daniel back from the brink of the major trouble he was heading toward.

The next year and a half was difficult for Andrea and Daniel. He still did not want to go to school and he asked her for all kinds of expensive things, which she had forewarned him she would not be able to afford if she returned to her job in Nicaragua.[111] Moreover, she was not all hugs and kisses but also assumed a firm stance with him in terms of what she would tolerate. Andrea insisted that if he was not going to attend school, he had to work and split the household expenses with her. Working in construction, Daniel was able to earn a reasonable salary. But he wanted to spend the money on himself rather than on the household. When faced with the position of his mother, he back-tracked and tried to enroll in school. Nonetheless, the deadline for enrollment had passed everywhere he tried to get into school in Managua. So, as mentioned earlier, Daniel ended up studying in the local school near the home of Andrea's parents in Chinandega. After completing the school year there, the next year Daniel again did not want to go to school. When Andrea starting looking for work for him in Managua, he realized that those were going to be his two options and he decided that school was the lesser of the two evils.

Although Daniel continued studying in Chinandega, he had not quite settled down. For a period, he was spending time with one of Andrea's younger brothers, and together they were taking drugs.[112] In her frustration, Andrea told him that she was going to let him decide how to live his life. However, subsequently Daniel shifted to socializing with a different group of young people and there he met Carolina, whom he would eventually marry. Given that Carolina's parents were not initially impressed by Daniel,[113] and that Carolina was quite a bit more mature than him (she was six years older), he gradually started to take school and finishing it more seriously. Before Andrea returned to work in Italy in mid-2007, she had identified a school in Granada[114] where he could complete his secondary education and get a technical diploma (as an industrial mechanic), and she paid the tuition for the following year. He finally graduated in 2010.

That outcome allowed Daniel to find the job he holds today (as discussed earlier). But it would seem that the years of his mother's absence were very hard for him and that certain aspects of that experience remained painful. As Andrea commented:

When I left my granddaughter, it was different—she said, "Grandma, don't go." My children never said that, ever. Daniel didn't [even] go to the airport to pick me up, nor to drop me off when I left. I always thought that it didn't matter to him . . . [But] it was that he couldn't stand to . . . I felt like what interested him was just the things [that I could bring back] . . . And at times when he came to pick me up [at the airport], he was so cool . . . And then I'd be there for my vacation . . . and it's not as if he gave me a lot of attention, as if he hung around . . . He was always like, "If you're here, it's okay, and if you're not here, it's okay." . . . Now that he is older, though, he says "Mamá, I didn't go to drop you off because I couldn't . . . Emotionally, I couldn't." But he didn't show me and he didn't tell me either . . . And I say, "If you had told me, even once, 'Mamá, don't go . . .' I'm sure I wouldn't have gone . . ."

So that's where I am always with Daniel, in a constant battle to understand what he is trying to tell me. Because he says one thing and he acts another way. It's tiring. It's tiring because at this point, I would think he would be old enough to tell me, "Mamá, I don't like this and this and this . . ." That's why I've proposed that we go to a psychologist [together] . . . even before I left I proposed it. He's totally rejected [that proposal] . . . [He says,] "A psychologist isn't going to cure me, I'll cure myself." I say [back to him], "One doesn't cure oneself on their own . . . perhaps a psychologist will give you ideas, or just the idea that [they are] listening, and you can reach your own conclusions, but at least you'll be talking [about things]" . . .

[He says,] "Mamá, leave it"—and with that tone—"Don't go around spending your money on things that are useless. Let me deal with it." I [always] say, "Well, at least find someone you can talk with." He talks with his wife . . . And it's because of her that I've realized how he felt. Because she has pushed him—saying, "Tell your *mamá* why you wouldn't go [to the airport]." . . . So he said, "Mamá, it was because I couldn't stand the idea of seeing you leave again. And I [thought], I wish I could grow up so that I could support her and she wouldn't have to go [away]." These are things that he wouldn't tell me if she didn't push him to.[115]

Andrea and her son are still grappling with these difficult feelings all these years after her first trip abroad.

Moreover, Andrea noted that her absences had coincided with a drop in her daughter's grades in secondary school.[116] Clara had been a stellar student in elementary school. Yet, as discussed further in Chapter 5, this changed as she moved on in school. Like many young people in secondary school, Clara became more interested in social and romantic relationships. So she may have been less focused on her schoolwork than in the past.

As noted in Chapter 1, research has observed that the likelihood of children falling behind in terms of their grade level and dropping out of school increases when a parent goes abroad to work (c.f. Démurger 2015; Dreby 2010). While Heymann and colleagues (2009) caution against assuming that this always occurs, they argue that a critical factor in determining the impact on children left behind when a parent emigrates is whether that parent had been the principal caregiver. In the case of Andrea's family, she had clearly always been the principal caregiver, so her absence would likely have made more difference to their children than that of their father.

Had Andrea remained at home in Nicaragua, her presence might have forced Clara to pay more attention to her studies and less to other distractions.[117] If that proved true, Clara's efforts to gain admission to college right out of high school might have been successful. But it is impossible to say definitively that this would have occurred.

Likewise, if Andrea had not left Nicaragua to work in Italy, Daniel might not have become involved with the local gang and she might have been able to exert more of an influence over him so that he would have stayed in school during the two years that he discontinued his studies. However, it is unlikely that all of the young people in Nicaragua who are gang members have parents who are working out of the country. Here again, we will never know if he would have stayed in school both of those years if Andrea had been present. Nonetheless, Andrea still bears the burden of these doubts on her conscience. And the knowledge of how bad Daniel felt each time she went away and the communications issues that arose between them as a consequence of it still weigh upon her.

ADVICE FOR OTHERS ABOUT EMIGRATING

The pain resulting from leaving behind loved ones, especially one's children, led each of these women to say that their advice for a fellow Nicaraguan who was considering emigrating was to stay home if it was at all possible.[118] They argued that one should explore every option in one's own country before leaving.

Certainly there were negative aspects about going abroad, but it also had its upsides. Andrea, Silvia, Ana, and Pamela all spoke of the economic benefits of working overseas. Most importantly, it allowed them to support their children's studies. It was what had made a university education a viable option. That is, they felt that their emigrating helped their family "get ahead." They also mentioned how valuable it was to meet new people and to get to know other places and other cultures.

But their list of disadvantages was significantly longer than that of advantages. First, they all mentioned missing their families. Silvia spoke of being away from the family that raised her.[119] Andrea talked of leaving for one of her stays abroad when her son, Daniel, was still a child, and returning to find him with mustache hair.[120] She spoke of "the years lost," in referring to not being there to see her children grow up. Ana mentioned having to start all over again, particularly with reference to her return to Italy after living off and on in Portugal for ten years.[121] Pamela spoke of the loneliness one experiences, which is an emptiness that nothing fills.[122]

Pamela also suggested that if one has to go away and leave one's children back home, it is essential to bear in mind that you are going to work.[123] One cannot be too demanding about the type of work you get. When one has responsibilities, one has to take the jobs that exist.[124] And, as Andrea said, "one isn't going to live the grand life, like everyone thinks . . . you have to sweat [for your salary]."[125]

Pamela also advised that one needs to find ways of staying connected with one's children. In commenting on a Nicaraguan friend in Milan who has a difficult relationship with her three children back home, Pamela implied that the woman was too caught up in her own life in Italy and did not stay in touch with her children. If one wanted that relationship to stay strong, and for one's children to stay out of trouble, then communicating with them was key:

> If one wants to work far away, which is worthwhile, one needs to stay close to one's children . . . to stay as close to one's children as you can. I'm not going to stop communicating with them just because I'm far away. No. One can't abandon one's children. Even more so now that there are so many means of communication. So one can't say, I couldn't communicate with my child, which is why my child ended up going down the wrong

path, and is involved with gangs. That can't be justified . . . The proof is I've always been present for my sons, even if I'm far away . . . [What is important is] having a presence, giving them love, and taking responsibility [for them].[126]

And, as Andrea learned, when communicating from afar is not enough, sometimes one needs to move back home and be physically present for one's children.

EXPERIENCING DISCRIMINATION

Something else that those contemplating emigrating must consider is the potential for experiencing discrimination in a country that is not one's own. Until the 1980s, Italy was largely a sending country in terms of immigration (Calavita 2005; Ambrosini 2013). Domestic immigration consisted of southern Italians moving north within the country. This meant that other than certain tourist destinations—such as Venice and Florence—most of those who dwelled in the country were natives. As of the 1980s, the situation in Italy has undergone a reversal, and it is now a major receiving country for immigrants (Calavita 2005; Ambrosini 2013; Devitt 2018). In fact, it has become a gateway to Europe, with hundreds of thousands arriving there every year. With the surge of immigration to Italy, some of the population has reacted negatively toward the new arrivals.[127] This attitude found an echo in Italy's political sphere, as became apparent when the Northern League party led by Matteo Salvini—a right wing, anti-immigrant politician—won a major victory in the parliamentary elections of 2018. As a result of that victory, Salvini became the country's deputy prime minister and minister of the interior. From those positions, he put in place a number of policies designed to slow the arrival of immigrants from the Global South.

Meanwhile, Andrea and Ana had both encountered that discrimination in their daily lives in Italy. Ana was quick to point out that it was mostly older Italians who expressed hostility toward foreigners. She recounted several experiences of discrimination:

Once, in a supermarket, I had an experience with a man . . . I would assume that he is that way with all foreigners, it wasn't only me. But it happened to me . . . I was at the checkout stand. I have the things I want to buy and I want to put them on the conveyor belt so that I can [eventually] pay for them. The man was before me . . . and he starts to say, "You wait, you shouldn't put your things there. Can't you see that I have my things on the belt." I said, "Yes, don't worry . . . I'll wait my turn" . . . [Then] he's on the other side of the register and I see that his things are gone, and I start to put mine on the conveyor belt. Even then [he starts in again,] "Can't you wait . . ." The cashier stares at him . . . and [finally] says, "Sir, pardon me, but she's there, and you're here. I'm done with your purchases." He's putting his things in the bag and saying to me, "How rude, she couldn't wait . . ."

Another episode that happened to me was . . . I was someplace and I didn't know where I was. I went up to a woman and asked her, "Where is such and such street," and she said to me. "I don't know . . . Go away . . . I don't know where that is. Please go away." It seemed that she was afraid that I was going to do something [to her] . . .

So I think they are rejecting [me] for being a foreigner. That's what I feel anyway. At a minimum, they're afraid . . . I don't know if it was that way before. But since I've been here . . . people mistreat you because you're a foreigner . . . As if you were ignorant . . . and aren't worth anything. As if you were a fly in the soup! It's more or less like that.

[Interviewer question: Is there a general ambience of discrimination?] [No,] I'd say it's specific people. Above all, older people. The youth accept people of color and immigrants who are here in the country. But older people, yes, they blame one for what's happening [in the country], for everything . . .[128]

So Ana did not see all Italians as discriminating against the immigrants who have gone to work in Italy, but rather it was individual Italians who did. In the two instances she related, both of the Italians involved were older people. Older Italians would remember a time when Italy was mostly populated by native Italians. Since Ana's skin is significantly darker in color than that of the average Italian, she would probably not have "passed" as a native of the country.[129] This may be why the several people she spoke of reacted to her in the way they did. In contrast, younger Italians would have grown up with much more diversity in their midst, so it would seem more "normal" to them.

Andrea also felt discriminated against in Italy. In discussing it, she compared the discrimination she had experienced during her several stays in the United States with what she had been subjected to in Italy:

> When I was in the United States, yes, [I felt discriminated against]. Above all in the buses . . . it was pretty blatant, but I think it was also because of the language . . . when one doesn't have a [strong] command of the [English] language, that's where I felt it, to tell you the truth . . . when you have problems communicating, people aren't very patient.
>
> But . . . at certain times, I have felt the racism here much more . . . because it is directed [right] at you. It's not just that you overhear it. It's directed right at you . . . I had Facebook for a time, a while ago, and I had as friends many people who I had met while I was moving around for my work here—and there they expressed their racism in a very violent and clear manner . . . [They would write things like:] "Foreigners come here . . . [to] our country. It's not even ours anymore, it's theirs." . . . [Mind you,] these weren't just people I met through social media. They were people I met personally. . . . they would engage with you personally, and then write those kinds of things . . . knowing that the majority of their friends were foreigners.[130]

Hence, Ana and Andrea found that confronting racism was periodically part of their lives in Italy.[131] Several types of inequality intersected to produce these expressions of discrimination: racial/ethnic, immigration status, and probably class distinctions as well. Such actions and attitudes embodied the structural violence that characterized their reception in Italy.

LONG-TERM PLANS

Despite the multiple disadvantages of their lives in Italy, Andrea, Silvia, and Ana do not foresee leaving the country anytime soon. When asked about their long-term plans, none of them could say that they definitely envisioned retiring in Italy. Yet this option was one they were certainly considering. Silvia and Andrea were both contemplating obtaining Italian citizenship, which suggested an inclination to stay in the country for the foreseeable future.[132] Pamela, however, hopes that in the medium term she will be able to reunite with her sons in Panama, where (as mentioned earlier) two of them are already working. Clearly, Pamela feels both less connected to Italy and a stronger pull to be near her five sons. But what might be the reasons for Andrea's, Silvia's, and Ana's lack of strong interest in returning home to Nicaragua when they are no longer working in Italy?

They have some specific reasons and some more general ones. Silvia is now married to an Italian man. And they have an apartment that they are in the process of buying, which is located close by his family. Her husband, Mauro, also has a steady job. He has expressed an interest in moving to Nicaragua when he retires, yet he has not accompanied her there on her trips "home."[133] And now that her mother has passed, Silvia no longer feels a real pull to return to Nicaragua to live. Moreover, she opined that the economic, political, and social situation there would need to undergo serious changes for her to want to build a life there again.

Two of Ana's children live in Portugal, and one lives in Nicaragua. But she now also has a partner of several years in Italy. Joaquín is Ecuadoran and has lived in Italy since 2001. With his earnings from working in Italy, Joaquín has bought a house back in Ecuador, which is occupied by one of his five children.[134] Yet because of the constant tensions between his children, most especially with regard to jealousies about the remittances he has sent them, he was not anxious to return there.[135] And Ana's relationship with her sisters, all of whom still live in Nicaragua, was such that she, too, was not drawn to "go home." Furthermore, with the inheritance she received from her most recent employer, she was buying an apartment for herself and Joaquín in Italy.[136] Such a purchase reflected her commitment to continuing to work in Italy for the medium term, although her long-term plans remained unclear.

Over time Andrea found that her health—most especially in terms of her allergies and asthma—was a lot better when she was living in Italy than in Nicaragua. As discussed earlier, the environment of Nicaragua was harmful for her allergies and asthma. On each trip home, they got worse the longer she was there. An essential condition for her to return to live there would be that she be able to obtain the ongoing vaccinations that she began to receive in Italy and that have radically improved her quality of life.[137] Those vaccinations were still unavailable in Nicaragua. But she is hopeful that in the medium term, they might become so.

However, should they choose to stay in Italy, all four of these women could look forward to receiving a government pension. All of them have been paying into the social security system there. If they do not work long enough to earn social security, they will receive what is called a *social pension*. A social pension is available to those who have at least a Permesso di Soggiorno, have reached retirement age and do not receive social security, and are relatively poor. It is not a lot of money—in 2016, it came to 460 euros a month, or roughly $500 US—and they would have to reside in Italy to receive it. Still, it is more money that any of these women could expect to receive in Nicaragua. And Silvia is also entitled to receive social security through her husband.[138] So whether it comes through the regular social security system or the social pension system, there are clear financial incentives to eventually retire in Italy. Nonetheless, Pamela, who intended to go back to Central America to retire, was using part of her salary in Italy to pay into the social security system in Nicaragua.[139] She planned to rely on the Nicaraguan social security system when she retired.

Hence, working in Italy has put Andrea, Silvia, Ana, and Pamela in a fundamentally distinct position than they would, in all likelihood, have been in had they stayed in Nicaragua. With the pensions they will earn in Italy they will be at least somewhat self-supporting in their old age. Although Pamela is aiming to do so through the Nicaraguan social security system, her salary from Italy is facilitating that. Thus, they will not have to follow in their parents' footsteps, nor those of most people in their social position in Nicaragua, of relying on their children to support them once they are too old to work.

CONCLUSION

For Andrea, Silvia, Ana, and Pamela, the decision to work overseas stemmed from the responsibility they felt to support their children and aging parents,[140] as well as to open up possibilities for their children to have futures distinct from their own. Although they came of age during a revolution in their country, which opened the way to thinking that the limitations of their "place in life" might be improved, the process of change in Nicaragua came to a halt in 1990. Moreover, even while the Sandinista government was in power in the 1980s, the prospects for a fundamental reshaping of their lives dimmed with each passing year of the Contra war and the deepening economic crisis that impacted the country. But the revolution had given them a new consciousness of what was possible. Emirbayer and Mische (1998) speak about such a possibility resulting from a situation of great change as exemplified by a revolution. This new consciousness would remain with them even after that process of change had been curtailed. In fact, while these women no longer had great expectations for themselves, they wanted their children to have different options than they had.

The revolution also bequeathed to them access to the network that made their emigration possible. That network meant that they were fortunate enough to be able to go abroad legally and to have jobs waiting for them at their destinations. This gave them an advantage over those who emigrate and then have to find work without legal documents. In these senses, their experience diverged from that of many immigrants discussed in the literature on immigration to Italy and elsewhere in the Global North (e.g., Boyd 1989; Parreñas 2015; Solari 2017; Gonzales et al. 2019). Yet Andrea and Ana experienced discrimination in their receiving country—Italy—because they were immigrants and people of color. And all of them felt the hardship of being far from home and their loved ones. They advocated for staying and working in one's home country if at all possible.

Nonetheless, their work abroad has enabled them to support their families in ways that it would not have been possible to do in Nicaragua, and they have been able to lay the foundations for taking care of their own needs as they age. In these senses, they have been agents of (small-scale) change vis-à-vis the prospects for themselves and their families given the social positions they occupied in Nicaragua prior to their emigration (à la Hays 1994). They *have* been constrained to working in the care sector of Italy's economy[141]—a sector that three of them had already been relegated to in Nicaragua—because of gender and immigration status inequalities. Moreover, Andrea, Silvia, Ana, and Pamela have not been able to share these years with their families back home. Yet they have seized the opportunities afforded them through emigration to shift the course of their own and their children's lives. It is to those distinctions in their children's lives that we now turn.

5 | THE CHILDREN OF ANDREA, ANA, AND PAMELA

Education is the passport to the future, for tomorrow belongs to those who prepare for it today.

Malcolm X

Let us sacrifice our today so that our children can have a better tomorrow.

A.P.J. Abdul Kalam

WITHIN THE CONTEXT OF STRUCTURAL violence that characterized the worlds of Andrea, Ana, and Pamela, these women made significant sacrifices so that their children would have less restricted options than they themselves had to decide what they would do with their lives. That is, rather than accept that their children would have to suffer in the ways they had from the multiple inequalities that marked their society, these women aspired to much more for them and were determined to do what they could to make those aspirations a reality. This chapter explores how their children's circumstances have differed from their own. In doing so, it examines the environment in which their children were raised, the opportunities they had in terms of schooling, and the fields in which they now study or work as young adults.

As we delve into the lives of this next generation of Nicaraguans, we also look at the factors that contributed to the differences between their children's experiences and those of these three women.[1] Because Andrea, Ana, and Pamela became adults during the revolution that took place in their country starting in 1979, and some of the benefits of that process of change fell to their families and themselves, we consider the extent to which this may have played a role in any of those differences. Nonetheless, other things augmented the resources available to these women. Those, too, are identified. When asked directly, each of the women attributed the distinctions between their children's lives and their own as largely being due to their years of hard work to make that possible. Therefore, we take a close look at this factor as well.

In order to explore these dynamics, we need to return to Nicaragua and go back in time, far from the present-day existence of these women in Italy. It is to these issues that we now turn.

THE BASIC CIRCUMSTANCES OF THE NEXT GENERATION

The children of Andrea, Ana, and Pamela always had their most basic necessities guaranteed, which represented a major contrast from the childhoods of these women. For example, they did not experience the hunger their mothers did. As Andrea stated:

> In the first place, my children didn't suffer from hunger . . . there were difficulties and all that, because, remember in the '80s, it was hard to get food . . . [But they didn't experience hunger] because I had the things from [my boss's ration] card.[2] [They] gave me the right to [use their] card. And then I had my own. This was not only different from how I was raised but also from so many people in the neighborhood.[3]

So having something in their stomachs was not a daily preoccupation for the children of these women, allowing them to concentrate on other things, like their schoolwork and playing with their friends. Having regular meals also meant that they were not subjected to the troubling effects of malnutrition on their health and physical and mental development.

They also had mothers who were attentive to their health more generally and could provide them with access to the care they needed. Andrea recounted: "When I saw the first . . . symptoms that Clara was also going to be asthmatic, I took her running [to the doctor] and I was always conscientious about her care until the asthma disappeared."[4] That concern with their care has continued to the present, as even from afar Andrea gathers medical information and advice to pass along to Clara about her autoimmune disorder and sends money to help with her health-related expenditures.

In addition, the children of Andrea, Ana, and Pamela benefited from having a roof over their heads. Moreover, the home they had—although not always from birth—belonged to their parents, as opposed to being the property of extended family members. Their parents came to be in possession of these homes through different means. But in at least two of these cases, that means was connected directly or indirectly with the process of change that was set in motion when the Sandinistas came to power in 1979.

In Andrea's case, the foreign couple she was working for in the 1980s joined with two of their friends to purchase a humble home for her and her family. This enabled them to move out of their rented one-room hovel. As Andrea recounted:

> This is a quite a story . . . Clara [my daughter] was four years old, so it was '88 . . . Clara couldn't believe it when we moved into the house and it had two doors. "Mamá, I'm going to eat outside, so that I can breathe the air!" I don't know . . . when [they] got the idea to buy me a house. I just remember that they told me . . . we've decided that between all of us, we're going to help you buy a house . . . I couldn't believe it, a house of my own . . . And we started to look . . . all over. . . . until we found that one . . . The lot was big and the house was small.[5]

Although their new house needed work, it was a vast improvement over where Andrea and her family had lived previously and, most importantly, it belonged to them. Her employers and their friends who had made this move possible had come to Nicaragua to work in distinct capacities in relation to the Sandinista government.

In Ana's case, she and her husband had received the land where they built their home after it was confiscated by the Sandinistas from someone who had been closely associated with the Somoza regime. Then they pooled together their earnings to construct that home. Ana's earnings came from working for a different foreign family, which was also in Nicaragua because its members were interested in working with or studying the process of change under way there. Her husband's earnings came from working for a foreign aid organization that was there to assist the government, both that of the Sandinistas and those that came after it.

Pamela was the exception in this regard, in that an EU assistance program, which was administered through the government, enabled her to purchase a home. The program was implemented in 2000, long after the Sandinista revolution. Pamela was fortunate to be able to access this program, given the lack of economic support she received from her husband. When I asked her about her husband's participation in keeping their family economically afloat, she said that he had provided her with "nothing." She went on to specify that he had given her

> nothing significant. In fact, this house that I have . . . I submitted my documents [for it] as a single mother . . . because it was only for single mothers. He asked me why I was going to [apply].[6] [So] I asked him, "Are you going to buy me a house?" . . . He asked me, "Why don't you say that I'm your husband?" "Do you think it's nice when a woman has to go out and ask her neighbor to borrow money . . . for that, one has a husband who is supposed to be responsible for the household." It was embarrassing to me to say that I had a husband . . . So I applied as a single mother. And thank God they were able to give me the house. When he left . . . his mother called me and said, "Pamela, how are you going to resolve the problem of the house?" . . . "This house is mine," I said. . . . because, in fact, my mom told me, "Never share expenses." I never permitted him, aside from the fact that he didn't have it, to give me even one payment toward the house. Never. Because I didn't want him to have any right to it. So I could say, "All of this is mine."[7]

Hence, this housing program for single mothers granted Pamela the possibility of having a home that was legally her own, which gave her and her sons a secure place to live. Meanwhile, this quote suggests that Pamela still had some belief in the ideal that one's husband should "be responsible for the household," although it had not worked out that way either with her mother and father or with her own husband. But she also absorbed from her mother that a woman must not rely on her husband, which her mother must have learned through long experience. At any rate, by mid-2018, Pamela had paid off what she owed for this house.[8] Her earnings from her work in Italy had also allowed her to purchase two lots nearby her house in Managua, so that her sons might eventually be able to build their own homes there.

Regardless of the source, for the children of Andrea, Ana, and Pamela, having parents who owned the family's home meant that they did not experience the dramatic insecurity concerning housing that Ana and Pamela had experienced as children.

THE POSSIBILITY OF GOING TO SCHOOL

The sons and daughters of Andrea, Ana, and Pamela also all had the possibility of going to school, rather than working, when they were children. They were not kept home to help with the work there, or forced to go out to work instead of going to school. That is, their mothers decided that ensuring their children's education would be a priority and figured out how to manage it financially.

For Andrea and Pamela, the fact that they lived in Managua by the time they had children would have facilitated this. However, even for Carlos (Ana's first child), who was the only one of this group of children to spend his early childhood in the countryside, access to education was not an issue. Carlos stayed in the hamlet where Ana had lived with her mother and stepfather when she went to work in Chinandega as a teenage mother. As mentioned in Chapter 2, he lived there until he was fourteen years old. Yet the community had a local public school, which Carlos attended. Then, once Ana was married and had her own home on the outskirts of Managua, he joined her there. His secondary education was not all completed in the same school:

> [Carlos] went to the public school in Monte Tabor [which was approximately a two-kilometer walk from our house on the outskirts of Managua]. He did secondary school there . . . [and] he went to Managua to finish—to a school in San Judas . . . After that, I took him out of San Judas and I put him [in a school that was] closer, because that was a long way to go [each day]. So I put him in a private school. At that point, I had the means . . . I put him in a school at 7 Sur . . .[9] He finished secondary school there, it was his last year. He graduated from there.[10]

Moving around from school to school may have been a less than ideal experience for Carlos.[11] Yet it did not impede him from gaining admission to, attending, and graduating from the country's premier university for engineering (see the discussion that follows).[12]

The rest of these women's children grew up in Managua or on its outskirts and attended a mixture of public and private institutions. For example, as mentioned in Chapter 2, Andrea's daughter went to a public daycare center/preschool that was opened in the 1980s for working mothers. It was relatively close to Andrea's house and allowed her to leave Clara in a safe place, which was also educational, while she went to work. When it came time to start primary school, Clara also shifted schools a fair amount. She started her studies in a Jesuit academy with financial assistance from Andrea's employer.[13] However, it quickly became clear that it was located too far from their home for it to be feasible for Andrea to get her back and forth to school with her newborn son in tow. Aside from the distance, bus strikes became a common phenomenon in the early 1990s, as there was significant resistance to the neoliberal economic policies of the Chamorro government at that time. Therefore, Andrea prioritized keeping Clara close to home when she selected a school alternative for her to avoid having to rely on public transportation. Clara attended first one then another local public school for her early years of elementary school. By the later years, though, and for all of her secondary education she went to a private religious school. It was run by an evangelical church and it was located in their neighborhood.[14]

Andrea's second child, Daniel, attended a Catholic preschool. Then he went to one of the same public schools that his sister had attended for the first few years of his elementary education before transferring with her to the private evangelical school for the rest of his primary instruction. But he also had the good fortune of participating in a neighborhood program that gave the youngest child in each family a backpack filled with school supplies, a school uniform and shoes, and toys every year.[15] They regularly had a piñata for the children in the neighborhood and occasionally they gave each of the participating families a Christmas basket filled with food. The program, called Plan Padrino, was a type of sister city project that operated within the Catholic Church.

Then, as described in Chapter 4, after starting and dropping out of school two years in a row, Daniel ended up studying for two years in the local public secondary school in the rural community of Andrea's parents. When he was nearing completion of his second year there, Andrea was trying to decide whether to return to Italy for a job. However, she was concerned that if she left, Daniel would drop out of school once again the following year. When he assured her that he would not, she sought admission for him to a private technical high school[16] in the city of Granada for the next year. He had a rough start there, though:

> It was very difficult for him because he had to get up at four o'clock in the morning, go, and then come back [to our home in Managua[17]] . . . [He went] to Granada every day . . . He came home very late [and] he studied a lot . . . He was always late [to school]. [So] I bought him a bike . . . He put it on the bus and then [when they got there], got off and took off on it [to get to school]. Sometimes he came home from Granada on the bike. It really scared me because [he rode on] the highway. He was more and more tired out. So he talked with [those who ran the school] and he became a boarding student. He was there from Monday to Friday. On Fridays when he got out in the afternoon, he got the bus and went to La Concepción [to his maternal grandparents' house]. He'd get there about midnight. He [did the last stretch] walking. I think he was looking for a warm, family environment.[18]
>
> . . . [But] he finished secondary school there and studied for a technical degree . . . [The program was] three years. He is [now] an industrial mechanic.[19]

Despite that difficult beginning, Daniel had clearly come around to the idea of being in school. He was interested enough in that particular school to petition for a room-and-board scholarship. Receipt of that scholarship enabled him to live at the school for the remainder of the three years he was there.[20] Needless to say, Andrea was greatly relieved when Daniel finally completed high school and had a degree that would enable him to find work.

By and large, Andrea and Ana preferred to send their children to private schools. For these mothers, private schools were a better option than the public schools because the latter were characterized by having very large classes (about sixty students each) and quite limited resources. The private elementary and secondary schools they sent their children to were mostly religious and not very expensive. For example, Ana's two younger children,

Pedro and Monica, went to preschool and then attended primary school at a very small Baptist institution close to their house. Eventually Pedro started secondary school at a Catholic school nearby before leaving with his sister to join their mother in Portugal.

Once in Portugal, where state investment in education was greater, the schools they attended were public. Their insertion in school there was challenging, though. As Ana reported:

> It was difficult [for Monica]. [But] it was more difficult for Pedro . . . Boys are more self-contained . . . Monica was always more open to friendships. She had just arrived . . . there were times when she felt discriminated against . . . because . . . in her mind, she thought she was the only foreigner in her school. But . . . at the school she attended there were many [kids] from other countries . . . Brazilians, [children] from Ghana, from Cape Verde, from other places. But at the beginning, she felt . . . rejected. But immediately, she found a professor who helped her a lot—I still remember her . . . She called me to a meeting and she said . . . "Monica is timid . . ." She had become more timid after arriving in Portugal . . . This teacher . . . said, "I want to help Monica. I want her to come to private classes at my house and her brother [Pedro] should come as well . . . I'll give them private classes so that she can get up to speed on the language and then she can recover her standing in her [other] classes. That's the only thing [she's weak in] . . . She's working hard, and has a lot of interest in learning, but she has problems with the language. I want to help her with that." And that's how it went. She didn't charge me anything . . . She called the kids to her house and [worked with them] in the afternoons when she had free time. [She was] a wonderful person.[21]

In spite of Monica's initial concerns about being the only foreigner in her school, she clearly was not. Moreover, she and Pedro were fortunate in finding people who supported them during their transition to studying in another language and living in a world very different from the one to which they had previously been accustomed.

Aside from their comprehensive schooling, these women encouraged their children to take extracurricular classes. For example, Pamela's second-youngest son, Héctor, was studying English at a private language school.[22] While telling me about him, she said:

> He's in his fourth year of secondary school . . . and he loves English . . . He also likes to work, [his older brother] Wilfredo taught him how to work [in construction]. And he loves soccer . . . So I said to him, "Look, would you like to go to Panama . . . to work there?" He said, "No, Mamá, I prefer to look for a job here that doesn't pay much, but keep moving forward in English. Because later on I'm going to work in anything that uses English." [He wants to go] to college. Meanwhile, this year he's studying English [alongside his classes in high school]. Because . . . that's his dream . . . I said, "That's fine . . . stay here. Finish. Because that's what you like [to do]."[23]

Pamela has effectively let Héctor decide what he will do, even if it means that he is not earning anything while he is finishing high school and preparing to go to college, and even if it means that she has to send him more money so that he can study a foreign language outside his classes for school.

In addition, at least one child in each of these households went to college, and in one of them, all three did. In the case of Andrea's children, Clara went on to study computer engineering at a private secular school.[24] She had yet to finish college by the time of our interviews (to be discussed shortly), but the fact that she had this opportunity was still noteworthy. Pamela's oldest son was studying architecture at the National Engineering University (UNI), where Ana's oldest son had gone to college.[25] And all three of Ana's children have attended a university. As mentioned earlier, Carlos completed his Licenciatura[26] in electrical engineering at the UNI. After completing high school in Portugal, Ana's middle child—Pedro—completed a university degree in economics at a public university in Lisbon; Monica, Ana's youngest, is currently studying nutrition at a private university in Lisbon. Andrea's younger child and Pamela's second and third child have each, for one reason or another, been less academically inclined. But their lack of pursuit of university studies was not caused by their mothers' unwillingness to find a way to finance them. Moreover, their mothers had gone to great lengths to make various educational opportunities—both formal education and extracurricular activities—available to their children that were far removed from their own experiences.

THEIR WORK TRAJECTORIES

Each of the women at the center of this study started to work when they were quite young, as described in Chapter 2. And the need to work interrupted, if not ended, their schooling. The situation for their children was quite distinct. Although they may have worked during summer vacations, their jobs did not conflict with their studies. And they did not start to work full time until they had left school, whether temporarily or permanently. Moreover, the choice to leave school was not imposed upon them by their parents.

For example, Andrea's son—Daniel—started to work in construction in his midteens, after dropping out of secondary school. However, when he decided to return to school, he ceased working.[27] Likewise, his sister Clara did not start to work until she had completed high school. Clara did not begin her university studies until two years after completing high school. As Andrea recounted:

> Clara lost two years [in her studies] . . . because she was irresponsible . . .
> In primary school, when I was routinely there working at home . . . Clara
> always, always got the highest grades . . . In secondary school, when I
> wasn't always keeping track of her,[28] she started to get interested in boys,
> it started like that, and her grades started to fall . . . They weren't terri-
> bly low, but they weren't as high as they had been before. And . . . when
> she graduated from high school, she went to take the [college entrance]
> exam[29] and she didn't pass it . . . Her godparents paid for . . . [a year of
> classes to prepare her to take the exam again], and her [only] responsibil-
> ity was to study . . . But even then . . . she didn't pass it. So, I was angry
> with her, and I said . . . how is it possible, that after all that money, all that
> time, and a year lost, she still didn't pass? I told her, "What you've done
> is a total disappointment . . . So I'm not willing to offer you [anything
> more] . . . Figure out what you're going to do." She didn't do anything,
> anything that whole year . . . she finally said to me, "Mamá, I don't have
> anything to do . . ." [And my response was,] "That's your problem, look for
> work . . . If you don't want to study, work. You're grown up now, work."[30]

In talking about the difference between her own work experience and that of her children, Andrea commented:

> When I would leave [to work overseas], I'd always have someone [there to take care of the household] . . . They didn't have to work like I had to work from when I was small. Their lives were totally different from mine. But . . . in wanting to protect them, I didn't teach them how difficult life is . . . Clara went to work, after she was with Mario[31] . . . There was a year in which I forgot about her . . . because she hadn't passed . . . the entrance exam to architecture school and at that point I was . . . disillusioned and, above all, angry . . . [So, she was eighteen or nineteen when she started to work.] But she wasn't there long . . . She was there for a little while until they fired her, because of [her aunt] Camila. Camila had a problem and Clara left the [ice cream] stand to help her. Both of them were fresh! . . . She said, "I have to go because my family needs me," and she went. And when she went back, there was someone else in her place.[32]

Andrea believed that perhaps she had "protected" her children too much from having to work while they were in school and as a result they did not fully appreciate the opportunity she had provided them to focus only on their studies. She was angry with both of them that they did not cherish what she had given them, which was something that she herself had never been offered.

What is most likely is that they had simply become distracted with other things, as happens with many adolescents. Young people who have to work in addition to studying would have less time for distractions. But having a parent nearby who can pull their children back from those distractions might also make a difference. As discussed in Chapter 4, Daniel's and Clara's difficulties with staying on track through school may have reflected the potential risks associated with parents leaving to work overseas (c.f. Démurger 2015; Heymann et al. 2009) more than the fact that they did not have to work while they were in school.

Regardless of the balance between these factors, Andrea eventually put her anger aside, and when she next returned to Nicaragua to visit, she offered to help her daughter go to college if she still wanted to study. At that point, Clara started studying computer engineering at a private university.[33] Hence, despite facing numerous challenges along the way, Andrea convinced both of her children that it was in their best interests to stay in school long enough to acquire the skills that would enable them to attain stable employment in jobs where they are in demand.

Ana's two younger children started their work life in a restaurant owned by Ana's employers during the summer vacation leading up to college. Given that:

> The [Portuguese state] doesn't permit people to work until they are eighteen years old . . . Pedro was eighteen when he started college, and Monica as well. They worked [the summer before that].[34]

With time, they also worked while they were in college. But the work they did while they were in school was part time and did not keep them from attending college.

Two of Pamela's sons left school in their midteens and started working in the construction industry. According to Pamela, school was not to their liking, and that is why they left it:

> [My second oldest son] is twenty-six years old . . . His name is Wilfredo. Look, school has been hard for him. But I think that . . . he's seen so many problems at home and all of the problems with his dad, who always treated him badly . . . He closed himself off . . . He didn't understand school. They were always calling me . . . because he didn't do his homework. He said to me, "Mamá, I want to learn a trade, so that I can start working. I don't want to study, because I don't like [school] . . ." So look, I did everything I could, he got through the third year . . . of secondary [school]. Later, he said to me, "Mamá, I want to wear good-looking pants, I want this thing . . . But you don't have [money] to buy it, so I'll go to work . . ." [I said,] "Okay, go to work." Because those were difficult times, and you know the kids went around in the streets looking for gangs . . . So . . . I preferred that he would go to work and come home really tired out and not have time to get into anything . . .
>
> The twenty-two-year-old is the same . . . [His name is] Tomás . . . he's always thinking of grandiose things. He had big dreams. He's the only one like me, with big dreams . . . He was always saying "I'm going to go . . . to

another country." . . . He had a difficult time at school as well. He couldn't seem to retain what he learned. I would say it was a family problem. But he does like to work . . .

I would say to them, are you going to study? "Mamá, we want to work." [I'd reply,] "Okay. But the day will come when you will see that you need to study . . . to not be doing that kind of heavy work . . ." Because by [working] they will see that things don't come easy and they'll value them more . . . Everything in its time.[35]

Clearly Pamela valued her sons' willingness to work, alongside her concern with their getting an education. That may have stemmed from her having been married to someone for fourteen years who did not contribute to the household through his work. Even more importantly, it may have also reflected her worries about the family's financial situation. After all, it was five years into her stay in Italy before she started earning enough to send home a substantial amount in remittances and to begin to save some of her wages. Nevertheless, when Pamela's eldest son decided to go back to school to study architecture after being employed in construction for quite a while, he did so with Pamela's support. Thus, while she allowed her sons to start working when she was worried about the alternative of their joining a gang, she continued to promote their pursuit of an education.

Moreover, several of the women's children now hold professional positions and/or positions in which they are much sought after. Ana's two sons both work in a professional capacity. Pedro, her middle child, was able to find a job in his field once he graduated with his degree in economics in Portugal.

Back in Nicaragua, Ana's older son had a more challenging time getting work. As she noted:

He found his first job almost a year after he had graduated . . . it wasn't as an engineer. He started as a . . . technician . . . more or less as an electrician. It wasn't the engineering he had studied . . . he's had two jobs since he started [working]. The one he has now is repairing the machinery in dental chairs . . . This isn't what he studied to do. He studied for something else . . . He . . . wanted to work in the control towers of the airport or on [something related to] the telephone [system] . . . but we don't have any connections. You know that [it's all to do] with connections . . . But, thank God, he's working steadily now. He's earning a living . . . Clearly, his diploma helped him a lot to get this job . . . He could aspire [to much more]. We'll see in the future. As he says, "I don't think of living my whole life here, Mamá . . . I'm always thinking about [how to] get ahead. To look for [a job] in what I studied."[36]

As Ana suggests, it is reasonable to conclude that Carlos's difficulty obtaining a more interesting job stemmed from the lack of a family or friendship network that could have opened the necessary doors for another kind of job. Given their class background, his family did not have the social and cultural capital that would have allowed him to make the kinds of connections that have become so important for finding a professional job in Nicaragua today. That is to say, the class inequalities that have impacted Ana's life continuously have also affected that of Carlos. Even so, the positions Ana's sons hold represent a strong contrast from her own history of employment, primarily as a domestic worker and care provider, as well as from that of her former husband as a security guard.

Andrea's two children have been steadily employed since they ended their studies. Clara was hired to teach at the high school associated with the university where she studied computer engineering, despite having yet to receive her Licenciatura. After teaching as a substitute many hours a day and weekends, she now teaches

part time . . . until noon[37] . . . She's at home in the afternoons . . . since last year . . . She earns practically the same and she works half the time. Because . . . she's no longer a substitute . . . Now that she has her own class, as you know, she has to plan [her lessons] . . . [so] she uses the time she's at home to plan [her classes], and to teach Belinda.[38]

After teaching computing to all grades within the secondary school for a number of years, more recently Clara was transferred to teaching in one of the elementary classrooms at the school.[39] She was more satisfied teaching computing. But the job has provided her with a stable income and health insurance for herself and her daughters.

Clara's brother Daniel found a job shortly after graduating with his technical degree. That first job was with the state energy company, INE.

But he has now been working for some years at a solar panel company. As Andrea said:

> He's a technician . . . in alternative energy . . . He's learned a lot . . . He loves his work [and] he picked it up [easily]. If that boy had [been willing] to study, he would have had a [real] future . . . I had to move my contacts . . . because he wasn't getting any work.[40]

Daniel has worked his way up in the company and now supervises the installation of solar panels all over the country. Aside from working too much, he is fortunate to have a job he likes. Moreover, the job provides him with a stable income and health insurance for himself and his children. Hence, both Daniel and Clara—whose mother has worked primarily as a domestic and care provider and whose father worked as a security guard and laborer—are in an enviable position compared to what most people with their socioeconomic background in Nicaragua could aspire to (Andersen 2001; Azevedo and Bouillon 2010).

As noted earlier, three of Pamela's sons have worked in the construction industry, with two of them having made it to the position of construction foreman (including Walter, who is now a student of architecture). Pamela helped her second and third oldest sons emigrate to work in this sector in Panama. They received a much higher salary there than they would in Nicaragua—with the first to emigrate earning $1,200 US per month—and were also able to send remittances home for their three brothers who were still studying there.[41]

Aside from having steady work and sending money home, according to Pamela, the experience has been very good for helping at least one of them to mature:

> My son Tomás was . . . he earned money, got his salary, and every payday he liked to go to parties with his girlfriends. He didn't bring any [of his earnings] home. So I said, "Okay . . . Don't bring anything home . . . It's okay." I didn't demand it. I said to my [other] son, Wilfredo . . . "Look, Tomás needs to learn how to be responsible. He needs to learn how much things in life cost." [So when Tomás] said he'd like to go to Panama, he didn't [have to] tell me twice. [I said], "You're going to Panama. I'll send

you the money for the ticket . . ." Because there, he'[d] have to pay for
everything he eats! Everything. It was a relief for me. Because he'd have
to learn about life . . . And once he was there, he started to send [home]
money . . . [He says,] "Buy this, buy that . . ." Now he organizes everything.
So I say that's what he needed.[42]

Hence, Pamela's two sons who have emigrated and are working in Panama
have surpassed their father in terms of earning a stable and relatively good
income given their level of education. They have also become responsible
about contributing to the economic well-being of their family. That is another important contrast with their father. And with their and their mother's
support, perhaps their brothers who are still studying will succeed in joining
the ranks of the professional workforce.

A SAFE HOME ENVIRONMENT

Given that two of these mothers experienced sexual violence as children,
they were very conscious about creating a home environment that would be
safe for their own children. That meant a number of things, including keeping the lines of communication open, talking with their children about what
is appropriate touching and what is not, being attentive for any symptoms of
abuse, providing some measure of sex education, and generally doing all in
their power to protect them.

Ana, whose oldest son was the outcome of such abuse, mentioned the
importance of always listening to what one's children are trying to say. In
talking about the fact that Ana's mother always believed her stepfather, as opposed to believing her, she commented: "When one has children, one has to
hear one's children as well. When my children were small, I always thought
that . . . so that no one would hurt them."[43] She went on to say:

I wanted to protect my daughter, I always tried to protect her, to defend
her. I [did my utmost] so that no one . . . would abuse her that way. Because, I said, . . . "Everything that happened, I wouldn't wish it on anyone . . ." [crying] . . .

Above all . . . [I tried] to instill in . . . [my children] that they have to
protect and listen to their [own] children when they have them . . . because I've told them some things, not exactly everything, some things . . .

I told them, "My *mamá* never listened to me; my *mamá* . . . said that I was a liar . . . I hope that someday [when you have children] . . . you teach them and you listen to your children. I've said that to Monica, Pedro, and Carlos. Respect and listen to them, when they come to tell you something . . . My granddaughter . . . is very restless and there are times when she's [a bit wild]. Her mother says, "She's a liar, she invents things." I respond, "No. Listen to the girl, always listen to her." [And] I say to Carlos, "If [your wife] won't listen to her, you listen to her, to your daughter . . . if your daughter comes to tell you something, please listen to her."[44]

Out of Ana's pain came a determination to ensure that the suffering she endured as a child would not be repeated in future generations. For her, a number of things were critical in this effort, with a parents' willingness to hear and believe what their child has to say being central to them. Ana is realistic that she will not be able to stop such abuse around the world. But she has done what she can within her family, so that her children and her grandchildren would have very different childhoods than she did.

Likewise, in raising her own children, Andrea consciously sought to prevent the sexual abuse she experienced from happening to them. As she recounted:

And in spite of everything, they had a father who was not a *papà padrone* (a father who conceived of himself as owning his family) like I had. And I was always attentive to Clara . . . that she wouldn't experience any kind of abuse . . . I did many things that were the total opposite of what my parents did . . . I was always very careful, looking for any [potential] symptoms, and I always asked her questions and explained what was normal and what was not . . . And the same when she bathed her daughter. Because when I had [Clara], I didn't know how to touch her, what was normal and what was not . . . She didn't have to experience any of that.[45]

From Andrea's point of view, educating her children about their bodies and about sex was important for preparing them for life, but also for protecting them from abuse. When I asked Andrea about her own knowledge of birth control before her first child was born, she responded:

> I don't think I knew anything about it . . . I wasn't in school at the stage
> where they teach this. The truth is that no one explained anything . . .
> And if they explained it, their explanations were wrong. Moreover,
> if it depended on my mother's explanations [. . . it would have left me
> knowing nothing] . . . in my own development, as they call it, I thought,
> "My God, what has happened to me now," because no one had told me
> anything.[46]

And, despite having her innocence taken away at a very early age, she grew
up "with a total ignorance"[47] about reproductive health and sex.

> The truth is that I learned a lot about birth control and all that . . . when
> [the North American woman I worked for] started to help me, because . . .
> even in the health centers, they gave you misinformation . . .
>
> In contrast, from a very young age my daughter knew about these
> things. Because I thought . . . I was always trying to make sure that she
> didn't grow up as ignorant as I did . . . And . . . Daniel, I explained every-
> thing to him, which his father should have explained, but I did.[48]

Andrea was committed to providing her children with the knowledge they
would need to live healthy lives. This meant that she talked with both of them
about human sexuality and reproduction, even though she thought it was
her partner's job to explain these things to their son.

In sum, Andrea's and Ana's children grew up in a very different environment from that of their mothers. This next generation was protected from
abuse and learned about what was and what was not appropriate touching as
children, and about reproductive health and sexuality more generally.

CHILD REARING IN THE NEXT GENERATION

Most of Pamela's, Ana's, and Andrea's children have not yet had their own
offspring. Of those who have, several started their families later than their
mothers did. Despite all of their children being at least eighteen years old
by the time I carried out the bulk of the interviews with their mothers, only
two of them (of a total of ten) had their own children. Two of Pamela's sons
had children within the following couple of years, though, as did Andrea's

son. Pamela's youngest son (who would have been about nineteen years old at the time) was living with a woman who had a child of her own, and several months after I completed the better part of the oral history with his mother he had a child with his partner.[49] More recently, his middle brother (who would have been about twenty-four years old at the time and had stable employment in Panama) had a baby with his partner. But their other three brothers remained childless. Only Ana's and Andrea's eldest children had their own children by the time I completed most of my interviews with these women.

Ana's oldest child, Carlos, has one child. His daughter was born after he finished college. Bearing in mind that his own mother had been thirteen years old when he was born, this was a significant difference in their experiences. In all likelihood, having waited to have a child until he was done with college enabled Carlos to complete his studies and go on to look for a better-paying job than he would have otherwise found.

In addition, it is unclear whether Ana would have been able to provide her son with sufficient funds to both pay for his studies and support a child of his. As things were, even when Carlos graduated from college, it took him some time to find a job that could fully maintain him. Until then, Ana kept sending remittances to help him out. As she recounted:

> He graduated the year I took [Pedro and Monica] to Portugal . . . after he graduated, he found his first job . . . But even then I continued to help him [financially]. He got married, and I kept helping him. His daughter was born, and I kept helping him. But later, when [Pedro and Monica] started college, I completely stopped helping him, because I had more things to pay for . . . I kept helping him because I felt . . . it's not as if he really needed it, but I sent it anyway. One day [he said], "You don't need to send any more. Take care of my siblings; look out for them like you took care of me. I don't need you to keep helping out." So I stopped sending money to him.[50]

Thus, although the support from Ana was clearly welcome before Pedro and Monica went to college, at that point Carlos recognized his mother's need to redirect her financial support to his younger siblings and began to stand fully on his own economically. This shift was facilitated by Carlos having been able to attain a steady job, which was greatly aided by his college degree, as Ana pointed out.

As described earlier, Ana's two younger children—Pedro and Monica— emigrated to Portugal to live with her after she had been working there several years. Although both of them have been living with partners for a few years, neither has a child. Ana commented:

> This is because they have a different culture . . . because of their emigration . . . Because if they had been in Nicaragua, I believe they would be different [people]. You know, if one stays in one's country . . . the culture remains the same . . . But they're here now and have changed . . . Their way of thinking . . . I see that they don't think the way kids of their age [who were] raised in Nicaragua think. . . For example, in Nicaragua there are many young women Monica's age [twenty-two] who already have children . . . I don't know if my daughter was in Nicaragua if she would already have a child, but she would be on that track . . . [But] the culture and the education they've received—that they've been given here in Portugal, that they might not have received there . . . this has opened up their minds for them to say, first they have to study and meet their goals, and [only] after that can [they] start to think about [having children]. In Nicaragua [people] don't think about meeting their goals. They simply fall in love . . . and the next thing, [they have] a child. The man says, "If you don't have my child, you're not worth anything." [And] the woman says, "That's right, I love him so I need to give him a child . . ." And then [the men] disappear, and there you are with his child . . .[51]

Ana is correct in her assertion about the early age at which women start having children in Nicaragua; about half of young women there give birth before age twenty (Lion et al. 2009: 91). In contrast, while Portugal's adolescent birth rate is high in the context of Europe, it is still well below that of Nicaragua; in 2010 it had "14.7 births per thousand females between the ages of 15 and 19 years" (Mendes et al. 2014: 7). Survey data suggests that Portugal's decreasing adolescent birth rate has coincided with rising levels of education and the desire on the part of young women to have a career. So it would seem that Pedro and Monica have been influenced by their surroundings to approach child rearing differently than they might have if they had remained in Nicaragua.

Ana went on to contrast the way of thinking of Pedro and Monica with that of Carlos, who had remained in Nicaragua. I pointed out to her that Carlos had waited to get married until he had completed college. Ana responded:

> But see, he got married . . . He had a Nicaraguan mentality from growing up there. He married the first young woman he went out with, and there he is with her. I can assure you that if he'd come to Portugal to study, even for a year, Carlos would still be single, he wouldn't have married. That's the difference in mentality.[52]

Ana concluded by saying that Carlos regrets that decision now.

Nonetheless, Carlos *is* distinct from many young people in Nicaragua in having waited until he finished college to marry and have a child. Perhaps what led him in this direction was the milieu that he encountered himself in once he was in college. Two of the factors that Katherine Lion and colleagues (2009) found to be associated with the age at which young women in Nicaragua had their first child were education and wealth. Their argument is that the younger a woman is when she first has sex is strongly indicative that she will have her first birth early, and young women with higher levels of education and from wealthier backgrounds tend to have their first sexual relationship later than other young women there. But Carlos is different from most of those attending college in Nicaragua, who are likely to be from the upper middle and upper class. Perhaps, despite his working-class background, his own and his mother's commitment to his going to college were what kept him from following the common path for his background.

Andrea's older child, Clara, had her first daughter just as she was finally starting college (following the gap of two years after her graduation from high school). She was nineteen years old. Earlier on, once Andrea was aware that Clara had a steady boyfriend, she took her daughter to start having birth control injections.[53] Andrea wanted to ensure that Clara would not have a child as a teenager, which had been her own experience. But her daughter was not careful about having her injections punctually—or perhaps she had decided that she wanted to have a child—and the possible became the inevitable. The timing was unfortunate. As Andrea commented, when Clara failed the college entrance exam the second time, she told her daughter:

> "If you do want to go back to school someday, let me know." [Then] when I came back that year, I found her pale, super pale, and emaciated . . . She said to me, "I want . . . I'm going to study, and I'm going to work hard . . ." She was already with Mario by then . . . "I'm going to do everything and I'm going to graduate . . . on time, you'll see . . ." But [her statements] didn't convince me. I said, "Go have some [medical] tests and see what you've got . . ." [Well, she was pregnant.] But I had already given my word to help her . . . She started to cry . . . and said to me, "Just when you had said that I . . . could start at the university . . . I want to study so much . . ." I said, "Let's do this . . ." If I give my word, I keep it. I've always been that way and I'm not going to change now. And I think that one shouldn't turn their back on their children. So I said, "Study all that you can now, and then we'll see what we can do . . ." So she studied that year . . . She was studying what she has always been studying . . . *computer engineering* is the name of her major . . . But I knew that after you have a child . . . you know how it is . . . But the idea [of saying] "Well, now that you're pregnant I won't help you" didn't come into [my head] . . . Belinda, as you know, was born in July [of 2004].[54] After that, sometimes [Clara] went [to school], and sometimes she didn't. She didn't finish some of her classes . . .[55]

Having a child did appear to complicate Clara's completion of college. As of 2015, when I conducted much of the oral history with Andrea, she had yet to obtain her Licenciatura.

As noted earlier, despite not having a degree in hand, Clara was able to attain and keep a job as a teacher. And in the aftermath of Belinda's birth, she apparently decided to be more careful about planning for further expansion of her family. Her second child, Sandra, was not born until 2015. In all likelihood, the gap between the birth of her first child and that of her second helped Clara get most of the way through her Licenciatura and to become firmly ensconced in her job before she had to assume the responsibilities that come with having a newborn baby.

Clara's brother Daniel got married in mid-2014.[56] His wife had already finished college by then, and he had been steadily employed for several years. He was twenty-three years old at the time of his marriage. After they had been married for a few years, the question arose of whether one or the other of them had a health issue that might be inhibiting a pregnancy. But without any medical intervention, by early 2018 Daniel and his wife were expecting a baby.[57] And, much as was true for Ana's eldest son, having not had a child earlier on meant that Daniel and his wife were able to gain some economic stability before they embarked upon this next stage of their lives.

In sum, whether they were in Europe or in Nicaragua, most of the children of Ana, Andrea, and Pamela had opted to postpone having children until they had completed their studies and/or were settled into steady employment. This represented a contrast from the pattern characterizing their mothers' lives and from that of many Nicaraguans of their mothers' and their own generation.

TO WHAT DO ANDREA, ANA, AND PAMELA ATTRIBUTE THEIR CHILDREN'S RELATIVE WELL-BEING?

When I asked Andrea, Ana, and Pamela what the differences between their own and their children's lives were due to, they pointed to a number of factors. Most importantly among these was their own hard work and their emigration to where they could earn higher wages. Interestingly, although their emigration had depended on networks that they had access to as a result of the Nicaraguan revolution and that their nuclear and birth families had benefited in diverse ways from the revolution, that was not what they thought of when asked to explain the distinct opportunities the next generation had.

We can see this understanding very clearly in Andrea's response to the question of what gave rise to the differences between her life and those of her children:

First . . . because of my work . . . In addition, because . . . when I was little, that is, when I wanted to study and couldn't, I said that my children . . . I'm not going to make them miss school. They will study what they want to study. I imagined them grown up . . . my children [would be] proud professionals and with so many more possibilities than I had until then because . . .

And, well, my emigrating was essential in all this. Because, surely if . . . I had stayed there, they would have studied in public schools. I'll be honest, public education now is no great thing, and it wasn't then [either. So] this was key in the change for them.[58]

When I went on to ask her directly about whether the revolution might have played a role in the difference, she said:

Yes, [in terms of] healthcare . . . and the schools. But I believe that even if we'd never had a revolution, my children would have studied because of me [and my determination about this.][59]

Andrea is a very strong woman and when she sets her mind to something—especially as she has gotten older and wiser about how the world works—her will to accomplish it often means that she achieves it. Her children have benefited enormously from her resolve that their lives would offer them more options than she had.

Ana also considered that her commitment to her children having different lives from her own and her emigration were the critical elements in this unfolding reality. While discussing the fact that her eldest son, Carlos, was able to graduate from college, Ana argued that it was because:

I supported him[60] . . . because he had me, and I pushed him to do this. Because maybe if he had been alone or he didn't have my support, he wouldn't have gotten to be what he is today . . . and he himself says, . . . "If you hadn't supported me, Mamí . . ."

Clearly, if I had someone supporting me, someone who—more than anything—pushed me to keep moving forward, and said "Do it!" . . . but I didn't . . . My mom didn't even listen to me, can you imagine her supporting me?[61]

Given that she had been talking earlier about the importance of emigration for changes in the "mentality" of Carlos's siblings, Pedro and Monica, I asked Ana if her emigration was not essential for the opportunities that opened up in the lives of all three of her children—even Carlos. Ana responded:

I think that if I had stayed in Nicaragua, it would have been possible with my sacrifices. I'm sure of it. I'm sure that I would have been biting my fingernails, I would have eaten fried eggs every day, but I would have made it possible for my son [Carlos] to study [at the university] . . . because what I wanted was to see my son as he is now, educated. And, well, I didn't [have to] get to the point of eating my nails, thanks to God and to [my employers] who gave me the chance to leave, so that I could work overseas.[62] But anyway, I'm sure I would have achieved it somehow.

Perhaps I wouldn't have helped the other two, because the weight of the load would have been heavy . . . I wouldn't have been able to help them in the sense of sending them to private schools [in Nicaragua], because Carlos was at the university. Pedro [had just started] attending . . . [a private Catholic school], and Monica was finishing primary school and [we] would have needed to look for a secondary school [for her]. So I think they wouldn't have been able to study in a good school . . . Perhaps I would have had to take [Pedro] out of the [private school] and put them both in Monte Tabor [the local public school], the younger two . . . But somehow I would have pushed them forward . . . the three of them. With struggle and sacrifice . . . But of this, yes, I'm sure that they would have studied. Because it was a goal of mine—I felt that I didn't achieve it and I wanted my children to.[63]

Although Ana spoke of the transformation brought about by the Nicaraguan revolution in a decidedly positive fashion, and pointed to her and her husband's ability to build a home on the outskirts of Managua that resulted from it, she did not connect this process with the differences between her life and those of her children.

When the question of what had brought about any differences between her sons' lives and her own was posed to her, Pamela responded in two contrasting ways. Initially, she talked about modifications in the nature of the job market that had made it a less hospitable environment for finding work:

The majority of businesses in Nicaragua that have [opened up in recent years] are in the Zona Franca [that is, the maquiladora zone]. So many young people who have trained, studied, and received technical degrees, done everything, and received their diplomas . . . But it's difficult because, to start out with, no one will give you a job contract, it's all temporary work . . . [Young people] have no other option besides going to work in the Zona Franca and it doesn't have anything to do with what they studied. Having studied doesn't help them at all.

Yes, the job market [has changed]. Before, when I worked . . . there wasn't [this business of] . . . connections, as they say . . . I went directly to the personnel [office] at the Ministerio de Finanzas and said, "Well, here's my diploma, I'm looking for work." . . . Immediately, they gave me a test, and I got 95 on [it] . . . The next week a telegram arrived at the house calling me [in] for a job.[64]

Thus, Pamela pointed out various aspects of the labor market that had been transformed, making it more difficult for young people to get a decent job.

Shortly thereafter, I asked Pamela if these transformations and any differences in her sons' options versus her own stemmed from the multiple shifts in the orientation (and policies) of the Nicaraguan government over her lifetime. Her response was that the circumstances in which one ended up were closely tied to one's own individual approach to that same labor market, and to life more generally. In her words:

I believe that all of this depends on each of us . . . There have always been limitations; poverty has always existed. As a young person of fourteen, fifteen years old, I liked to study . . . it's not that at that time, it was impossible to study—that's untrue . . . Because I had so many limitations . . . but I studied because I wanted to. So I believe that it's something personal, that you have to be motivated. But now [people] aren't. Now people are complacent and look for someone else to blame. And they say, "because of the government, I can't" . . . [But] now there are more opportunities. Because before, for example, . . . my mother was very poor and I had to go out and sell tortillas. My children have not had to go out to sell anything . . . and if they don't study, it's because they don't want to . . . It wasn't [as if] because my mother sent me [out] to work, I couldn't study . . . It's [all about taking] initiative. I believe that everyone has to have initiative; a spirit of getting ahead in life.

. . . Because . . . no government is going to maintain me. No one knows if I eat or if I don't, they're not even interested . . . It's me, everything depends on me, that's what I believe . . . People are accustomed to placing blame on others . . . They vent, saying that "because of the government, I don't have . . ." It's not true. Rather, the government is responsible for there being so many people now who don't worry about buying anything because it's given to them . . . the government has spoiled them . . . [and] the NGOs . . . which have made life easier, as much as possible . . . And that's bad, because one should start out [facing] difficulties, so that [later on] one feels satisfied and can say, "I've achieved this alone . . . I've done this [myself]."[65]

Hence, despite using somewhat different language, each of these three women emphasized the importance of their strong determination to accomplish what they have accomplished, whether in their own or their children's lives. Pamela did briefly mention the structural changes in Nicaragua's labor market. But other than that they considered their own initiative, whether with regard to emigrating or simply working hard and pushing themselves and their children to get ahead, the key to this puzzle. This is the other side of the consciousness that was discussed in Chapter 2, which has become increasingly common within the neoliberal context. While in that discussion I noted that this consciousness led them to accept difficult times and debt as their own responsibility, here it leads them to fully credit their own initiative with any advancement in their family members' experiences.

Andrea, Ana, and Pamela had indeed worked very hard to support their families and to garner the resources they would need to provide their children with the option of attending college. This was an option they had not had. Consequently, they were tenacious in ensuring that their children not be limited in the same ways they had been. And they strategized—that is, they expressed agency—to find the means to open the path forward for their children.

Moreover, the strategy they ultimately adopted—of working overseas—enabled them to provide for their children in ways that their parents were not able to provide for them.[66] Undoubtedly, the markedly higher wages they can earn overseas make a major difference in their own and their families' lives. Whereas Andrea earns 1,200 euros a month as a live-in care provider for an elderly woman in Italy, she would probably not be able to earn much more than \$200 US a month as a domestic worker in Nicaragua, and that would be a good salary for the job there. Given their meager earning power in Nicaragua, it would have been much harder for the aspirations Andrea, Ana, and Pamela had for their children to be realized had they remained there. Hence, the importance of their overseas wages cannot be denied.

However, it is crucial to highlight several things when pointing to the essential role that emigration has played in their own and their children's economic well-being. These things go beyond the efforts and agency of the four women, to the structure of the society they were raised in and lived their lives in prior to emigrating. The first thing that must be noted is that the network of connections that made it possible for them to emigrate was firmly rooted among people who had moved to Nicaragua because they sympathized with the revolution that was underway there. That is to say, emigrating legally was one of the by-products of the effort that took place in Nicaragua in the 1980s to transform the country's social structure.

It is also important to underline the strong link between the reversal of that social transformation effort in the 1990s—in the form of the neoliberal structural adjustment that was implemented during this latter period—and the upsurge in emigration from Nicaragua. Although economic reform was begun even during the Sandinista government, especially as of 1988,[67] full-blown structural adjustment of the economy was not imposed until the 1990s. It was also then that emigration from Nicaragua escalated.[68] Some of that emigration was to countries within the region, most especially to Costa Rica, and large numbers of Nicaraguans went to the United States. Nonetheless, the present study suggests that they went to wherever networks and economic opportunities made it possible for them to "get ahead," even if that meant going to less traditional locations such as Italy.

In emigrating to Italy, Andrea, Silvia, Ana, and Pamela became agents insofar as they made the choice to go, out of the "structurally provided alternatives" they were presented with (to draw on Hays 1994: 63). Those alternatives arose from several distinct "structures": that pertaining to the period of social transformation in Nicaragua; that emerging during the country's neoliberal period; and Italy's own social structure, which facilitated their incorporation into its labor force as domestic workers and care providers. As Hays (1994: 63) argues, this course of action typically accomplishes "the reproduction of existing social structures." In this case, it did not undermine those structures in either Nicaragua or Italy (and would have only reinforced them). However, simultaneously, it played a major role in creating the tangible differences that this chapter has described between their own and their children's lives.

CONCLUSION

The children of Andrea, Ana, and Pamela have, by and large, led very distinct lives from those of their mothers. They have suffered significantly less from the structural violence—and not at all from the sexual violence—that their mothers experienced. They did not face hunger, they had much more secure and safe home lives, they were offered the opportunity to study, and they were not forced into the labor market before they had gone as far in their studies as they desired.

Several of them have already achieved professional jobs, while others are still completing their college or secondary educations. The remainder have entered the labor force in advantageous positions relative to the average Nicaraguan worker without a college degree or a high school diploma. Several of them have found their career trajectories constrained, however, by their lack of the social connections that might open doors to better jobs (offering higher pay or status, or speaking more to their substantive interests). These kinds of social connections are commonly associated with one's social class, giving those with a higher-class background advantages in terms of this assistance in the labor market. In some cases, racial/ethnic inequalities may have also contributed to this dynamic, at times interacting with the social connection limitations stemming from economic inequalities. High youth unemployment rates, especially in Nicaragua, have also made their job options more restricted than their educational achievements have warranted.[69] Yet these young adults have still been able to attain positions in the labor market that represent an improvement over those of their parents.

Moreover, they have been able to take advantage of the greater openness within their families with regard to discussions of birth control, so as to move into adulthood less encumbered than their mothers had been. That is, the knowledge their mothers imparted to them about sexuality and reproduction has enabled them to approach decisions regarding marriage and the birth of children in a more conscious way than that of Andrea, Ana, and Pamela. In the process, their mothers have given them an additional means to prepare for supporting themselves in the future.

In sum, all of the differences in experience between these two generations that have been described in the preceding pages provide evidence of social mobility occurring between them. Hence, even within the context of more generalized obstacles to this social dynamic in Latin America, the children of Andrea, Ana, and Pamela have had notably more options than their mothers and have been able to achieve some measure of social mobility, both of which represent a major accomplishment.

CONCLUSION

History will judge us by the difference we
make in the everyday lives of children.

Nelson Mandela

As long as poverty, injustice, and gross
inequality persist in our world, none of us can
truly rest.

Nelson Mandela

OVER THE COURSE OF THE preceding chapters we have
seen how structural violence, in its varied forms, has conditioned the lives of
Andrea, Silvia, Ana, and Pamela. It expressed itself throughout their childhoods, their adolescence, and the years of adulthood they have experienced
thus far. Yet it was moderated by both the revolution during which they came
of age and their own efforts to realize the dreams that were fostered by that
larger process of change. The combination of these latter two dynamics has
generated a distinct situation for their children, enabling this next generation
to achieve some degree of social mobility, and for their mothers—the women
at the center of this book—to be able to look forward to a measure of economic independence in their later years that is far removed from what was
true for their parents. That is to say, while structural violence has certainly
colored these women's lives, they have employed agency in ways that have
meant that it has not fully defined their own and their children's existence.

In the pages that follow, we briefly review the nature of that structural violence and the ways in which it was evident in the lives of Andrea, Silvia, Ana,
and Pamela. We also analyze the extent to which their histories—and this
account of them—coincide with and diverge from what the literature tells us
about the experiences of poor women in Latin America as a whole, whether
or not they engage in emigration. Finally, we consider the implications of

those coincidences and divergences for our understanding of structural violence and distinct efforts to redress it.

STRUCTURAL VIOLENCE IN THE LIVES OF
ANDREA, SILVIA, ANA, AND PAMELA

As described in Chapter 1, structural violence is expressed in the constraints that arise from the inequalities contained within a society's social structure that keep certain groups from reaching their full potential. Those inequalities are multiple and, in this case, include at least those generated by class, gender, racial/ethnic, and immigration status distinctions. We will briefly examine how each of these inequalities played out in the lives of these four women, as well as how they intersected with one another.

Within the social sciences, class distinctions were the first to be studied extensively, and they have been a central component in the generation of structural violence. For Andrea, Silvia, Ana, and Pamela, the poverty they grew up in was evidenced in their often unstable living circumstances and in their educational experience. Hence, we saw that the families of Ana and Pamela moved around a fair amount, given that finding a more permanent place to live was compromised by their restricted financial resources. At the same time, the education of all four women was impacted by the class position of their parents. The disadvantaged situation of rural dwellers, especially those who could not afford to send their children to urban areas to study, was particularly clear in the intermittent and incomplete studies of Andrea and Silvia. Yet even for Ana, who was forced to leave her education behind when she became pregnant, and Pamela, who had to attend a different session of classes from her sisters to be able to use their shoes to go to class, economic limitations affected their educational prospects.

With a stunted educational experience and social connections that brought them into the world of service to those with more resources, Andrea, Silvia, and Ana were incorporated into that sector of the economy at an early age. Coming from an urban background and with more education, Pamela was able to find employment within the state bureaucracy until it contracted with the spread of neoliberalism in the 1990s. After that point in time, the advantages she previously held vis-à-vis the other women became more tenuous.

Nonetheless, until well into adulthood these women attempted to build a life for themselves and their children in Nicaragua. But each of them eventually found that because of their limited income and—for Andrea, Ana, and Pamela—the lack of support from the fathers of their children, their ability to sustain their families and open up new prospects for their children was constrained. That lack of support was not uncommon within the prevailing gender inequalities that characterized Nicaragua, and it worked hand in hand with their class position to place these women in an untenable situation if they wanted to assist their children's pursuit of a future distinct from their own lives. Moreover, by the time their children were approaching the end of secondary school, the financial obligations of these women vis-à-vis their aging parents were growing well beyond what they had been from their earliest years of employment, given the latter's lack of access to the national social security system. Hence, they found themselves with little in the way of options beside emigrating to where they might earn higher wages. While Andrea, Silvia, and Ana initially explored this option on a short-term basis, all four of these women ultimately concluded that working overseas was the only means they had to help their children take advantage of educational opportunities that would allow them to have employment prospects outside the service sector and/or to fulfill their responsibilities to their parents.

The insertion of these four women into their destination country's service sector was a relatively fluid process. Given Italy's "care deficit," it permitted the importation of labor from elsewhere to fill this need. Moreover, the prevailing gender inequalities in both their country of origin and their destination country had led to care provision being gendered labor, which fell overwhelmingly to women to carry out. Here we see at least three spheres of inequality intersecting—class, gender, and immigration status. However, an additional sphere of inequality also needs to be taken into account, that of race/ethnicity. In Latin America, given racial/ethnic inequalities, those with darker skin tend to be largely concentrated in the lower rungs of the social structure. Hence, class, gender, and racial/ethnic distinctions often intersect to channel darker-skinned women into the service sector in that region.[1] These dynamics described Andrea's, Silvia's, and Ana's experience in Nicaragua. In Italy, those who provided care to the wealthiest in the past were often women from poorer rural areas and the southern part of the country (see, e.g., Notari 1998). But the demand for such workers expanded to also come from the middle and upper middle classes starting in the 1970s. The immigrant women employed to meet that demand were often women of color. Pamela's experience is emblematic here in that, despite her employment background including long periods of white-collar work, once she immigrated to Italy she joined her Nicaraguan friends in this disadvantaged occupational category. That is to say, racial/ethnic inequalities also characterized Italy's service sector.

In the 1960s and 1970s, inequalities in the areas of gender, race/ethnicity, and immigration status started to gain traction as topics of study in the social sciences. The inequalities in each of these areas and their intersections were evidenced in multiple ways in the stories of Andrea, Silvia, Ana, and Pamela. Aside from the previously mentioned issue of their area of employment, we also saw the ways in which gender inequalities played out in terms of the sexual abuse they were subjected to as children and the sexual harassment they experienced in their jobs in the service sector. Gender inequalities were also present in the less than equitable relationships they had with their partners and in their having to assume responsibility for their children's well-being despite the undisputed nature of the latter's parentage. In Andrea's case, we also saw how racial distinctions were part and parcel of the problematic nature of her relationship with the father of her children. Nonetheless, he was not alone among the fathers of these women's children in failing to contribute to their economic sustenance. As noted earlier, that failure led these women to conclude that their only alternative was to emigrate if their children were to have the possibility of university studies.

Aside from experiencing the negative effects of racial distinctions with the father of her children, Andrea also spoke of experiencing discrimination in Italy. Ana faced discrimination in Italy as well. That discrimination was twofold, and the two parts were inextricably bound. Because they were darker-skinned than most Italians, they were assumed to be immigrants. This dual positionality distinguished them from native-born Italians and led some of the latter to mistreat them. Ana's children also initially felt discriminated against in Portugal. The assumption of their immigrant status, which stemmed from their skin color and their limited command of the language in their destination country, also brought these two areas of distinction together for Ana's two younger children. However, the challenges that Ana's elder son, Carlos, had in gaining professional employment in Nicaragua that was commensurate with his educational level once he had his Licenciatura likewise pointed in the direction of inequalities stemming from racial/ethnic and class distinctions.

Yet in all likelihood, Carlos would never have had the chance to attend college had he not been born at the point in Nicaraguan history that he was. Despite its many shortcomings, the revolution the country experienced between 1979 and 1990 brought some material benefits to the families of at least three of these women. Carlos's mother, Ana, was one of them. In addition to those benefits, it brought the women employment with foreigners who had come to work in Nicaragua precisely because of the revolution that was under way there. That employment further solidified the economic situation of these households. As importantly, the revolution also provided sustenance for these women's belief that they and their children might not be "predestined" to live in poverty.

Later on, in the context of neoliberal Nicaragua, the reality Andrea, Ana, and Pamela faced vis-à-vis the prospect of aiding their children in progressing on a path distinct from their own was not bright. And it was in this same period that Silvia joined the other women in assuming a growing responsibility for supporting her parents. However, the revolution had also provided these women with the network that opened up the possibility of emigrating legally. Over time they came to see emigration as a way to realize the dream of seeing their children attend college.

Emigration did prove to be the solution to many of their economic woes. For each of these women it took some time to find an employment situation that would allow them to accumulate relatively significant savings. But even prior to that, they were able to earn more than they had in Nicaragua, and that meant that they could provide more support for their families back home. At least one of the children of each of these women[2] seized the opportunity this afforded to attend college. And as a result of the educational opportunities their mothers have been able to offer them, they have found employment that gives them both satisfaction and relative job security (and benefits). Hence, some measure of social mobility has been achieved between these two generations.

Disadvantages have also arisen with their emigration. Requests for increased financial support came from a widening pool of relatives and acquaintances. Moreover, their absence from home took a toll on some of their children who remained in Nicaragua. But they have learned to grapple with those dilemmas, and they are proud of their children's achievements. They are also pleased that they themselves will have greater economic security as they age, something that would have been unthinkable had they remained in Nicaragua.

SITUATING THEIR HISTORIES

The experiences of Andrea, Silvia, Ana, and Pamela coincide in a number of ways with those of poor women all over Latin America. In fact, many of the aspects of structural violence that were illustrated in their lives can be seen in the experiences of the Guatemalan and Salvadoran women described by Menjívar (2011) and Walsh and Menjívar (2016), respectively; the Brazilian women described by Nancy Scheper-Hughes (1992); the Mexican women at the center of Lourdes Benería and Martha Roldan's (1987) study; and so forth. Likewise, poor women have relied heavily on the service sector for employment all over Latin America, as the academic literature documents (e.g., Babb 1989, 1996a; Draper 1985). Moreover, the other elements of the structural violence these women experienced, such as sexual violence and discrimination based on their race/ethnicity, also characterize the lives of many women in the region (as noted in the preceding chapters).

Nonetheless, the four women whose life histories we have become acquainted with differed from those elsewhere, as described in these other studies, in several important ways. First, they lived through a revolution and the prospects of several of their families were expanded by the change it wrought. Along with the material benefits they received, the revolution provided them with a new sense of possibilities for the future. There is, of course, a significant body of literature on the social impact of the Nicaraguan revolution (e.g., Booth 1985; H. Williams 1987; Lancaster 1988, 1992; Macintosh 2016), and on the topic of women's participation in it (e.g., Kampwirth 1993, 2004, 2011; Stoltz Chinchilla 1990; Collinson 1990; Molyneux 1986). Yet most of these studies focus on the period from 1979 to 1990 and do not go beyond that point.[3] Therefore, they do not provide a longer-term vision of change at the micro level including before, during, and after the revolution. Given the promise of the revolution to redress the effects of structural violence, our examination of the lives of Andrea, Silvia, Ana, and Pamela allows for an understanding of the evolving nature of that violence during these distinct periods of Nicaraguan history.

Another way in which this account of the lives of these four women differs from the general discussion of structural violence and its manifestations in the lives of poor women in Latin America is with regard to the decision the former women made in the neoliberal period to emigrate. They have not been alone in making that choice: tens of millions of Latin Americans—a pool that has included Nicaraguans—have emigrated since 1990,[4] in search of a means to a better life for themselves and their families. A vast literature on immigration addresses a host of issues related to this topic. The components of it that are particularly relevant for the purposes of this study are those that look at the immigrants' reasons for leaving Latin America;[5] the networks they use to move to their new "homes" (e.g., Menjívar 2000; Boyd 1989; Winters et al. 2001); the relationships they maintain with their families—especially their children—back home (e.g., Parreñas 2005; Hondagneu-Sotelo and Avila 1997; Dreby 2010; Pratt 2012); and their status and reception in their country of destination (e.g., Parreñas 2015; Solari 2017; Davidov and Semyonov 2017; Barbulescu 2019; Jaret 1999).

The present study portrays the ways in which all of these dynamics came together and expressed themselves in the lives of a small group of immigrant women. One example of this is the connection between the revolution and their emigration, in the sense that the former brought them in touch with the network that would be their pathway to working overseas. Without the network of foreigners who had come to Nicaragua because of the revolution, in all likelihood they would never have ended up working in Italy. This is, after all, not one of the predominant paths of migration in the world today.[6]

Their path of emigration has had both positive and negative features for Andrea, Silvia, Ana, and Pamela. They were able to immigrate to Italy legally, which gave them a variety of advantages, including having greater earning potential than those who do not.[7] Once these women arrived in Italy, they were required to apply for residency. But as others have shown, obtaining it was a much more likely prospect in Italy than in most other northern countries.[8]

Moreover, simply submitting their documents to apply for residency provided them with access to the Italian public health system. That system offered them free, high-quality healthcare. On the negative side of the scale, all four women are stuck working in the country's service sector. As discussed in Chapter 1, this is true for many immigrants to Italy from the Global South, especially those who receive legal documentation to be in the country.[9] Yet as we have seen, that had already been the fate of Andrea, Silvia, and Ana in Nicaragua. In addition, the distance between Italy and Nicaragua—as opposed to the United States and Nicaragua, for example—may have meant that they have had to wait longer between trips home, and those trips cost much more. Perhaps there was also a psychological element to this issue of distance, in that they feel much farther away from their loved ones.

But besides illustrating the ways in which these various social dynamics may work together to produce particular outcomes, this account of their history also starts decades before their emigration. And it puts in evidence that the social change resulting from the Nicaraguan revolution was not sufficient to present these women with an alternative to leaving their country of origin if they wanted to ensure that their children would have more options than they had themselves.

We also saw that their children did have more opportunities than Andrea, Ana, and Pamela had to study and find satisfying jobs. This was largely the product of the consistent hard work of these women over many years, both in Nicaragua and abroad. This finding suggests that emigration enables some degree of social mobility for family members left at home.[10]

The initiative these women have taken to emigrate has facilitated these changes in their own and their children's lives. Yet even as Andrea, Ana, Pamela, and Silvia expressed contentment about those changes, given the nature of Nicaragua's labor market, the children of the first three still need some degree of economic support for their own children's education and when health and other crises arise. So at a time in their lives when these women should be thinking about their own financial futures, given that they are no longer young, they are still unable to do so in an exclusive fashion.

In sum, through their imaginations and actions these four women have pushed the boundaries of the structural violence they were born into. That is, their coming of age and becoming young adults during the Nicaraguan revolution—a process that expressed *structurally transformative* agency on a societal level—helped to modify their consciousness about what it might be possible to achieve in their lifetimes. Andrea was the most explicit in acknowledging the alteration in her point of view regarding what women might be able to do. But each of them demonstrated a notably wider frame of reference and greater aspirations than those of their mothers. These aspirations were evident in their seeking intimate relationships and family dynamics that were distinct from those accepted by their mothers. The four women also sought to achieve a higher level of education and a different position in life. Eventually, though, when it became clear it would be difficult for the women to achieve these goals for themselves, they shifted their focus to ensuring that their children would have them within reach.

Much of the agency expressed in the actions of these women was not meant to, and did not, contribute to the transformation of their societies.[11] As a consequence, it constituted *structurally reproductive* agency on a societal level. Yet it did bring about changes in their own and their children's lives. Hence, their histories illustrate the lasting impact of a society-wide process of *structurally transformative* agency, even for those not politically engaged on a continuing basis. That impact was noteworthy even though the four women, like most other members of their society, were ultimately left with little other outlet than efforts to refashion individual lives.

Yet the contexts in which Andrea, Ana, Pamela, and Silvia have made those efforts—Nicaragua and Italy—are still very much characterized by structural violence. Thus, even though the children of the first three of these women have experienced some social mobility, the lives of these women continue to be delimited by it.

BROADER IMPLICATIONS AND REFLECTIONS

The life stories of Andrea, Silvia, Ana, and Pamela illustrate many of the challenges faced by those who occupy a disadvantaged position in the social structure of their societies in the Global South. As the term *structural violence* indicates, they have great difficulty reaching their full potential because of the multiple inequalities that constrain them from birth onward. For much of this population, emigration remains one of the few, if not the only, means of social mobility for them and/or their children.

Yet in engaging in the agency implied in emigrating from their country of origin—which typically comes at a notable cost, financially and/or emotionally—those who leave release pressure on the economy and society that is failing to sustain them. Moreover, if they send back remittances, which is their likely reason for going abroad, they are helping to support the economy in that same country of origin. Thus, even as their loved ones may see an improvement in their well-being at the level of their family, in some senses the overall social structure of their country of origin is being reinforced.

At the same time, without major transformation in the country they immigrate to, in all likelihood their actions—as embodied in the work they undertake—also reinforce the existing social structure there. That is, as we have seen, they are absorbed into the society there in order to fulfill a need for a particular kind of labor. That labor is not attractive to the local population because of the low wages and low status associated with it. Hence, when this immigrant labor force is "fortunate enough" to be able to stay in their country of destination, they are inserted into a new set of social inequalities. And their insertion most likely places them in a disadvantaged position.

Moreover, despite the clear need for certain kinds of labor—most especially for the agricultural and service sectors—in the societies/economies of the Global North, we are witnessing a growing resistance to the presence of immigrant workers. Whether it takes the form of the presidency of Donald Trump in the United States, the rise of Matteo Salvini to become the dominant voice in the governing coalition in Italy, or the prime ministership of Viktor Mihály Orbán in Hungary, each of these administrations gained power, at least in part, because their anti-immigrant rhetoric found a resonance in the sectors of their population that have been hurt by the economic changes of recent decades.[12] The sentiments held by these constituencies make the presence of immigrants that much more tenuous and challenging. In Italy, hate crimes against immigrants increased significantly following the installation of the government that Salvini was at the pinnacle of (e.g., Montalto Monella 2018; Gosteli 2018; Speak 2018). This represented both a lessening of inhibitions vis-à-vis the expression of hostility toward immigrants and a sense that the government—at least in the form of Salvini's control over the Ministry of the Interior—was committed to reducing the presence of immigrants in the country. Aside from an apparent increase in expressions of discrimination against immigrants, the language employed by those at the helm of these three governments reduced any sense of security immigrants might have felt about being able to remain in their countries of destination. In a poignant example, Salvini called for a census of the Roma people, stating that those who had been born in Italy would be permitted to stay there, while those who were foreign born would be deported (Kirchgaessner 2018; Euronews 2018). However, the message contained in his "call" and general anti-immigrant stance was felt beyond the Roma population, with many in the immigrant population experiencing growing unease (Segreti 2018; Uyangoda 2018).

A logical conclusion one might reach given the more and more inhospitable nature of the environment in their receiving countries is that staying in their countries of origin may be less stressful for immigrants. In fact, that was the response of Andrea, Silvia, Ana, and Pamela when I asked them what advice they might have for their compatriots back home.[13] That opinion appears to be reflected in data about the decrease in migration of Mexicans to the United States (Gonzalez-Barrera and Krogstad 2017; Zong et al. 2018). Remaining in their home country would enable them to stay with their families and to not uproot their lives. As indicated by my findings, as well as those of others (e.g., Parreñas 2005; Dreby 2010; Yarris 2017), their emigration put a strain on their families back home, even as their families may have benefited materially from their work abroad.

Yet being able to stay home would require that these emigrants have better opportunities in their countries of origin. That is, it would require a lessening of the structural violence at home. A lessening of the degree of structural violence would, in all likelihood, only be made possible through a serious modification of the social structure. As Yarris (2017, quoting Rocha 2006) stated, those who emigrate—such as these women—are being forced to do so because their states are failing them. Their home states are not enacting policies that enable those who ultimately leave to not only survive but also to thrive while employed within the country's labor force.

Hence, until the governments in immigrants' countries of origin change their priorities to take into account those at the bottom of their social structure, we can only expect the numbers of emigrants from them to increase—whether their destination is to the Global North or elsewhere in the Global

South where their labor will be absorbed. Yet by and large, the pattern of governments in power in Latin America does not appear to be oriented in that direction. In the 2000s there was a strong wave of change in this region—embodied in the so-called Pink Tide—which brought to power governments that prioritized reducing structural violence (Beasley-Murray et al. 2010; Reygadas and Filgueira 2010). Social indicators in at least some of these countries put in evidence that commitment (Reygadas and Filgueira 2010; Enríquez and Page 2018). That wave has been weakened in recent years, though, as political parties on the right side of the spectrum have gained new momentum.

The result is that the policies that conservative governments in the Global South pursue—which are supported by conservative governments in the Global North[14]—reinforce the structural violence that propels emigration. At the same time, conservative governments in the Global North are not bringing about any kind of social change that would fill the labor deficits in their own countries, such as making employment in the undersupplied sectors of the economy—most especially agriculture and domestic service—more attractive to the local labor force. It would take this kind of shift to reduce the objective need for an immigrant labor force in these sectors. Without such a need, immigrants would not find the jobs that draw them to leave their own countries. In sum, *structurally transformative agency* is required in both areas of the world if the goal is to permit people in the Global South to remain there and thrive, and to find a way out of the economically hard times in the Global North that incite people to react against immigrants.

Notes

1. These names, along with those of their home communities, relatives, and employers, are pseudonyms, which I have used to protect their privacy.

2. Hays (1994: 64); italics in the original.

3. This term comes from Ehrenreich and Hochschild (2003).

4. Menjívar and Abrego (2012) also bring the concept of violence to bear on the legal categories that describe inequalities in immigration status. These scholars argue that what they call "legal violence," which stems from those inequalities, works in concert with other types of violence in conditioning the life chances of Central American immigrants to the United States. These other types of violence include those derived from class, racial, and gender inequalities.

5. See also Burrell and Moody (2015).

6. See also ECLAC (2021: 49). I included figures from 2019, rather than 2020, as the latter were distorted by the pandemic that expanded across the globe in 2020. Meanwhile, the figures for poverty in Latin America had fallen since 1980, when poverty affected 40.5 percent of the population and extreme poverty affected 18.6 percent (ECLAC 2016: 10).

7. This data points to an increase in poverty since 2015, when the first figure was 39.0 percent and the second was 7.6 percent (ECLAC 2016: 13).

8. Some other sources, including the World Bank (https://data.worldbank.org/indicator/SI.POV.GINI?end=2014&locations=NI&start=2014, accessed June 1, 2021) place this figure at .462 for 2014. I have cited ECLAC's figure to be consistent

in my sources. The figure for 2014 is the most recent one available describing Nicaraguan income inequality. FIDEG (2020: 14) presents a Gini index for 2019 based on consumption. That figure has been stable since 2015. But a Gini index based on consumption is not directly comparable to a Gini index based on income, the latter of which is used by the United Nations and the World Bank and is the more common measure of inequality.

9. See also Azevedo and Bouillon (2010).

10. For discussions of the racial caste system that permeates Latin America, see Wade (2008) and Telles (2014); for discussions of the patriarchal structure of society in the region, see Paulson (2016) and Dore (1997).

11. Chapter 3, which addresses the sexual and physical violence that overshadowed the childhoods of Andrea, Silvia, and Ana, will also include a discussion of the literature specifically focused on these two types of violence.

12. For example, Menjívar's (2011) fine book.

13. Elements of this discussion will be further developed in subsequent chapters where they are relevant for the retelling of these women's lives.

14. See also R. Williams (1994) and Bulmer-Thomas (1995).

15. See Langley (1983) and Macaulay (1998).

16. For discussions of the Somoza dynasty—which started with Anastasio Somoza García (the father), who was succeeded by Luis Somoza Debayle (the elder son) and eventually by Anastasio Somoza Debayle (the younger son)—see Booth (1985), Walter (1993), and Dunkerley (1988).

17. Booth (1985: 67) notes that one scheme Anastasio Somoza García used to bolster his annual income was to grant concessions to both foreign and local companies, for which he "received 'additional contributions,' 'executive levies,' and 'presidential commissions.' Associates estimated his take from gold mining alone at from $175,000 to $400,000 per year during the 1940s."

18. See also R. Williams (1986) and Bulmer-Thomas (1987).

19. See also R. Williams (1986), Brockett (1998), and Bulmer-Thomas (1987).

20. Booth (1985) and Vilas (1986) provide comprehensive accounts of the various sectors of society that participated in the struggle to overthrow the Somoza regime and the agenda of the Sandinista-led government.

21. See Johns (2012) and La Botz (2016).

22. See Booth (1985) and H. Williams (1987) for further discussion of this topic.

23. See also Close (1988).

24. H. Williams (1987: 249–250).

25. H. Williams (1987: 252).

26. Stahler-Sholk (1990) and Conroy (1987) both speak to this issue.

27. See also Conroy (1990) and Enríquez (1997) on this topic. Aside from the role the U.S. government played in the various elements contributing to Nicaragua's economic crisis, it actively sought to influence the outcome of these elections, among other ways by publicly promising significant economic aid if the opposition coalition won.

28. Stahler-Sholk (1997) and Acevedo Vogl (1998) discuss the Chamorro government's structural adjustment.

29. See also Enríquez (2010) and Catalán Aravena (2001).

30. See Gill (2008) and Türken et al. (2016) on this issue.

31. Some social programs to assist the poor were put in place there under this FSLN administration, and the poverty rate declined for a while (Martí i Puig and Baumeister 2016; FIDEG 2020). However, the downturn in the economy of Nicaragua's key benefactor, Venezuela, started to be felt there in the middle of the 2010s. At that point in time, the subsidized oil exports that the Venezuelan government had initiated after Daniel Ortega's reelection in Nicaragua became unsustainable, and the social programs that had brought some relief to the poor in the latter country were curtailed.

32. See also Stahler-Sholk (1997) and Catalán Aravena (2001).

33. With regard to the incorporation of intersectional analysis in the study of entrepreneurship see, for example, Valdez (2015) and Romero and Valdez (2016); with respect to social activism, see Zavella (2017), whose work insisted on the need to incorporate analysis of race/ethnicity into studies of the ways in which gender and class interact even before the concept of intersectionality was introduced (c.f. Zavella 1987); and with respect to domestic service see Ray and Qayam (2009) and Lutz (2011).

34. Yarris (2017: 8) refers to the argument of Luis Rocha that, rather than thinking of such emigration as stemming from choice within a "sending" country context, we should actually consider the context to be one in which the population is being "expelled." The population is expelled because of "state failure to provide economic opportunity and protect social security for their populations." I would agree that this is certainly the larger milieu in which women such as those at the center of this study contemplate their options. However, ultimately, they do make a choice as to how best to resolve the dilemmas such state failure presents them with.

Here, too, I would like to underline the differences between Nicaragua and Central America's "Northern Triangle" countries of El Salvador, Guatemala, and Honduras. At least until the uprising of 2018, Nicaragua was the safest country in

Central America and, for most people there, being forced to flee for one's life was not an issue. This is important to note because the daily reality for many people in the Northern Triangle countries has been so dangerous that *choice* has not been the correct word to describe their thinking before their departure from the region. I am grateful to Marjorie Zatz (personal correspondence, April 27, 2019) for calling this to my attention.

35. Further divisions could certainly be made—such as between the 1990–2006 period and the Central America Free Trade Agreement (CAFTA) period. But for the sake of brevity, this history will be separated into these three periods.

36. For example, the 1960s were a heyday for the export of certain key crops—such as cotton. Yet the expansion of its production hit subsistence farmers especially hard as cotton growers took over more and more area that the former had previously cultivated.

37. Figures regarding emigration from Nicaragua (and elsewhere in Latin America) should be taken as estimations, and different sources provide quite distinct estimations depending on their own sources and the methodology employed for arriving at them.

38. Lundquist and Massey (2005) make a strong case that the Contra war was critical in stimulating the flow of Nicaraguans to the United States, as opposed to it being a result of the economic situation in the country at the time.

39. Jonakin (2018) speaks to the pattern of expanding neoliberal economic policies leading to growing emigration throughout Latin America. Despite this relationship between economic policy and emigration, I would not make the case that the Nicaraguan state is a labor broker state for those emigrating in the sense that Rodriguez (2010) argues that the Philippine state is. My rationale is that the Nicaraguan state has not established an apparatus similar to what she describes, but has instead simply allowed emigration to take place.

40. See United Nations (2020a: Table 1—International Migrant Stock 2020: Migrants by Destination and Origin).

41. See United Nations (2020a: Table 1—International Migrant Stock 2020: Migrants by Destination and Origin). See cautionary note in footnote 37.

42. The principal recipient of Nicaraguan émigrés in Europe is Spain, with an estimated 42,784 of them (United Nations 2020a: Table 1—International Migrant Stock 2020: Migrants by Destination and Origin).

43. Given an estimated total overall population of 6,625,000 in 2020 (United Nations 2019: File POP/1-1—Total Population by region, subregion, and country), and the UN estimates presented earlier, it would appear that approximately 11 percent of the Nicaraguan population resided outside the country in 2020.

44. Ehrenreich and Hochschild (2003) speak of the four predominant regional paths of migration worldwide: (1) from Southeast Asia to the Middle and Far East; (2) from the former Soviet bloc countries to western Europe; (3) from Mexico northward to the United States and Canada; and (4) from Africa to Europe. Likewise, the United Nations (2020b: 23), presents the ten largest migration corridors worldwide, and migrating from Latin America to Europe is not one of them.

45. With the shift in administration from the Trump to the Biden presidency, and the promise of adopting new immigration policies on the part of the latter, it became conceivable that Central Americans would find it less difficult to emigrate to the United States. However, the Biden administration's position emphasized putting resources into foreign aid to the three northern countries in the region (Guatemala, El Salvador, and Honduras) to make it possible for potential émigrés to stay in their country of origin, rather than welcoming them to the United States. This had ostensibly been the approach taken by former president Barack Obama, to little effect. Hence, it remained to be seen whether Joe Biden's stated policy would make a difference in the number of people emigrating. If it did not, and if the United States did not enact a more permissive immigration policy, then Central Americans might well continue to follow the path opened by people like these four women.

46. See United Nations (2020b: Figure 5 and Annex Table—International Migrant Stock 2020).

47. See United Nations, "International Migrant Stock 2019: Country Profiles," https://www.un.org/en/development/desa/population/migration/data/estimates2/countryprofiles.asp, accessed May 31, 2021.

48. Calculated from data posted by Italy's official statistics agency (http://stra-dati.istat.it/Index.aspx, accessed May 31, 2021). It is critical to note here that these data only take into account the documented population.

49. See, for example, Istat (2015: 5). The most important destinations, in order of importance, have been Germany, the UK, Switzerland, and France. See also Bartolini et al. (2015) and Labrianidis and Pratsinakis (2016).

50. Several scholars note that cultural/religious characteristics may also make Italy a more attractive destination than some others: for example, Chell-Robinson (2000) and Orsini-Jones and Gattullo (2000) speak about the importance of Christianity—and especially Catholicism—being shared between one's home and receiving country.

51. Burawoy's (1976) analysis is meant to theorize the reasons for, and elements central to, long-running migration streams. Its viewpoint is that of the

migration system as a whole, rather than that of the individual migrant, the latter of whom may decide to leave their homeland because of extremely problematic circumstances there regardless of whether a job awaits them.

52. However, many working-class women—especially African American women—always had to work to generate income for their households (e.g., Brenner and Luce 2006).

53. Meanwhile, its birth rate has been falling since the late 1960s. See also Reuters (2017) and Schwartz (2016).

54. Bonizzoni (2013: 137) notes that while hiring foreign outside help was a privilege of Italy's urban upper-middle and upper classes in the 1970s, by 2009 one out of ten Italian families had outside domestic help (most of which was foreign). She argues that it had shifted from being a luxury to being a necessity for many families over this period of time. Colombo (2005) also speaks to this issue.

55. This is the case at least for the local population that has the luxury of choosing which sector of the economy they might enter in search of a job. That is, local women of color from the working class, who may not be considered for other more remunerative positions, have often found themselves seeking employment in the homes of their white, middle- and upper-class compatriots (see Roberts 1992; Romero 2002; Trotz 1996).

56. Sciortino (2004) defines the Italian state as a "conservative" welfare state in that it looks to the family to provide a lot of the services and care needed by its members, and for many areas of need, it provides cash transfers to the family instead of services. Ginsborg (2003) also highlights the extent to which the family is expected to take responsibility for its members in Italy. Healthcare is a major exception to this rule.

57. On the neoliberal turn in Italian economic policy, see also Ginsborg (2003) and Berend (2016).

58. According to Gagliardi et al. (2012: 96), the state provided 7 percent of households with such money transfers to assist with paying for migrant care workers between 2005 and 2008. See also Sciortino (2004) and Barbiano di Belgiojoso and Ortensi (2015) on the economic logic behind the approach taken by the state in this regard. This logic was also mentioned in an interview with an Italian who had formerly worked for a decade at a NGO that provided services for immigrants in Turin (August 8, 2017). He argued that the state saved about 40 billion euros in 2015 by helping to keep elders in their homes. This calculation was based on what it would have cost the state to subsidize the price of their stay in assisted living facilities versus the assistance it gave to those in need

to pay the much less costly immigrant laborers to provide support for elders in their homes.

59. Tognetti Bordogna and Ornaghi (2012) discuss the relatively inflexible nature of Italy's welfare system—which "meets overt needs [such as for health-care and a pension] but not the multifaceted needs of the elderly and their families." Locating the site of this care in the family ensures that those needs will be met, although no longer by family members but instead by immigrant women.

60. Lutz (2011: 160) speaks of a similar dynamic emerging in Germany, in which under a new, more restrictive immigration law, the only legal form of en-try for unskilled workers was through arrangements to work for up to three years providing in-home care for German citizens.

61. Lutz (2011) and Gonzales et al. (2019) present the multifaceted nature of the vulnerability that immigrants face when they are not legally documented; Zatz and Rodriguez (2015) speak to the "dreams and nightmares" of the undocu-mented in the United States. Menjívar and Lakhani (2016) illustrate the ways in which immigrants are willing to transform their lives to become legally docu-mented. Meanwhile, Borjas and Tienda (1993) and Abrego (2014) discuss the fact that legal documentation leads to greater earning potential for migrants to the United States; Solari (2017) speaks to this issue with regard to Italy.

62. This dynamic represents a strong contrast with a major destination coun-try for Nicaraguans—the United States. Aside from some very specific cases (see Repak 1995), immigrants who enter the care sector of the U.S. economy are not given any preferential treatment in their efforts to obtain documenta-tion (c.f. Parreñas 2015; Abrego 2014). In contrast, there have been periods in U.S. history when the entry of foreign workers destined for other sectors of the economy has been fostered by the U.S. government. Calavita (1992) analyzes one such case: that of the millions of Mexican agricultural workers who entered the United States through the Bracero program between 1942 and 1964.

63. This has not always been the case. Solari (2017: 54) observes that in the 1700s domestic servants in Italy were primarily men, but this pattern began to change in the 1800s as men were increasingly absorbed into the budding indus-trial sector. By the time that immigrants started to fill this role, it was decidedly a position for women. Ehrenreich and Hochschild (2003) and Hondagneu-Sotelo (2001), among others, write about domestic work as female migrants' work more generally. Interestingly, Ray and Qayum (2009: 25) speak about the ideal do-mestic worker in India being the "family retainer," which is a category of worker who has been employed by the same family for generations. These retainers have

typically been men. But they have a decreasing presence in the landscape of domestic servants in "modernizing" India.

64. Calculated from Istat data (http://stra-dati.istat.it/Index.aspx), accessed June 1, 2021).

65. Calculated from Istat data (http://stra-dati.istat.it/Index.aspx), accessed June 1, 2021).

66. See especially Solari (2017).

67. As stated earlier, Peru is Italy's sixteenth most important sending country, and Ecuador is Italy's eighteenth most important sending country. Catanzaro and Colombo (2009) identify the key migration streams for Italy's domestic labor force as being from Latin America, Eastern Europe, Asia, and the Horn of Africa. Meanwhile, Bonizzoni (2013: 2) states that "eight out of ten [registered foreign domestic] workers [were] women" in 2010.

68. Interview, the first Salvadoran immigrant to arrive in Italy, July 6, 2016. She arrived in 1968.

69. See also Parreñas (2015). In comparing wages cross-nationally, Parreñas refers specifically to the other destination countries of Filipina migrant domestic workers, which include several Asian countries (e.g., Hong Kong and Singapore) and the Gulf Cooperation Council nations (including the United Arab Emirates [UAE], Kuwait, and Saudi Arabia). However, wages in Italy, Canada, and the United States are also substantially better than they are in the immigrants' home countries.

70. For example, Lutz (2011) mentions that domestic workers and care providers in Germany are not granted labor contracts, so they have no rights or obligations (beyond that of actually doing the job they are hired to do). And there are no federal laws in the United States that regulate domestic and care work (Solari 2017).

71. In fact, Barbiano di Belgiojoso and Ortensi (2015) show that mobility out of this type of work is *very* limited.

72. In a study of the well-being of immigrants working in Italy's care sector, Boccagni (2016: 298) argued that this concept needs to be expanded to include the well-being of the immigrants' family back in their country of origin, as immigrants often identify how they themselves are in terms of how their families are doing. In response to Boccagni's questions, the answer that seemed to capture this idea best was "As long as they are well, so am I."

73. Silvia does not have children, so this issue was not central to her decision.

74. On the negative side, remittances can, however, at least for a time, lead to increased inequality within sending communities, because those with family members overseas are at an advantage over those without.

75. Dreby's (2010) findings from a study of Mexican families in which one or both parent(s) migrate to work in the United States coincide with Démurger's (2015) in these senses.

76. Parreñas (2005) also insists on the need for us to assess the impact of the departure of each parent separately. She argues that given traditional gender roles, children are more likely to accept their fathers leaving than their mothers leaving. And this dynamic may have implications for how the children fare—including at school—in their absence. Dreby (2010) concurs with Parreñas (2005) in many of these senses. However, Dreby (2010) finds that children's aspirations regarding education coincided with which parent it was who emigrated; those whose mothers emigrated had higher educational aspirations than those whose fathers emigrated.

77. I moved to Nicaragua in 1982 to conduct the research for my PhD dissertation on the country. I ended up staying for seven years, completing my PhD in 1985 and going on to work as an advisor for the Nicaraguan Food Program (PAN-MIDINRA) and as a member of the research/teaching faculty at the Universidad Centroamericana (UCA). But my connection with the country continued even after assuming a postdoctoral position and then a faculty position in the United States, as my husband remained there to work as an architect and planner.

78. Speaking of a similar dynamic, Omi and Winant (1986) highlight the fact that even though the civil rights movement in the United States did not achieve all of its objectives, it fundamentally changed the consciousness of Black people in the United States vis-à-vis their rights and their identity.

79. This wording is a paraphrasing of Hays (1994: 64).

CHAPTER 2

Portions of this chapter first appeared in the Springer Nature publication *Qualitative Sociology*, "Everyday Violence in Central America as Seen Through the Life of One Woman." Enríquez, Laura J. © 2017. Reprinted by permission from Springer Nature.

1. Departments are roughly the equivalent of counties.

2. Interview, September 10, 2015.

3. Interview, September 10, 2015.

4. This is a little over half a hectare (1 *manzana* = 0.7 hectares) or 1.3 acres (1 manzana = 1.7 acres).

5. The children in the immediate household of Andrea and Silvia were born to and/or raised by their mother and father together. But their father and mother, with their various partners including each other, had a total of twenty-seven children. Their father had come into their parents' partnership having already had

five children, and their mother had already had two children. Interview, Andrea, September 10, 2015. Stephens (1989: 139) notes that Nicaraguan families tend to be large, with the average birth rate per woman approximating six children.

6. This shift in their "family structure" will be discussed at greater length in Chapter 3.

7. She had four additional pregnancies that did not make it to full term.

8. The relationship between Ana's mother and father was complicated, and her mother chose not to accept support from him for their child.

9. Interview, October 11, 2015.

10. Three of her stepfather's perhaps ten children with his previous "wife" also lived with them off and on while Ana was still at home (interview, October 11, 2015).

11. Interview, October 11, 2015.

12. Interview, October 11, 2015.

13. Here, Ana seems to be referencing groups or movements of "landless" workers, perhaps even the Landless Workers' Movement of Brazil.

14. Interview, October 11, 2015.

15. Interview, October 24, 2015.

16. Interview, October 11, 2015.

17. State farms controlled 13.3 percent of the agricultural land; cooperatives and individual agrarian reform beneficiaries controlled 15.7 percent (calculated from CIERA 1989: vol. 9, p. 56; Dirección General de Reforma Agraria, MIDINRA, unpublished data, 1988). The area that was distributed to cooperatives and individuals continued to grow after 1987, but arriving at calculations about how much land these distinct actors controlled after 1987 is complicated by the fact that the government agency charged with land distribution (MIDINRA) began to use a new system to describe the structure of land tenure in 1988.

18. In fact, one of the siblings she grew up with is a half brother, as her mother gave birth to him before she became the common-law wife of Pamela's father. Pamela recently discovered that she also has two half sisters from a relationship that her father had prior to meeting her mother. These two half sisters did not form part of her family's life (interview, November 4, 2015).

Common-law relationships are very widespread in Nicaragua and elsewhere in Central America. Formalizing a relationship in marriage has frequently coincided with one's class position in that the more advantaged are more likely to (be able to) seek recognition from the state and/or church for their relationships.

19. Interview, November 4, 2015.

20. Interview, November 4, 2015. Belli (2002: 57) also refers to the food rations that were made available following the earthquake, which included "meager amounts of rice, beans, potatoes, and sugar."

21. See also Southerland (1985), who describes the process of reconstructing the city.

22. Nonetheless, this initiative was grossly marred by massive corruption on the part of the Somoza regime and highly speculative economic activity on the part of some members of the private sector (Higgins 1990; Booth 1985). This would eventually be a turning point in the life of the regime, in that its corruption was so apparent that the movement in opposition to it began to expand and reach sectors of the population—like businesspeople—who had previously turned a blind eye to its illicit actions.

23. Personal correspondence, March 24, 2020.

24. Interview, November 4, 2015.

25. Interview, November 4, 2015.

26. Interview, November 4, 2015.

27. Calculated from United Nations Population Division Data cited at https://www.indexmundi.com/facts/nicaragua/indicator/SP.URB.TOTL.IN.ZS.

Miller (1982: 245–246) argues that the lack of educational facilities in rural areas was a result of the country's underdevelopment and, simultaneously, reflected the needs of the country's political and economic systems. That is, the economy did not need the rural areas to be populated by educated people, who would then have to go on to be farmhands and poor peasants; the more highly educated the rural population was, the greater the likelihood that they would protest the abysmal conditions in which they were generally forced to live and work.

28. Interview, September 24, 2015.

29. Interview with Silvia, September 11, 2015. Through correspondence with a colleague who took part in the Literacy Crusade of 1980 and was posted in the mostly rural Department of Jinotega, I learned that the school in the community she lived in there was not functioning. She stated that "there were a lot of other [rural] places with no school at all" and that the size of a school would depend on the remoteness of it. She herself grew up in a rural community next to the border with Honduras. Her elementary school there had four classrooms, for six grades of students. She hypothesized that it might have had greater access to teachers than more isolated areas since the community had regular transportation to it given that it was a border crossing point (personal communication, former Literacy Crusade participant, March 29, 2020).

30. Interview with Andrea, September 24, 2015.

31. Menjívar (2011), in contrast, found that it was more often girls than boys who were taken out of school.

32. Interview, September 24, 2015. The woman Andrea is referring to was her father's other common-law wife, Ada.

33. Interview, September 24, 2015.

34. In Nicaragua, as in most of Latin America, there is a close relationship between class, status, and skin color. Generally, lighter-skinned people tend to be located higher up the social hierarchy—in an intersection of inequalities (class and race) that form part of the structural violence existing there. For a discussion of the coincidence of racial and class inequalities in Latin America as a whole, see Wade (1997, 2008) and Telles (2014).

35. Interview, September 24, 2015.

36. Interview, September 24, 2015.

37. See also Enríquez (1991), R. Williams (1986), and Brockett (1998).

38. Interview, November 5, 2015.

39. Interview, October 11, 2015.

40. See also Enríquez (1991).

41. Interview with Andrea, September 10, 2015.

42. Interview, October 8, 2015.

43. This is a relatively common experience for domestic workers in other countries as well, and for domestic workers who are immigrants (c.f. de Souza and Cerqueira 2008 and Welsh et al. 2006).

44. Interview, October 11, 2015.

45. Wade (2013: 187) argues that racial/ethnic inequalities are also at issue in the sexual harassment experienced by so many domestic workers in Latin America. He posits that domestic workers in that region embody not only class and gender inequalities but also racial/ethnic inequality—to the extent that they are "marked by blackness or indigeneity"—and consequently become exoticized and sexualized. Although Ana was not Afro-Nicaraguan, nor self-identified as indigenous, her skin color was dark brown. Therefore, this dynamic could have contributed to the harassment she was frequently subjected to on the job. This might well have also factored into the harassment Andrea and Silvia experienced (see later discussion), as they, too, had dark brown skin.

46. Interview, October 11, 2015.

47. Interview, October 11, 2015.

48. The topic of remittances is discussed at length in Chapter 4.

49. Interview, October 11, 2015.

50. The daughter in this household was born in Nicaragua, so she had dual—German and Nicaraguan—citizenship.

51. Interview, October 18, 2015.

52. Interview, October 8, 2015.

53. Interview, October 8, 2015.

54. Interview, October 8, 2015.

55. Interview, September 24, 2015.

56. Interview, October 8, 2015.

57. Interview, September 24, 2015.

58. Interview, November 5, 2015.

59. Interview, September 24, 2015.

60. Interview, October 8, 2015.

61. Interview, September 24, 2015.

62. Jurik (2005) and Davutoğlu (2013) found the same for other populations of less well off people. See also Banerjee (2013) for a general review of the literature on microfinance.

63. It is infamous for being a locale where one can find absolutely anything (legal and illegal) for sale, and where it is also somewhat dangerous to go because of thievery.

64. Interview, September 11, 2015.

65. Interview, September 25, 2015.

66. See Bickham Mendez (2005: 3). She argues that the overwhelming presence of female workers within these assembly plants stems from the desire of the companies that own them to have a docile and cheap labor force. Hence, the composition of the workforce embodies and reinforces the devaluation of women's labor that is an expression of the gender inequalities within the societies in which they operate.

67. The workers previously employed in the state-owned garment industry had also been primarily women. But this labor force was distinct in an important sense: it was unionized.

68. See Bickham Mendez (2005: 11). Van Wunnik (2011/2013) and Vukelich (1994) also analyze Nicaragua's Zona Franca.

69. Interview, September 11, 2015.

70. Interview, September 25, 2015.

71. For general histories of this sector, see E. Colombo et al. (2017) and Dipartimento di Comunicazione e Ricerca Sociale (2012).

72. Interview, November 4, 2015.

73. Interview, November 4, 2015.

74. González-Rivera (2011) uses the term "maternal breadwinners" to describe the strong connection between being a mother and assuming financial responsibility for the household in Nicaragua, given the commonality of the lack of such responsibility being practiced by the father of her children.

75. Interview, November 4, 2015. The husband she is describing is the father of four of her children; the oldest of her children was born before she met him (see her family tree).

76. For a sampling of this literature, see Chant (2002), Townsend et al. (1999), Wilson (2013), and Casique (2010). Other reactions mentioned included withdrawing financial support from the household, and desertion of their spouses and children (see especially Chant 2002). These latter reactions are considered in subsequent chapters.

77. See, for example, Schickedanz et al. (2015), Larson and Halfon (2010), and S. Cohen et al. (2010).

78. See, for example, Schickedanz et al. (2015), Currie (2009), and Case et al. (2005).

79. See, for example, Schickedanz et al. (2015) and Kozyrskyj et al. (2010).

80. Interview, October 30, 2015.

81. See also Bossert (1985). As was the case with public education, the Somoza regime invested very little in public health facilities in rural areas.

82. Interview, October 30, 2015.

83. She was also treated innumerable times for asthma on an outpatient basis. Interview, October 30, 2015.

84. Andrea's eventual emigration to Italy provided her with access to Italy's public health system. But a recent allergy/asthma crisis had led her to pay for the shots rather than wait the estimated six months to receive them free of charge through the system. Each shot cost her 250 euros or approximately a fifth of her monthly salary in Italy (Interviews, November 5, 2015, and October 22, 2015).

85. Interview, October 9, 2015.

86. Interview, September 10, 2015.

87. A likely cause of this disorder is discussed in Chapter 3.

88. Interview, October 30, 2015.

89. Interview, October 30, 2015.

90. Interview, November 19, 2015.

91. Interview, November 19, 2015. Trigeminal neuralgia can be triggered by stress.

92. Pamela experienced another very difficult period later on, while she was living in Italy. She was unemployed at the time and therefore had no way to send

money home to her children. The associated stress triggered another outbreak of the neuralgia:

> When I came to Italy and was living in Margarita's house and couldn't find work . . . it started again, and my face started to swell up again. Look, the thing is, it happened again and I'm talking about at two o'clock in the morning. Across the street there was a *pronto soccorso*, what they call an emergency room here. So I went, at two o'clock in the morning. I went over there and I said, "Look, do you have a pill [for me], I can't take the pain in my face." They said, "No, but if you'd like, we can take you to the hospital." That was at the time when they were grabbing "illegals." [Interviewer question: You were undocumented then?] Yes. So I said, "No . . . it would be better not" [to go]. So they said, "Here's something else you can do . . . go to the Centrale [train station]. There's a pharmacy that is open twenty-four hours [a day there]. Buy yourself some pills, the strongest you can get, and take them." With what money was I going to buy them? (Interview, November 19, 2015)

Since she could not access any medical assistance, Pamela went home and took large quantities of headache medicine and put bottles of cold water on her face until the pain died down.

93. Interview, October 24, 2015.

94. Interview with Andrea, November 5, 2015.

95. Interview with Silvia, September 11, 2015.

96. Interview with Andrea, October 8, 2015.

97. Interview, October 24, 2015.

98. Interview, November 5, 2015.

99. Interview, November 5, 2015.

100. Kampwirth (1993) speaks to this point. Montoya (2002: 72) analyzes changes that took place in gender ideologies—and practices associated with them—in a small rural town in southwestern Nicaragua and argues that the numerous visits to the town of feminists from national organizations (including AMNLAE) had contributed to this process. Those visits "promoted women's right to work outside the home, live free of domestic violence, refuse sexual intercourse with their husbands, and participate in decisions concerning birth control."

101. It became possible to obtain a safe abortion in a legally operating health clinic during the 1980s. The government simply ignored its practice rather than fight for legalization of the procedure. However, shortly before the Sandinista Party won back the executive branch of government in 2006, it supported the passage of legislation making abortion illegal under any circumstances.

102. These kinds of opposition operated at the "public" level. Yet general opposition from men was certainly an obstacle to women engaging in all kinds of activities that were oriented toward changing their role in society and in the family. Much of this latter type of opposition was enacted in the home and local community. See, for example, Montoya (2003) and Kampwirth (1993).

103. Stoltz Chinchilla (1990) analyzes AMNLAE's efforts to promote a feminist agenda in Sandinista policy making early on in the revolution and how they got tempered over time. Heumann (2014) is more critical about that "tempering" process, arguing that the FSLN went so far as to adopt an antifeminist discourse that sidelined those pushing for more radical change, especially in terms of reproductive rights. Meanwhile, Isbester (2001) provides a periodized account of the distinct forces at play and the various ups and downs with regard to feminist initiatives in Nicaragua between 1977 and 2000.

104. See also Molyneux (1986). For discussion of this larger historical pattern, see Molyneux (1981) and Kruks et al. (1989).

105. For discussion of Nicaragua's post-1990 independent women's movement, see Isbester (2001) and Ewig (1999).

106. Interview, September 24, 2015. Those self-defense classes served her well when the father of her children, with whom she was living at the time, tried to hit her on one occasion. Given that she had learned to kickbox, he was the one who ended up hurt.

107. Interviews, October 9, 2015, and November 5, 2015, respectively.

108. Interview, October 9, 2015.

109. This is to say nothing of the tens of thousands of Nicaraguans who suffered because of the war more generally speaking, including the approximately thirty thousand who lost their lives as a result of it (Prevost and Vanden 1997: 2).

110. Interview, October 9, 2015.

111. See Acevedo Vogl (1998), Enríquez (2010), and Stahler-Sholk (1997) with regard to their impact on the general population; see Babb (1996a, 1996b) and Fernández Poncela (1996) vis-à-vis their impact on women.

112. Interview, October 24, 2015.

113. Interview, April 2, 2016.

114. Interview, November 5, 2015.

115. See also Türken et al. (2016) and Brown (2003) on this issue.

CHAPTER 3

Portions of this chapter first appeared in the Springer Nature publication *Qualitative Sociology*, "Everyday Violence in Central America as Seen Through the Life of One Woman." Enríquez, Laura J. © 2017. Reprinted by permission from Springer Nature.

1. Underreporting by boys may be even greater than by girls (Collin-Vézina et al. 2013).

2. Traditional family structures are quite diverse across cultures. However, the risk of children experiencing sexual abuse increases with deviations from whatever traditional family structure may exist in a given society.

3. The authors of this study characterize it as exploratory because of its limitations, including the lack of specification in the definition of the term *sexual abuse* used with the research participants and its nonrepresentativeness vis-à-vis the entire population given the subject pool.

4. These figures are similar to those cited earlier for Costa Rica and Peru.

5. See also Stephens (1989) and Engle (1995) on this topic.

6. Kampwirth (1993: 37) notes that "paternal power 'sparkled in its absence.'" But she also goes on to say, much like Stephens (1989), that he was always "free to return to assert control."

7. Similarly, Yarris (2017) describes "Nicaraguan family and kinship patterns" as "matrifocal but patriarchal."

8. Ramírez et al. (2011) refer to patriarchy as "machismo" and point to the mother's belief in it as being another risk factor.

9. Interview, September 10, 2015.

10. Interview, September 11, 2015.

11. Their father had one additional child that they knew about, with another, married woman. Interviews with Andrea and Silvia, September 10 and 11, 2015, respectively.

12. Interview, September 10, 2015.

13. Interview, September 10, 2015.

14. Interview, September 10, 2015.

15. According to Polanczyk et al. (2003), children who witness sexual abuse are more likely to become victims of such abuse themselves.

16. Interview, September 10, 2015. Andrea became aware later on that Roberto was also abusing her brother's daughter.

17. Some potential reasons for this will be discussed shortly.

18. Interview, November 19, 2015.

19. It bears noting that it was the children of this grandfather who had abused Andrea and several of her siblings.

20. The word she used here was *molestarme*. That word can mean "bother me" or "molest me" in Spanish. Throughout this long quote, I've chosen to translate it

as "bother me." This is because in general, Silvia was implicit rather than explicit in her description. However, she could have meant "molest."

21. Interview, September 11, 2015.

22. A later section of this chapter focuses on why the mothers of these three women may have chosen not to confront their partners about the abuse.

23. As noted in Chapter 2, Andrea turned to a maternal aunt who helped her to find a job in Chinandega so that she could leave home and escape this traumatic situation.

24. Interview, October 11, 2015. After moving into their household, Don Raúl adopted Ana's younger sister Carmen. But he chose not to adopt Ana. Ana hypothesized that perhaps her mother was pregnant with her younger sister Carmen when she met her future partner. This kind of timing would have allowed them to present Carmen as his daughter. Whereas, given that Ana was already a small child when he came into their lives, it would have been impossible to sustain such a "myth" about her.

25. Interview, October 11, 2015.

26. Interview, October 11, 2015.

27. Interview, October 11, 2015.

28. Interview, October 11, 2015.

29. Interview, October 11, 2015.

30. Interview, October 11, 2015.

31. Interview, October 11, 2015.

32. Interview, October 11, 2015.

33. Interview, October 11, 2015.

34. Interview, October 11, 2015.

35. Here she is referring to before he was born.

36. Interview, October 11, 2015.

37. Interview, October 11, 2015.

38. Pamela spoke of her father threatening once to hit her. She was twenty years old, pregnant with her first child, and unmarried at the time. Given the threat, which she did not suggest was acted upon, she moved out of her parents' house to live with her brother. Interview, November 4, 2015.

39. Interview, September 11, 2015.

40. Interview, September 10, 2015.

41. Interview, September 10, 2015.

42. Interview, October 11, 2015.

43. Interview, October 11, 2015.

44. Interview, September 10, 2015.

45. As mentioned in Chapter 2, she started secondary school again once she was married and working in Managua. However, this later period of study ended very quickly when she became pregnant with her second child.

46. In Ana's case, her childhood was also cut short by the birth of her son.

47. Interview, October 8, 2015.

48. His harassment of her when she was an employee in this family's household is described in Chapter 2.

49. Interview, October 8, 2015.

50. As discussed in Chapter 5, Andrea had not received any education about sex, so protecting herself from a pregnancy was not something she was familiar with at this point in her life.

51. See also Baldwin (2006) and Swann (1996).

52. Many young (and some not so young) people joined the Militia at this point in time.

53. Interview, October 8, 2015.

54. Interview, October 22, 2015.

55. Interview, October 8, 2015.

56. They had a common-law marriage and referred to each other as husband and wife.

57. This is equivalent to approximately 70 hectares, which would have made him a medium- to large-sized peasant producer.

58. Andrea is a very beautiful woman with dark brown skin.

59. Interview, October 22, 2015.

60. In the following pages I describe several kinds of behavior that Juan engaged in that reflected his identification with the patriarchal relations that characterized Nicaragua, which suggests that he also thought he was more worthy than Andrea because he was a man.

61. Interview, October 22, 2015.

62. The literature referred to in Chapter 2, which described the potential reaction of men to withdraw their financial support in response to their diminished role as household breadwinner (c.f. Chant 2002 and Safilios-Rothschild, 1990), may suggest this as the impulse behind Juan's ceasing to provide child support to Andrea at this point in time. However, as Andrea noted, his contribution to the household income had always been limited regardless of what Andrea was earning. His inclination in that regard may have begun when he decided to have a second family (discussed shortly). The prevailing gender inequalities in Nicaragua simultaneously fostered the polygamy that was common there as well as the ideology of the male provider. But given the likelihood that men who were

not wealthy would have a difficult time supporting multiple families, this com- bination of gendered dynamics would have had as its end result that the women they had children with would not be able to count on them for the support they needed. Chant's (1997) findings would support this assertion. This would seem to coincide with a finding Engle (1995) had in a comparative study of Guatemalan and Nicaraguan families: that more Nicaraguan men failed to provide support for their children than was true of Guatemalan men.

63. This company makes car batteries.

64. Interview, October 22, 2015.

65. Interview, September 25, 2015.

66. Interview, September 25, 2015.

67. This is a literal translation. However, as can be seen in her following com- ments, Silvia means that it was not a committed relationship.

68. Interview, September 25, 2015.

69. Interview, October 18, 2015.

70. Pedro is the first child of Ana and Rafael. He was born in 1992, when Ana was twenty-two.

71. Interview, October 18, 2015.

72. Ana was a faithful member of the Pentecostal church in her neighborhood.

73. Monica is Ana and Rafael's daughter and Ana's youngest child. Monica was born in 1995, when Ana was twenty-five years old.

74. Interview, October 18, 2015.

75. Interview, October 18, 2015.

76. Rafael's emigration to the United States will be discussed in the following chapter.

77. Interview, October 18, 2015.

78. Interview, October 18, 2015.

79. A clear example of this was the Ley de Patria Potestad that was in place in Nicaragua until 1979. As discussed in Chapter 2, this law gave fathers virtual property rights over their children.

80. Lancaster (1992) and Sternberg (2000) talk about the phenomenon of pa- triarchy in the Nicaraguan context in terms of *machismo*. Stevens (1973) presents these characteristics as true of *machismo* throughout Latin America.

Meanwhile, in the early 1990s, Kampwirth (1993) conducted a survey of men's and women's attitudes toward marital infidelity in a working-class neigh- borhood in Managua. She compared her results to a large survey that had been carried out in that city in 1975. Kampwirth (1993: 286) found that whereas in 1975 "not only was de facto bigamy a reality in Somoza's Nicaragua but it was accepted by the majority of the nearly 1000 women interviewed. In the 1990s, the sexual double standard continues to hold, but much more tenuously." The earlier survey would have coincided with the period in which Andrea, Silvia, and Ana were growing up at home with their parents, while they would have been young adults when the latter was conducted.

81. Abrego (2014) makes a similar argument with regard to men in El Salvador. Kampwirth (1993) argues that this reality may have contributed to the resistance of Nicaraguan men to abortion being legalized in the 1980s, as it would have the potential of undercutting their ability to show how manly they were if women were able to end an unwanted pregnancy.

82. In a classic piece, Stevens (1973) describes *marianismo* as the counterpart phenomenon of *machismo*. Without using the term *marianismo*, Kampwirth (1993: 244–268, especially p. 246) relates multiple situations that exemplify it in discussing case studies of distinct types of household gender relations in Nicaragua in the early 1990s.

83. It is important to clarify here that I am not arguing that *machismo* and *marianismo* are what give rise to child sexual abuse (CSA). Instead, I believe that CSA has distinct origins, including perpetrators often having been a victim of such practices themselves and then expressing their own emotional disturbance in a replication of the experience, but this time as perpetrator, as well as other sources of emotional and psychological disturbance. For further information on this topic, see Smith (1991).

84. Andrea also made reference to their mother's move to this house on the cooperative, which occurred after she and Silvia had left home, as a turning point in their parents' relationship (interview, September 10, 2015).

85. Interview, September 11, 2015.

CHAPTER 4

Portions of this chapter first appeared in the Springer Nature publication *Qualitative Sociology*, "Everyday Violence in Central America as Seen Through the Life of One Woman." Enríquez, Laura J. © 2017. Reprinted by permission from Springer Nature.

1. The population figures for Chinandega and Managua are drawn from República de Nicaragua (1977: 21). These numbers are projected estimations based on data from the 1971 census. There was no census conducted in 1980.

2. As described later, in 2012 Ana moved back to Italy from Portugal, where she had been working off and on with a family since 2002.

3. Interview, October 24, 2015.

4. As noted, Rafael's effective abandonment of Ana and their children coincided with the loss of his job in Managua, his marital crisis, and his decision to emigrate. Although Ana stepped into the role of principal breadwinner when he was laid off from his employment, it is probable that once he found work in the United States he was earning more than she was. Hence, I would argue that her being thrust into that role while he was still in Nicaragua does not explain his unwillingness to take any responsibility ever again for the family's well-being once he was able to find work overseas, despite what one might conclude from the literature on the reactions of men to losing their breadwinning role (e.g., Chant 2002). Clearly, there was more going on in this situation than any feelings of threat to his role as breadwinner that Rafael may have experienced at the time.

5. This was a different Italian NGO from the one Pamela and Silvia worked for in Managua. However, the woman was friends with the coordinator of that NGO, the latter of whom was Ana and Andrea's employer.

6. Interview, October 18, 2015.

7. Interview, October 24, 2015. As described in Chapter 3, Rafael had left the previous year for the United States, with their marriage in tatters.

8. Interview, October 18, 2015.

9. Interview, October 18, 2015.

10. Interview, October 24, 2015. They had agreed that Carlos would join them in Portugal once he graduated from college. But by that time he was contemplating marriage with a woman in Nicaragua. So he continued his life there.

11. Romero (2011) and Hondagneu-Sotelo (2001) speak to the tensions that arise when the expectations of employers vis-à-vis nannies conflict with the needs of the latter to care for their own children.

12. Interview, October 18, 2015.

13. Personal communication, June 26, 2017.

14. Interview, October 24, 2015.

15. Half in jest, Ana characterized this arrangement as yet another "inheritance"—this time to her former employer's son. But she chose to accept the arrangement. Personal communication, June 26, 2017.

16. Interview, October 22, 2015.

17. Interview, November 5, 2015.

18. Unlike her work arrangement with this family in Nicaragua, where she went home to her own family at the end of each work day, the plan for the time in the United States was that she would live with them but keep roughly the same hours she had held in Nicaragua. However, within a few months of arriving in the United States she moved in with a Guatemalan man with whom she was in a

relationship. This new arrangement held for each of her subsequent stays in the United States.

19. Personal communication, June 23, 2017.

20. She also traveled elsewhere in Latin America with them for a shorter period of time. Interview, October 22, 2015.

21. Interview, October 22, 2015.

22. The story of Silvia's emigration to Italy will follow that of Andrea's. Silvia had gone to work for the same family that had originally offered Andrea a job in Italy, after Ana had completed the six-month stint with them in Andrea's stead.

23. Interview, October 22, 2015.

24. Her salary stabilized at 600 euros a month during this period.

25. At that point, his wife and son were spending nine to ten months of the year in the United States, where their son was in elementary school. But Ana was now working in Portugal year-round and so her position with this family in Nicaragua had opened up.

26. Andrea had requested that she be paid extra for working on her days off, instead of taking them to rest. However, these kinds of long, daily hours are not uncommon for live-in maids.

27. Andrea and Pamela, as well as many in Italian society, refer to workers who are care providers for the elderly and infirm as *badante*. However, the term is, at least to some extent, racialized (being associated with *extracomunitari*—those from outside the European Union) and gendered (being predominantly women) and therefore should only be used bearing these allusions in mind. (I am grateful to Professor Laura Zanfrini of the Università Cattolica del Sacro Cuore for stressing this to me [Interview, June 27, 2016].)

28. Interview, October 9, 2015.

29. I have found that whether in Nicaragua or in Italy, facilitating the entry of a relative or friend to one's domestic service position when leaving it is common when there is a relatively high degree of trust that the replacement will reflect well on the person leaving the position. In the case of domestic and care work in Italy, this dynamic cuts across distinct Latin American nationalities, although one is probably familiar with more women of one's own nationality and therefore more likely to recommend them.

30. Interview, October 9, 2015.

31. Interview, September 25, 2015.

32. Drawing on her interview data, Bonizzoni (2013) presents accounts of the terribly exploitative conditions experienced by a number of live-in domestic workers who were immigrants to Milan. In describing the conditions of Filipina

women who participate in Canada's Live-In Caregiver Program (LCP), Pratt (2012: 40) says that the program "creates the conditions of serfdom under the terms of the United Nations Supplementary Conventions on the Abolition of Slavery, the Slave Trade, and Institutions and Practices Similar to Slavery." The LCP is growing, even though Canada agreed to work toward abolishing such conditions when it signed on to the conventions.

33. Interview, October 9, 2015.

34. Interview, October 9, 2015.

35. Interview, October 9, 2015.

36. Interview, October 9, 2015.

37. Interview, September 25, 2015.

38. Interview, September 25, 2015. As of this point in time Silvia worked twenty-nine hours a week for them, spread over six days a week.

39. Silvia and Mauro were married in May 2014.

40. This was during Silvia's almost eight-year hiatus from working in Italy.

41. Interview, November 19, 2015.

42. The behavior of Pamela's husband in abandoning their family would seem to embody the pattern described in the literature on the potential reactions of men when their partners become the principal breadwinner in the household (see especially Chant 2002 and Moser and McIlwaine 2000). Although it is unclear that he had ever really fulfilled this role, which the predominant ideology had designated for men, he may have felt more and more threatened over time as each new initiative on his part failed to result in increasing the family's income as he had promised and when Pamela finally attained her receptionist position at the Italian NGO, which provided her with a stable income that was higher than she had had in a long time. Nonetheless, she ultimately divorced him.

43. Interview, November 4, 2015.

44. Interview, November 4, 2015.

45. Pamela's eldest was about twenty-three years old when she left for Italy.

46. Interview, November 19, 2015.

47. The woman in the Rossi couple.

48. See the discussion of her legal situation that follows.

49. Interview, November 4, 2015.

50. Interview, November 19, 2015.

51. Her landlady in this *posto letto* was a Peruvian woman who was responsible for the overall rental unit.

52. See also Boyd (1989) and Menjívar (2000). Repak (1995) describes a network of Central American immigrants to the United States that represents

an exception to this norm. In a study of Salvadorans in Washington D.C., she found that women were predominant among the earlier migrants in this national group. This phenomenon had its roots in their having been the domestic employees of families that had worked in the U.S. foreign service or international organizations in El Salvador. When those families returned to work in the U.S. capital, they brought these women with them to continue in their employment. Repak (1995) also speaks about Central American migrants who were recruited to work with diplomats stationed in Washington.

Two distinctions between this "diplomatic" network and that on which the Nicaraguan women in this study relied should be noted: the former dated back at least as far as the 1960s, and it consisted of people who were aligned with the U.S. government or international organizations closely associated with it, and who were, therefore, of quite a different political outlook. With regard to migrants working for diplomats stationed in Washington, it seems reasonable to presume that these diplomats may have been from the region. Here again, aside from diplomats from Nicaragua in the 1980s and post-2006 (and El Salvador between 2009 and 2019), diplomats from this region would likely have tended to have ideas more in sync with those of the U.S. government than the people who formed the network through which Andrea, Silvia, Ana, and Pamela traveled to Italy.

53. In contrast, Parreñas's (2015) Filipina interviewees in Rome had, by and large, entered Italy clandestinely. Yet the Filipina domestic workers she interviewed in the U.S. had mostly entered the country legally. In another study, the majority of the Ukrainian women whom Solari (2017: 61) interviewed remained undocumented during the time they worked in Italy, despite having entered the country legally on a ten-day tourist visa. They typically purchased these tourist visas from travel agencies in Ukraine, rather than obtaining them because they had a real letter of invitation from someone who wanted to employ them. Meanwhile, the comments of Repak's (1995) domestic worker interviewees suggested that those among them who migrated to the U.S. with job offers were able to obtain legal documents, although it is not stated how many went with job offers.

More generally speaking, Bonizzoni (2013: 139) notes that in 2009 half of all undocumented workers in Italy—who numbered almost four hundred thousand—were employed in domestic work. Meanwhile, in a study for the Pew Hispanic Center, Passel (2005: 3–4) mentions that close to a third of the immigrants in the U.S. at that time were undocumented, and that most of those undocumented were from Latin America.

54. A Permesso di Soggiorno authorizes its holder to remain in the country legally. One must renew it periodically for it to be valid.

55. Interview, November 4, 2015.

56. Interview, November 19, 2015.

57. Italy's immigration authorities have had periods of offering the *flusso* option and periods of offering *sanatorias*. These began with the ratification of the first comprehensive immigration law in 1986 (c.f. Calavita 2005). Parreñas (2015), Vianello et al. (2019), and Barbulescu (2019) note that multiple amnesties have been implemented. Bonizzoni (2013) comments that Italy had offered more amnesties than any other country in Europe.

58. Interview, September 25, 2015.

59. Footnote 68 highlights that this constraint may not have technically existed.

60. Bonizzoni (2013) also comments on the power dynamics at play between immigrant domestic workers and their employers when it comes to applying for documentation for the former in Italy.

61. Pojmann (2006: 26) studied organizing among immigrant women in Italy. In discussing the setting for their organizing, she noted the large number of groups that identified as "immigrant associations" (893 of which were listed in a 2001 study she drew upon) and that many of them were connected with labor unions.

62. Pojmann (2006: 33) notes that unions also mediate conflicts between Italian and migrant workers, facilitate the entry of immigrants into the legal workforce, and "offer [immigrants] opportunities for training and job growth, including language classes and leisure-time activities."

63. In contrast, after sending her a letter of invitation so that she could enter Italy legally, Ana's employers during her first stint there (in 2001)—the Rossi family—did not bother to apply for a work permit for her once she had arrived. Their logic may have been that her stay was going to be relatively short, just six months, but it meant that she was undocumented after her first three months there. Interview, October 24, 2015.

64. Interview, October 18, 2015. The delay was due to the fact that she had not arrived in time to actually be included in this *sanatoria*. *Sanatorias* typically only include people who enter Italy during a specified time period, and Ana had arrived after the end of this particular measure's period. But, as noted, her employer eventually found a means of having her included in the *sanatoria*.

65. Based on her study of Mexican migration to the United States, Dreby (2010) notes that for single mothers who migrate—which was, effectively, the

situation of Andrea, Ana, and Pamela when they left Nicaragua—having their children's consent is very important.

66. Interview, October 22, 2015.

67. Interview, October 22, 2015. In this case, a *fluzzo* was used to amnesty undocumented workers in Italy, as opposed to a *sanatoria* or *saneamento*.

68. A year into the wait for her second Permesso di Soggiorno, Andrea learned that once her application was submitted, she was free to change employment if she so desired. It would appear that Silvia had also been unaware of this option (see earlier discussion).

69. See, for example, Parreñas (2015).

70. See also Sciortino (2004).

71. See also Abrego (2014) and Borjas and Tienda (1993).

72. Interview, October 24, 2015.

73. Hondagneu-Sotelo and Avila (1997) would characterize this as an expression of "transnational mothering." This concept is discussed further shortly.

74. Interview, October 24, 2015. Ana commented that the $150 US she sent home each month was a little more than what she had been earning in Nicaragua. She was able to return home with some savings, which helped her—in combination with her wages there—to keep the family afloat until she left for Portugal the following year. However, this less than enormous difference in wages between what she earned in Nicaragua and in Italy underlines that there was more to her accepting this job overseas than simply economics.

75. Parreñas (2005) notes that daughters of migrant mothers often fulfill some of their mother's responsibilities in their absence. In Ana's case, though, it was her son who did so. But this particular task—of managing the household's finances—is not as gendered as, for example, providing care for younger siblings. This latter task probably fell more to Ana's mother and sister, who formed part of the household.

76. Ana's mother moved in with her in 1993, shortly after she built her house in Managua. Ana's stepfather had passed while Ana was on her first sojourn abroad in Germany.

77. Interview, October 24. 2015.

78. Interview, October 18, 2015.

79. Interview, October 24, 2015.

80. Interview, October 22, 2015.

81. Interview, October 30, 2015.

82. Interview, October 22, 2015. The woman he was living with was the person who had been his longtime companion, as described in Chapter 3.

83. Interview, October 22, 2015.

84. In fact, Clara experienced a blood clot in her leg about a month after her baby was born. Personal communication, December 2016.

85. Multiple personal communications, 2016.

86. Interview, October 30, 2015.

87. Interview, October 30, 2015. One of these sisters is Silvia and the other is her half sister, Camila. Camila is married and living and working in Sardinia.

88. Interview, November 5, 2015. Undoubtedly, Andrea is reflecting back on her own limited opportunities to study and, to the extent possible, she does not want her younger siblings and nieces and nephews to have these same constraints.

89. Interview, October 9, 2015. When Silvia initially returned to Italy she was earning 750 euros a month; and this later dropped to 450 euros a month. Hence, her remittances to her parents represented a sizable part of her earnings.

90. Interview, November 19, 2015.

91. Boccagni (2016) also found that the financial assistance that immigrants who work as care providers send to their families often impacts their own well-being while they work in Italy, in the sense of leaving them with little in the way of resources to take care of their own needs.

92. Andrea's mother was referring to her own grandchild and Andrea's nephew here.

93. Interview, October 30, 2015.

94. Interview, October 18, 2015.

95. Interview, April 2, 2016.

96. Interview, October 23, 2015.

97. Dreby (2010) and Pratt (2012) write at length about the pain, the trials and tribulations, and the gendered expectations facing women who are trying to mother their children from abroad, where they have gone in search of employment that will help them to support their families "back home." Meanwhile, Baldassar and Merla (2014) speak of the "circulation of care" that operates within transnational families, just as it does within nontransnational families. They highlight that the former include not only members of the working class but also of the middle class.

98. Interview, November 19, 2015.

99. In describing the changes that occur in relations within Filipino families when the mothers go to Canada to work as care providers, Pratt (2012) writes about how the long time between visits can mean that the mothers have difficulty recognizing their children when they return home.

100. They would have been about thirteen and fifteen years old, respectively, at the time.

101. Interview, November 19, 2015.

102. Pamela was generally concerned about the increasing incidence of terrorism in Europe. But she was also worried about her sons being at loose ends in Italy and being lured into something. Independent of the terrorism, there was a growing problem in Milan and Genoa of violence among gangs, which mostly consisted of young men from Latin America. These were the sons of women who had gone to work there. Undoubtedly, the difficulty these young men had with integrating into Italian society, particularly in the face of high unemployment, has fed into this problem. See also Esbensen and Maxson (2012) and Queirolo Palmas and Torre (2005).

103. As discussed in Chapter 1, Campani (2010: 145) calls our attention to the Mediterranean Model, which operates so that new migrants to this region are largely destined for work in specific sectors of the economy. Domestic work is one such sector. She notes that care and domestic work tend to be highly gendered, employing primarily women. Yet to the extent that men migrate to Mediterranean countries, they may end up in niches similar to those of women migrants.

Pratt (2012) describes the "failure" of many of the children of Filipina migrants to Canada, when those children are finally able to join their mothers there. That is, many of them are unable to continue their studies there, despite their educational success back home, and end up in jobs that do not represent the dream situations their immigrant mothers had envisioned when they sought family reunification in Canada.

104. Interview, October 24, 2015.

105. Monica was seventeen and Pedro was twenty years old.

106. Interview, October 24, 2015.

107. Interview, October 24, 2015.

108. Daniel was still in the early years of secondary school at the time.

109. This period of Andrea's life was discussed in Chapter 3.

110. Interview, October 22, 2015.

111. Interview, October 22, 2015.

112. Interview, October 22, 2015.

113. The fact that he was sporting a mohawk, a haircut which was not particularly common in rural areas in Nicaragua at that time, did not endear him to them. Interview, October 22, 2015.

114. Although the school was private, it was affiliated with the state-run National Technological Institute (INATEC) and received aid from Spain and France.

115. Interview, November 5, 2015. Parreñas (2005) recounts that one of her interviewees also mentioned not communicating to his mother the unmet emotional needs that her work abroad had created for him.

116. Interview, October 22, 2015.

117. Parreñas (2005: 153) recounts the experience of "Jeek Pereno," who dropped out of school during his mother's prolonged sojourn abroad. He believed that the lower level of discipline he received at home in his mother's absence had an impact on him.

118. The idea for asking my interviewees if they had any such advice came from Abrego's (2014) fine book about what emigration meant for the families of Salvadorans who emigrate to work in the United States.

119. Interview, October 23, 2015.

120. Interview, November 13, 2015.

121. Interview, October 24, 2015.

122. Interview, April 2, 2016.

123. Interview, April 2, 2016.

124. This would seem to be a reflection on her experience with the Rossi family, and the fact that her deciding to leave that job had been followed by a period of unemployment and job instability during which she found it hard to send money home to her sons in Nicaragua.

125. Interview, November 13, 2015.

126. Interview, April 2, 2016. Parreñas (2005) notes that communication eases children's emotional difficulties, as well as helping to build a feeling of family unity even though their parent(s) are far away.

127. Barbulescu (2019) writes of the hostility of Italy's native population toward immigrants of a distinct race and religion, although noting that this varies by region of the country. Davidov and Semyonov (2017) and Jaret (1999) speak about this dynamic occurring in several places in the world where large numbers of immigrants have arrived.

128. Interview, October 24, 2015.

129. That is to say, for older Italians, those who are native are thought of as white in terms of skin color. This, of course, disregards the long history of differences and differential treatment between those of southern Italian and northern Italian descent; with southern Italians having been perceived to be darker in skin color than those in the north (c.f. Stanley 2015). But Sniderman et al. (2002) argue that any point of difference—whether of color, nationality, or language—marks the immigrant as an outsider in Italy, not just color.

130. Interview, November 13, 2015.

131. When asked directly, Silvia and Pamela said that they had not found themselves to be the target of discrimination during their time in Italy. While Pamela's skin *is* lighter in color than that of Ana and Andrea, Silvia's is not. So it

would seem skin color alone is a not sufficient explanation of why some people experience such discrimination and others do not.

132. Personal communication, January 26, 2018, and July 12, 2017, respectively.

133. Interview, October 9, 2015.

134. His oldest child lived in this house with her husband. Personal communication, July 21, 2017.

135. Interview, October 18, 2015.

136. Personal communication, November 14, 2017.

137. Interview, November 5, 2015.

138. Interview, October 9, 2015. In 2011 Andrea set up a bank account for her retirement, which was growing with automatic deductions from her pay check each month (interview, October 30, 2015). These funds would complement what she earned through the Italian social security system and could go with her wherever she retired.

139. Interview, November 4, 2015.

140. They coincide with the Filipinas at the center of Parreñas's (2005) study in this sense.

141. As discussed in Chapter 1, this is true for many immigrants to Italy from the Global South. However, immigrants also get channeled into Italy's agricultural and manufacturing sectors (see especially Calavita 2005: 59). See also Barbiano di Belgiojoso and Ortensi (2015) on the lack of mobility out of domestic and care work in Italy once immigrants have entered into it. Barbulescu (2019: 75) notes that migrants are "overrepresented in the lower-skilled segments of the labor market" in Italy more generally. Meanwhile, Yarris (2017) notes that most Nicaraguan women who emigrate work in the care sector of their destination country, wherever that is.

CHAPTER 5

Portions of this chapter first appeared in the Springer Nature publication *Qualitative Sociology*, "Everyday Violence in Central America as Seen Through the Life of One Woman." Enríquez, Laura J. © 2017. Reprinted by permission from Springer Nature.

1. This chapter focuses only on these three women, as the fourth—Silvia—did not have children of her own to support.

2. Given the shortages and inflation that affected most consumer goods in Nicaragua's mid-1980s wartime economy, each household received a ration card and with that card was entitled to purchase basic goods—such as rice, beans, sugar, and cooking oil—at subsidized prices.

3. Interview, November 5, 2015.

4. Interview, November 5, 2015.

5. Interview, October 8, 2015.

6. They were still living together at the time. However, Pamela clearly felt that her husband would never carry his weight with regard to the family's expenses and, therefore, that it would always be on her shoulders to do so. Her eventual response was to start to carve out a life for herself independent of him, as we can see in this instance.

7. Interview, November 4, 2015.

8. Interview, July 20, 2018.

9. This is a reference to a location on the Carretera Sur (the Southern Highway) that is considered one of the city's borders. Carlos took the bus the roughly 5 kilometers from their house to the school and back each day.

10. Interview, October 18, 2015.

11. In the United States, research has shown that "school switching" can be associated with numerous negative consequences, including making it more likely that children will drop out of high school before they finish. See, for example, Gasper et al. (2012) and Grigg (2012). However, shifting from one school to another was not uncommon among these children. Constancy in a school in Nicaragua may be a "privilege" reserved for the upper middle and upper class, who would only consider having their children choose from a small pool of private schools and would not lack the means of paying for them.

12. Interview, October 18, 2015.

13. Interview, October 22, 2015. When Clara attended private school, her tuition was paid for by her godparents, who were the foreign couple that Andrea had worked for off and on since 1984. They also assisted her with expenses related to school supplies throughout her education.

14. Interview, October 22, 2015. As noted earlier, Andrea had selected this school for Clara because of its proximity to their house. Neither she nor Juan were members of an evangelical church. In fact, they had baptized their daughter in the Catholic Church.

15. Interview, July 17, 2018.

16. As noted in Chapter 4, this school had close links with several state institutions and was at least partially funded with foreign assistance. Hence, while tuition there was more than for a public school, it did not cost very much.

17. Daniel probably spent about two hours traveling each way on the several buses he would have had to take, despite Granada only being 42.5 kilometers from Managua. Most schools in Nicaragua start at 7:00 a.m.

18. By the time he started studying there, Andrea had returned to work in Italy. Parreñas (2005) noted that children of migrants who have the support of extended kin suffer somewhat less from feelings of abandonment. It would seem that this kind of support was what Daniel sought in his weekly treks to his grandmother's home.

19. Interview, October 22, 2015.

20. Interview, June 5, 2018.

21. Interview, October 18, 2015.

22. Interview, April 2, 2016.

23. Interview, November 4, 2015.

24. Interview, October 22, 2015.

25. Interview, November 4, 2015.

26. A Licenciatura is a five-year degree that, in a number of respects, is like a combined BA and MA, given that it entails focused study in one area over that period of time and completion of a thesis on a given topic in the chosen area.

27. Interview, October 22, 2015.

28. By then, Andrea was working overseas for extended periods of time.

29. Clara had wanted to study architecture at the UNI, and passing this entrance exam would have allowed her to do so.

30. Interview, October 22, 2015.

31. Her companion and the father of her two children.

32. Interview, November 5, 2015.

33. Interview, October 22, 2015.

34. Interview, October 18, 2015.

35. Interview, November 4, 2015.

36. Interview, October 18, 2015.

37. In many (most especially, public) schools in Nicaragua there is a morning session/group of students (from 7:00 a.m. to noon) and an afternoon session/group of students (roughly noon to 5:00 p.m.), because there are not enough schools for the number of school-age children in the country. So Clara actually teaches for the entirety of one of those sessions.

38. Interview, October 22, 2015. Belinda is one of Andrea's granddaughters and Clara's daughter.

39. Personal communication, February 10, 2018.

40. Interview, October 22, 2015. Here again, contacts were a critical factor in gaining employment.

41. Interview, November 4, 2015.

42. Interview, November 4, 2015.

43. Interview, October 11, 2015.

44. Interview, October 11, 2015.

45. Interview, November 5, 2015.

46. Interview, October 30, 2015.

47. Interview, October 30, 2015.

48. Interview, October 30, 2015.

49. Interview, July 20, 2018.

50. Interview, October 18, 2015.

51. Interview, October 24, 2015.

52. Interview, October 24, 2015.

53. Personal communication, February 13, 2018.

54. This was midway through Clara's first year in college, as the Nicaraguan academic year runs from February through November.

55. Interview, October 22, 2015.

56. Personal communication, February 14, 2018.

57. Personal communication, February 10, 2018.

58. Interview, November 5, 2015.

59. Interview, November 5, 2015.

60. Ana is talking about providing him with emotional support, perhaps even more than financial support, although the latter was clearly critical.

61. Interview, October 24, 2015.

62. As noted in Chapter 4, the first time Ana went to Italy and the first several years that she worked in Portugal, it was for approximately half the year; the rest of the year she returned to Nicaragua to resume her job there.

63. Interview, October 24, 2015.

64. Interview, April 2, 2016.

65. Interview, April 2, 2016.

66. Interviews, November 5, 2015, and 24 October, 2015, respectively. Andrea also spoke of the difference that several others made in their lives, including the assistance provided by several of her employers.

67. See especially Stahler-Sholk (1990).

68. See also Waters et al. (2007) and Barahona Portocarrero and Agurto (2001). Alvarado and Massey (2010) add violence to the equation including neo-liberal structural adjustment and emigration.

69. See also World Bank (2012).

CONCLUSION

1. Blofield and Jokela (2018) note that most domestic workers in Latin America come from the region's racial and ethnic minorities.

2. Excepting Silvia, who did not have children. However, as noted in Chapter 4, Silvia did support her younger sister so that she could attend college.

3. Excepting Kampwirth (1993 and 2011) and Macintosh (2016).

4. Calculated from UN Population Division, http://www.un.org/en/development/desa/population/migration/data/estimates2/estimates17.shtml, accessed August 10, 2018.

5. For several overviews of this literature, see Massey et al. (1993), De Haas (2010), and Gheasi and Nijkamp (2017).

6. Although, as noted in Chapter 1, it may become one for Central Americans.

7. Researchers studying immigrants to the United States have demonstrated the major difference in earning potential between those who are legally documented in this receiving nation and those who are not. See Abrego (2014) and Borjas and Tienda (1993).

8. See, in particular, Parreñas (2015). One of the implications of the relative ease of becoming documented in Italy is that they were less subjected to the "legal violence" that undocumented Central American immigrants in the United States have to contend with, as described by Menjívar and Abrego (2012). However, Andrea and Ana did feel the effects of the symbolic violence these two scholars speak of, in the form of the anti-immigrant discrimination they experienced on multiple occasions. Moreover, in the anti-immigrant environment fostered by, and reflected in, the policies of the Italian politician who became deputy prime minister in 2018, Matteo Salvini, even immigrants who were documented began to feel more vulnerable to the distinct types of violence about which Menjívar and Abrego (2012) wrote.

9. As noted in that chapter, the channeling of immigrants into Italy's service sector has been described by a number of scholars. But the literature discussing this pattern is separate from the literature on participation in the service sector in the immigrants' countries of origin. So the present study is also distinguished by bringing their history of participation in this sector in Nicaragua together with it in their country of destination, Italy.

10. My finding confirms the arguments of Hondagneu-Sotelo and Avila (1997) and Parreñas (2015) in this respect.

11. This is the case even though one could argue that the "taking of land" in which Ana participated alongside the rest of her family even before 1979, and her and her husband's receipt of a plot of land that had been confiscated from people

associated with the Somoza dynasty, represented small pieces of a larger effort to transform Nicaraguan society, and that even Andrea's membership in the neighborhood militia in Managua and attendance at the activities of the Sandinista women's organization were part and parcel of the activism associated with a commitment to the process of change that the revolution promoted.

12. This latter social dynamic is discussed in Hochschild (2016) and Cohen (2018).

13. It should be restated that they expressed this opinion in interviews in 2015 and 2016.

14. Those policies—which I have referred to as being of neoliberal orientation—have been promoted by the multilateral lending agencies and what became known as the Washington Consensus in the 1990s (the label of which underlines the physical location of the headquarters of those agencies as well as the U.S. government). See, for example, Williamson (1990) and Drake (2006).

Bibliography

Abbasi, Maryam Ajilian, Masumeh Saeidi, Gholamreza Khademi, Bibi Leila Hoseini, and Zahra Emami Moghadam. 2015. "Child Maltreatment in the Worldwide: A Review Article," *International Journal of Pediatrics* 3, 1–1: 353–365.

Abrego, Leisy J. 2014. *Sacrificing Families: Navigating Laws, Labor, and Love Across Borders.* Stanford, CA: Stanford University Press.

Acevedo Vogl, Adolfo. 1998. *Economía política y desarrollo sostenible.* Managua, Nicaragua: BITECSA.

Ackerman, Peggy T., Joseph E. O. Newton, W. Brian McPherson, Jerry G. Jones, and Roscoe A. Dykman. 1998. "Prevalence of Post Traumatic Stress Disorder and Other Psychiatric Diagnoses in Three Groups of Abused Children (Sexual, Physical, and Both)," *Child Abuse and Neglect* 22, 8 (August): 759–774.

Alvarado, Steven Elías, and Douglas S. Massey. 2010. "In Search of Peace: Structural Adjustment, Violence, and International Migration," *Annals of the American Academy of Political and Social Science* 630, 1: 137–161.

Ambrosini, Maurizio. 2013. "Immigration in Italy: Between Economic Acceptance and Political Rejection," *Journal of International Migration and Integration* 14, 1: 175–194.

Andall, Jacqueline. 2000. *Gender, Migration and Domestic Service: The Politics of Black Women in Italy.* Aldershot, UK: Ashgate.

Andersen, Lykke E. 2001. "Social Mobility in Latin America: Links with Adolescent Schooling." Research Network Working Paper #R-433, Latin American Research Network, Inter-American Development Bank.

Andersen, Lykke E., and Bent Jesper Christensen. 2009. "The Status and Dynamic Benefits of Migration and Remittances in Nicaragua." Development Research Working Paper Series 05–2009, Institute for Advanced Development Studies, La Paz, Bolivia.

Andersen, Lykke, E., Bent Jesper Christensen, and Oscar Molina. 2005. "The Impact of Aid on Recipient Behavior: A Micro-Level Dynamic Analysis of Remittances, Schooling, Work, Consumption, Investment and Social Mobility in Nicaragua." Development Research Working Paper Series 02/2005, Institute for Advanced Development Studies, La Paz, Bolivia.

Anthias, Floya, and Gabriella Lazaridis. 2000. "Introduction: Women on the Move in Southern Europe." In *Gender and Migration in Southern Europe: Women on the Move*, edited by Floya Anthias and Gabriella Lazaridis, pp. 1–13. Oxford, UK: Berg.

Antillón, Camilo. "Línea de base sobre concepciones, actitudes y prácticas de madres, padres y maestros respecto al castigo físico y humillante en los territorios de intervención de Save the Children." Informe Preliminar. Save the Children, Managua, Nicaragua.

Azevedo, Viviane M. R., and Cesar P. Bouillon. 2010. "Intergenerational Social Mobility in Latin America: A Review of Existing Evidence," *Revista de Análisis Económico* 25, 2 (December): 7–42.

Babb, Florence E. 1989. *Between Field and Cooking Pot: The Political Economy of Marketwomen in Peru*. Austin: University of Texas Press.

———. 1996a. *After Revolution: Mapping Gender and Cultural Politics in Neoliberal Nicaragua*. Austin: University of Texas Press.

———. 1996b. "After the Revolution: Neoliberal Policy and Gender in Nicaragua," *Latin American Perspectives* 23, 1: 27–48.

Baldassar, Loretta, and Laura Merla (eds.). 2014. *Transnational Families, Migration and the Circulation of Care: Understanding Mobility and Absence in Family Life*. New York: Routledge.

Baldwin, Mark W. 2006. "Self-Esteem and Close Relationship Dynamics." In *Self-Esteem Issues and Answers*, edited by Michael H. Kernis, pp. 359–366. New York: Psychology Press.

Banerjee, Abhijit Vinayak. 2013. "Microcredit Under the Microscope: What Have We Learnt in the Last Two Decades, What Do We Need to Know?" *Annual Review of Economics* 5: 487–519.

Barahona Portocarrero, Milagros, with Sonia Agurto. 2001. "Household Study of Nicaraguan Women Who Have Emigrated to Costa Rica Seeking Employment: Final Report." International Labor Organization Project INT/oo/M62/NET, "Promoting Decent Employment for Migrant Women and Improved

Welfare for their Families in Nicaragua. Managua, Nicaragua. http://www
.ilo.org/wcmsp5/groups/public/---ed_emp/documents/publication/wcms
_117956.pdf, accessed February 9, 2016.

Barbiano di Belgiojoso, Elisa, and Livia Elisa Ortensi. 2015. "Female Labour Seg-
regation in the Domestic Services in Italy," *Journal of International Migration
and Integration* 16: 1121–1139.

Barbulescu, Roxana. 2019. *Migrant Integration in a Changing Europe: Immigrants,
European Citizens, and Co-Ethnics in Italy and Spain*. Notre Dame, IN: University of Notre Dame Press.

Barndt, Deborah. 1985. "Popular Education." In *Nicaragua: The First Five Years*,
edited by Thomas W. Walker, pp. 317–345. New York: Praeger.

Barrios, Yasmin V., Bizu Gelaye, Qiuyue Zhong, Christina Nicolaidis, Marta B.
Rondon, Pedro J. Garcia, Pedro A. Mascaro Sanchez, Sixto E. Sanchez, and
Michelle A. Williams. 2015. "Association of Childhood Physical and Sexual
Abuse with Intimate Partner Violence, Poor General Health and Depressive
Symptoms among Pregnant Women," *PLoS One* 10(3): e0122573. https://doi
.org/10.1371/journal.pone.0116609.

Barthauer, Linda M., and John M. Leventhal. 1999. "Prevalence and Effects of
Child Sexual Abuse in a Poor, Rural Community in El Salvador: A Retrospective Study of Women After 12 Years of Civil War," *Child Abuse and Neglect* 23, 11: 1117–1126. http://www.sciencedirect.com/science/article/pii/S0145
213499000782.

Bartolini, Laura, Anna Triandafyllidou, and Ruby Gropas. 2015. "Escaping the
Crisis and Emancipating Oneself: Highly Skilled Mobility from Southern Europe," *Altreitalie* (July–December): 36–52.

Basa, Charito, Rosalud Dela Rosa, Dona Rose Dela Cruz, and Aubrey Abarin-
tos. 2017. "From Personal to Political, and Back: The Story of the Filipino
Women's Council," Open Democracy: Free Thinking for the World (June 19).
https://www.opendemocracy.net/en/beyond-trafficking-and-slavery/from
-personal-to-p/.

Beasley-Murray, Jon, Maxwell A. Cameron, and Eric Hershberg. 2010. "Latin
America's Left Turns: A Tour d'Horizon." In *Latin America's Left Turns: Poli-
tics, Policies, and Trajectories of Change*, edited by Maxwell A. Cameron and
Eric Hershberg, pp. 1–20. Boulder, CO: Lynne Rienner.

Belli, Gioconda. 2002. *The Country Under My Skin: A Memoir of Love and War*.
New York: Anchor Books.

Benería, Lourdes, and Martha Roldán. 1987. *The Crossroads of Class and Gender:
Industrial Homework, Subcontracting, and Household Dynamics in Mexico
City*. Chicago: University of Chicago Press.

Berend, Ivan, T. 2016. *An Economic History of Twentieth Century Europe: Economic Regimes from Laissez-Faire to Globalization*, 2nd ed. Cambridge, UK: Cambridge University Press.

Bickham Mendez, Jennifer. 2005. *From the Revolution to the Maquiladoras: Gender, Labor, and Globalization in Nicaragua*. Durham, NC: Duke University Press.

Blofield, Merike, and Merita Jokela. 2018. "Paid Domestic Work and the Struggles of Care Workers in Latin America," *Current Sociology* 66, 4: 531–546.

Boccagni, Paolo. 2016. "Searching for Well-Being in Care Work Migration: Constructions, Practices and Displacements Among Immigrant Women in Italy," *Social Politics* 23, 2: 284–306.

Bonizzoni, Paola. 2013. "Undocumented Domestic Workers in Italy: Surviving and Regularizing Strategies." In *Irregular Migrant Domestic Workers in Europe: Who Cares?*, edited by Anna Triandafyllidou, pp. 135–160. Burlington, VT: Ashgate.

Booth, John, A. 1985. *The End and the Beginning: The Nicaraguan Revolution*. Boulder, CO: Westview Press.

Borjas, George J., and Marta Tienda. 1993. "The Employment and Wages of Legalized Immigrants," *International Migration Review* 27, 4: 712–747.

Bossert, Thomas John. 1985. "Health Policy: The Dilemma of Success." In *Nicaragua: The First Five Years*, edited by Thomas W. Walker, pp. 347–363. New York: Praeger.

Bourgois, Phillipe. 2001. "The Power of Violence in War and Peace: Post-Cold War Lessons from El Salvador." *Ethnography* 2 (1): 5–24.

Boyd, Monica. 1989. "Family and Personal Networks in International Migration: Recent Developments and New Agendas," *International Migration Review* 233: 638–680.

Brenner, Mark, and Stephanie Luce. 2006. "Women and Class: What Has Happened in Forty Years?" *Monthly Review* 58, 3 (July–August). https://monthlyreview.org/2006/07/01/women-and-class-what-has-happened-in-forty-years/.

Brockett, Charles. 1998. *Land, Power and Poverty: Agrarian Transformation and Political Conflict in Central America*. Boulder, CO: Westview Press.

Brown, Wendy. 2003. "Neo-liberalism and the End of Liberal Democracy," *Theory and Event* 7, 1. https://doi.org/10.1353/tae.2003.0020.

Bulmer-Thomas, Victor. 1987. *The Political Economy of Central America Since 1920*. Cambridge, UK: Cambridge University Press.

———. 1995. *The Economic History of Latin America Since Independence*. Cambridge, UK: Cambridge University Press.

Burawoy, Michael. 1976. "The Functions and Reproduction of Migrant Labor: Comparative Material from Southern Africa and the United States," *American Journal of Sociology* 81, 5: 1050–1087.

Burrell, Jennifer, and Ellen Moody. 2015. "The Post-Cold War Anthropology of Central America." *Annual Review of Anthropology* 44: 381–400.

Calavita, Kitty. 1992. *Inside the State: The Bracero Program, Immigration, and the INS*. New York: Routledge.

———. 2005. *Immigrants at the Margins: Law, Race, and Exclusion in Southern Europe*. Cambridge, UK: Cambridge University Press.

Campani, Giovanna. 2010. "Gender and Migration in Southern Europe: A Comparative Approach to the Italian and Spanish Cases." In *Women in New Migrations: Current Debates in European Societies*, edited by Krystyna Slany, Maria Kontos, and Maria Liapi, pp. 143–170. Krakow: Jagiellonian University Press.

Carlo, Gustavo, Silvia Koller, Marcela Rafaelli, and Maria Rosario de Guzman. 2007. "Culture-Related Strengths Among Latin American Families: A Case Study of Brazil." University of Nebraska, Faculty Publications, Department of Child, Youth, and Family Studies. 64. https://digitalcommons.unl.edu/famconfacpub/64, accessed August 6, 2021.

Case, Anne, Angela Fertig, and Christina Paxson. 2005. "The Lasting Impact of Childhood Health and Circumstance," *Journal of Health Economics* 24: 365–389.

Casique, Irene. 2010. "Factores de empoderamiento y protección de las mujeres contra la violencia/Factors of Women's Empowerment and Protection from Violence," *Revista Mexicana de Sociología* 72, 1 (enero–marzo): 37–71.

Catalán Aravena, Oscar. 2001. "Structural Adjustment and the Impact on Income Distribution in Nicaragua," *International Journal of Political Economy* 31, 2 (Summer): 18–43.

Catanzaro, Raimondo, and Asher Colombo. 2009. *Badanti & Co: Il lavoro domestico straniero in Italia*. Bologna, Italy: Società editrice il Mulino.

Chant, Sylvia. 1997. *Women-Headed Households: Diversity and Dynamics in the Developing World*. Houndmills, UK: Macmillan.

———. 2002. "Researching Gender, Families and Households in Latin America: From the 20th into the 21st Century," *Bulletin of Latin American Research* 21, 4 (October): 545–575.

Chell-Robinson, Victoria. 2000. "Female Migrants in Italy: Coping in a Country of New Migration." In *Gender and Migration in Southern Europe: Women on the Move*, edited by Floya Anthias and Gabriella Lazaridis, pp. 103–123. Oxford, UK: Berg.

CIERA (Centro de Investigaciones y Estudios de la Reforma Agraria). 1989. *La Reforma Agraria en Nicaragua, 1979–1989*. Managua, Nicaragua: CIERA.

Close, David. 1988. *Nicaragua: Politics, Economics and Society*. London: Pinter.

Cohen, Patricia. 2018. "Even in Better Times, Some Americans Seem Farther Behind. Here's Why." *New York Times*, September 14. https://www.nytimes .com/2018/09/14/business/economy/income-inequality.html

Cohen, Sheldon, Denise Janicki-Deverts, Edith Chen, and Karen A. Matthews. 2010. "Childhood Socioeconomic Status and Adult Health," *Annals of the New York Academy of Sciences* 1186: 37–55. https://doi.org/10.1111/j.1749-6632 .2009.05334.x.

Coleman, Gerald D. 2015. "Pregnancy After Rape," *International Journal of Women's Health and Wellness* 1, 1. https://doi.org/10.23937/2474-1353/1510004.

Collins, Joseph. 1982. *What Difference Could a Revolution Make?* San Francisco: Institute for Food and Development Policy.

Collinson, Helen (ed.). 1990. *Women and Revolution in Nicaragua*. London: Zed Books.

Collin-Vézina, Delphine, Isabelle Daigneault, and Martine Hébert. 2013. "Lessons Learned from Child Sexual Abuse Research: Prevalence, Outcomes, and Preventive Strategies," *Child Adolescent Psychiatry and Mental Health* 7: 22. Published online July 18, 2013. https://doi.org/10.1186/1753-2000-7-22.

Colombo, Asher. 2005. "Il Mito del Lavoro Domestico: Struttura e Cambiamenti in Italia (1970–2003)," *Polis* 3: 435–466.

Colombo, Asher, and Giuseppe Sciortino. 2003. "Italian Immigration: The Origins, Nature, and Evolution of Italy's Migratory Systems," *Journal of Modern Italian Studies* 9, 1: 49–70.

Colombo, Emanuela, Maria Chiara Pastore, and Susanna Sancassani. 2017. *Storie di Cooperazione Politecnica, Stories of Cooperation at Polimi. 2011–2016*. Milan: Politecnico Milano-POLISAL. http://www.polisocial.polimi.it/wp -content/uploads/2016/12/libro_bianco.pdf.

Connell, R.W. 1987. *Gender and Power: Society, the Person, and Sexual Politics*. Stanford, CA: Stanford University Press.

Conroy, Michael E. 1987. "Economic Aggression as an Instrument of Low Intensity Warfare." In *Reagan vs. the Sandinistas*, edited by Thomas W. Walker, pp. 57–79. Boulder, CO: Westview Press.

———. 1990. "The Political Economy of the 1990 Nicaraguan Elections," *International Journal of Political Economy* 20, 3 (Fall): 5–33.

Cortés Ramos, Alberto. 2006. "Nicaragua's Indispensable Migrants and Costa Rica's Unconscionable New Law," *Revista Envío* 297 (April). http://www.envio .org.ni/articulo/3253.

Crenshaw, Kimberlé. 1989. "Demarginalizing the Intersection of Race and Sex: A Black Feminist Critique of Antidiscrimination Doctrine, Feminist Theory and Antiracist Politics," *University of Chicago Legal Forum* 1: 139–167.

Currie, Janet. 2009. "Healthy, Wealthy, and Wise? Socioeconomic Status, Poor Health in Childhood, and Human Capital Development," *Journal of Economic Literature* 47, 1: 87–122.

Daly, Martin, and Margo Wilson. 1999. *The Truth About Cinderella: A Darwinian View of Parental Love*. New Haven, CT: Yale University Press.

Da Roit, Barbara, Amparo González Ferrer, and Francisco Javier Moreno-Fuentes. 2013. "The Southern European Migrant-Based Care Model," *European Societies* 15, 4: 577–596.

Davidov, Eldad, and Moshe Semyonov. 2017. "Attitudes Toward Immigrants in European Societies," *International Journal of Comparative Sociology* 58, 5: 359–366.

Davutoğlu, Ayten. 2013. "Two Different Poverty Reduction Approaches: Neoliberal Market Based Microfinance versus Social Rights Defender Basic Income," *International Journal of Social Inquiry* 6, 1: 39–47.

De Haas, Hein. 2010. "Migration and Development: A Theoretical Perspective," *International Migration Review* 44: 227–64.

Démurger, Sylvie. 2015. "Migration and Families Left Behind," *IZA World of Labor* 144 (April). https://wol.iza.org/articles/migration-and-families-left-behind/long.

DeSouza, Eros R., and Elder Cerqueira. 2008. "From the Kitchen to the Bedroom: Frequency Rates and Consequences of Sexual Harassment Among Female Domestic Workers in Brazil," *Journal of Interpersonal Violence* 24, 8: 1264–1284.

Devitt, C. 2018. "Shaping Labour Migration to Italy: The Role of Labour Market Institutions," *Journal of Modern Italian Studies* 23, 3: 274–292.

Dipartimento di Comunicazione e Ricerca Sociale (Sapienza, Università di Roma). 2012. *Libro Bianco della Cooperazione Italiana. I documenti del Forum della Cooperazione Internazionale*. Milan, 1–2 ottobre 2012. https://www.coris.uniroma1.it/sites/default/files/180113_Libro_Bianco_Cooperazione_2.pdf.

Domínguez, Silvia, and Cecilia Menjívar. 2014. "Beyond Individual and Visible Acts of Violence: A Framework to Examine the Lives of Women in Low-Income Neighborhoods," *Women's Studies International Forum* 44: 184–195.

Dore, Elizabeth (ed.). 1997. *Gender Politics in Latin America: Debates in Theory and Practice*. New York: Monthly Review Press.

Drake, Paul, W. 2006. "The Hegemony of US Economic Doctrines in Latin America." In *Latin America After Neoliberalism: Turning the Tide in the 21st*

Century, edited by Eric Hershberg and Fred Rosen, pp. 26–48. New York: New Press.

Draper, Elaine. 1985. "Women's Work and Development in Latin America," *Studies in Comparative International Development* 20, 1 (Spring): 3–30.

Dreby, Joanna. 2010. *Divided by Borders: Mexican Migrants and Their Children.* Berkeley: University of California Press.

Dunkerley, James. 1988. *Power in the Isthmus: A Political History of Modern Central America.* London: Verso.

Durrant, Joan, and Ron Ensom. 2012. "Physical Punishment of Children: Lessons from 20 Years of Research," *Canadian Medical Association Journal* 184, 12 (September 4): 1373–1377.

ECLAC (Economic Commission for Latin America and the Caribbean). 2000. *Social Panorama of Latin America, 1999.* Santiago, Chile: ECLAC.

———. 2016. "Social Panorama of Latin America: 2015." Briefing paper. http://www.cepal.org/en/publications/39964-social-panorama-latin-america-2015-briefing-paper.

———. 2018. *Social Panorama of Latin America, 2017.* LC/PUB.2018/1-P. Santiago, Chile: ECLAC.

———. 2021. *Social Panorama of Latin America, 2020.* LC/PUB.2021/2-P/Rev.1. Santiago, Chile: ECLAC.

Ehrenreich, Barbara, and Arlie Russell Hochschild. 2003. *Global Woman: Nannies, Maids, and Sex Workers in the New Economy.* New York: Owl Books.

Emirbayer, Mustafa, and Ann Mische. 1998. "What Is Agency?" *American Journal of Sociology* 103, 4 (January): 962–1023.

Engle, Patrice L. 1995. "Father's Money, Mother's Money, and Parental Commitment: Guatemala and Nicaragua." In *Engendering Wealth and Well-Being: Empowerment for Global Change*, edited by Rae Lesser Blumberg, Cathy Rakowski, Irene Tinker, and Michael Monteon, pp. 155–179. Boulder, CO: Westview Press.

Enríquez, Laura J. 1991. *Harvesting Change: Labor and Agrarian Reform in Nicaragua, 1979–1990.* Chapel Hill: University of North Carolina Press.

———. 1997. *Agrarian Reform and Class Consciousness in Nicaragua.* Gainesville: University Press of Florida.

———. 2010. *Reactions to the Market: Small Farmers in the Economic Reshaping of Nicaragua, Cuba, Russia, and China.* University Park: Pennsylvania State University Press.

Enríquez, Laura J., and Tiffany L. Page. 2018. "The Rise and Fall of the Pink Tide." In *The Routledge Handbook of Latin American Development*, edited by Julie

Cupples, Marcela Palomino-Schalscha, and Manuel Prieto Montt, pp. 87–97. London: Routledge.

Esbensen, Finn-Aage, and Cheryl Lee Maxson (eds.). 2012. *Youth Gangs in International Perspective: Results from the Eurogang Program of Research.* New York: Springer.

Euronews. 2018. "Salvini Pushes for Census of Roma People in Italy." June 19.

Evans, Trevor. 1995. "Ajuste estructural y sector público en Nicaragua." In *La transformación neoliberal del sector público: Ajuste estructural y sector público en Centroamérica y El Caribe*, edited by Trevor Evans, pp. 179–261. Managua, Nicaragua: Latino Editors.

Ewig, Christina. 1999. "The Strengths and Limits of the NGO Women's Movement Model: Shaping Nicaragua's Democratic Institutions," *Latin American Research Review* 34, 3 (January): 75–102.

Farmer, Paul. 2004. "An Anthropology of Structural Violence." *Current Anthropology* 45, 3: 305–325.

Fernández Poncela, Anna M. 1996. "The Disruptions of Adjustment: Women in Nicaragua," *Latin American Perspectives* 23, 1: 49–66.

FIDEG (Fundación Internacional para el Desafío Económico Global). 2020. "Informe de resultados de la encuesta de hogares para medir la pobreza en Nicaragua 2019, Fundación Internacional para el Desafío Económico Global." http://fideg.org/investigaciones-y-publicaciones/medicion-de-la-pobreza-nicaragua-informe-de-resultados-2019/, accessed May 31, 2021.

Fields, Abbie Shepard. 2002. "Abuso Sexual Infantil en Nicaragua: Manifestaciones Clínicas e Impacto de un Tratamiento Terapéutico a Corto Plazo." MA thesis, University of Barcelona and University of El Salvador.

Finkelhor, David, and Larry Baron. 1986. "Risk Factors for Child Sexual Abuse," *Journal of Interpersonal Violence* 1, 1 (March): 43–71.

Fonseca, Claudia. 1991. "Spouses, Siblings and Sex-Linked Bonding: A Look at Kinship Organization in a Brazilian Slum." In *Family, Household, and Gender Relations in Latin America*, edited by Elizabeth Jelin, pp. 133–160. London: Kegan Paul International and UNESCO.

Forjuoh, Samuel N., and Anthony B. Zwi. 1998. "Violence Against Children and Adolescents: International Perspectives," *Pediatric Clinics of North America* 45, 2 (April): 415–426.

Funkhouser, Edward. 1992. "Migration from Nicaragua: Some Recent Evidence," *World Development* 20, 8: 1209–1218.

Gagliardi, Cristina, Mirko Di Rosa, Maria Gabriella Melchiorre, Lianna Spazzafumo, and Fiorella Marcellini. 2012. "Italy and the Aging Society: Overview of Demographic Trends and Formal/Informal Resources for the Care of Older People," *Advances in Sociological Research* 13: 85–104.

Galtung, Johan. 1969. "Violence, Peace, and Peace Research," *Journal of Peace Research* 6, 3: 167–191.

Gasper, Joseph, Stefanie DeLuca, and Angela Estacion. 2012. "Switching Schools: Reconsidering the Relationship Between School Mobility and High School Dropout," *American Educational Research Journal* 49, 3 (June): 487–519. https://doi.org/10.3102/0002831211415250.

Gheasi, Masood, and Peter Nijkamp. 2017. "A Brief Overview of International Migration Motives and Impacts, with Specific Reference to FDI," *Economies* 5, 31. http://dx.doi.org/10.3390/economies5030031.

Gill, Rosalind. 2008. "Culture and Subjectivity in Neoliberal and Postfeminist Times," *Subjectivity* 25: 432–445. http://www.palgrave-journals.com/sub/journal/v25/n1/full/sub200828a.html.

Ginsborg, Paul. 2003. *Italy and Its Discontents: Family, Civil Society, State.* New York: Palgrave Macmillan.

Gonzales, Roberto G., Nando Sigona, Martha C. Franco, and Anna Papoutsi. 2019. *Undocumented Migration: Borders, Immigration Enforcement, and Belonging.* Medford, MA: Polity Press.

González-Barrera, Ana, and Jens Manuel Krogstad. 2017. "What We Know About Illegal Immigration from Mexico." Fact Tank, Pew Research Center. 2 March.

González-Rivera, Victoria. 2011. *Before the Revolution: Women's Rights and Right-Wing Politics in Nicaragua, 1821–1979.* University Park: Pennsylvania State University Press.

Gosteli, Ylenia. 2018. "In Post-election Italy, Violent Racist Attacks Becoming Routine," Al Jazeera, August 7.

Gould, Jeffrey L. 2014. *To Lead as Equals: Rural Protest and Political Consciousness in Chinandega, Nicaragua, 1912–1979.* Chapel Hill: University of North Carolina Press. Project MUSE. muse.jhu.edu/book/40382.

Grigg, Jeffrey. 2012. "School Enrollment Changes and Student Achievement Growth: A Case Study in Educational Disruption and Continuity," *Sociology of Education* 85, 4 (October): 388–404. https://doi.org/10.1177/0038040712441374.

The Guardian. 2019. "As Trump Closes US Doors to Migrants, Latin Americans Look to Europe." July 10.

Gustafson, T. B., and D. B. Sarwer. 2004. "Childhood Sexual Abuse and Obesity," *Obesity Reviews* 5, 3 (August): 129–135.

Hays, Sharon. 1994. "Structure and Agency and the Sticky Problem of Culture," *Sociological Theory* 12, 1 (March): 57–72.

Herman, Judith, and Lisa Hirschman. 1977. "Father-Daughter Incest," *Signs* 2, 4 (Summer): 735–757.

Heumann, Silke. 2014. "Gender, Sexuality, and Politics: Rethinking the Relationship Between Feminism and Sandinismo in Nicaragua," *Social Politics* 21, 2: 290–314.

Heymann, Jody, Francisco Flores-Macias, Jeffrey A. Hayes, Malinda Kennedy, Claudia Lahaie, and Alison Earle. 2009. "The Impact of Migration on the Well-Being of Transnational Families: New Data from Sending Communities in Mexico," *Community, Work and Family* 12, 1: 91–103.

Higgins, Bryan R. 1990. "The Place of Housing Programs and Class Relations in Latin American Cities: The Development of Managua Before 1980," *Economic Geography* 66, 4 (October): 378–388.

Hillis, Susan, James Mercy, Adaugo Amobi, and Howard Kress. 2016. "Global Prevalence of Past-Year Violence Against Children: A Systematic Review and Minimum Estimates," *Pediatrics* 137, s3: e20154079.

Hilton, N. Zoe, Grant T. Harris, and Marnie E. Rice. 2015. "The Step-Father Effect in Child Abuse: Comparing Discriminative Parental Solicitude and Antisociality," *Psychology of Violence*, 5, 1: 8–15.

Hochschild, Arlie Russell. 2016. *Strangers in Their Own Land: Anger and Mourning on the American Right.* New York: New Press.

Hondagneu-Sotelo, Pierrette. 2001. *Doméstica: Immigrant Workers Cleaning and Caring in the Shadows of Affluence.* Berkeley: University of California Press.

Hondagneu-Sotelo, Pierrette, and Ernestine Avila. 1997. "'I'm Here, But I'm There': The Meanings of Latina Transnational Motherhood," *Gender and Society* 11, 5: 548–571.

Houck, Christopher D., Nicole R. Nugent, Celia M. Lescano, April Peters, and Larry K. Brown. 2010. "Sexual Abuse and Sexual Risk Behavior: Beyond the Impact of Psychiatric Problems," *Journal of Pediatric Psychology* 35, 5 (June): 473–483.

Hussey, Jon M., Jen Jen Chang, and Jonathan B. Kotch. 2006. "Child Maltreatment in the United States: Prevalence, Risk Factors, and Adolescent Health Consequences," *Pediatrics* 118, 3 (September): 933–942.

Isbester, Katherine. 2001. *Still Fighting: The Nicaraguan Women's Movement, 1977–2000.* Pittsburgh, PA: University of Pittsburgh Press.

Istat. 2015. "Migrazioni Internacionali e Interne della Popolazione Residente." Statistiche Report 2014. November 26. http://www.istat.it/it/files/2015/11/Migrazioni-_-Anno-2014-DEF.pdf.

Jaret, C. 1999. "Troubled by Newcomers: Anti-Immigrant Attitudes and Action During Two Eras of Mass Immigration to the United States," *Journal of American Ethnic History* 18, 3 (Spring): 9–39.

Johns, Michael. 2012. *The Education of a Radical: An American Revolutionary in Sandinista Nicaragua*. Austin: University of Texas Press.

Jonakin, Jon. 2018. *Market Liberalizations and Emigration from Latin America*. New York: Routledge.

Jonakin, Jon, and Laura J. Enríquez. 1999. "The Non-traditional Financial Sector in Nicaragua: A Response to Rural Credit Market Exclusion," *Development Policy Review* 17, 2 (June): 141–169.

Jurik, Nancy J. 2005. *Bootstrap Dreams: U.S. Microenterprise Development in an Era of Welfare Reform*. Ithaca, NY: Cornell University Press.

Kaimowitz, David, and Joseph R. Thome. 1982. "Nicaragua's Agrarian Reform: The First Year (1979–80)." In *Nicaragua in Revolution*, edited by Thomas W. Walker, pp. 223-240. New York: Praeger.

Kampwirth, Karen. 1993. "Democratizing the Nicaraguan Family: Struggles over the State, Households, and Civil Society." PhD dissertation, University of California at Berkeley.

———. 2004. *Feminism and the Legacy of Revolution: Nicaragua, El Salvador, Chiapas*. Athens: Ohio University Press.

———. 2011. *Latin America's New Left and the Politics of Gender: Lessons from Nicaragua*. New York: Springer.

Kilpatrick, Dean G., Ron Acierno, Benjamin Saunders, Heidi S. Resnick, Connie L. Best, and Paula P. Schnurr. 2000. "Risk Factors for Adolescent Substance Abuse and Dependence: Data from a National Sample," *Journal of Consulting and Clinical Psychology* 68, 1 (February): 19–30.

Kirchgaessner, Stephanie. 2018. "Far-Right Italy Minister Vows 'Action' to Expel Thousands of Roma." *The Guardian*, June 19.

Kleinman, Arthur. 1997. "The Violences of Everyday Life: The Multiple Forms and Dynamics of Social Violence." In *Violence and Subjectivity*, edited by Veena Das, Arthur Kleinman, Mamphela Ramphele, and Pamela Reynolds, pp. 226–241. Berkeley: University of California Press.

Kozyrskyj, Anita L., Garth E. Kendall, Peter Jacoby, Peter D. Sly, and Stephen R. Zubrick. 2010. "Association Between Socioeconomic Status and the Development of Asthma: Analyses of Income Trajectories," *American Journal of Public Health* 100, 3: 540–546.

Krugman, Scott, Leonardo Mata, and Richard Krugman. 1992. "Sexual Abuse and Corporal Punishment During Childhood: A Pilot Retrospective Survey of University Students in Costa Rica," *Pediatrics* 90, 1: 157–161.

Kruks, Sonia, Rayna Rapp, and Marylyn B. Young. 1989. *Promissory Notes: Women in the Transition to Socialism*. New York: Monthly Review Press.

La Botz, Dan. 2016. *What Went Wrong? The Nicaraguan Revolution.* Leiden, Netherlands: Brill.

Labrianidis, Lois, and Manolis Pratsinakis. 2016. "Greece's New Emigration at Times of Crisis." GreeSE Paper No. 99, Hellenic Observatory Papers on Greece and Southeast Europe, London School of Economics and Political Science (May).

Lancaster, Roger, N. 1988. *Thanks to God and the Revolution: Popular Religion and Class Consciousness in the New Nicaragua.* New York: Columbia University Press.

———. 1992. *Life Is Hard: Machismo, Danger, and the Intimacy of Power in Nicaragua.* Berkeley: University of California Press.

Langley, Lester D. 1983. *The Banana Wars: An Inner History of American Empire, 1900–1934.* Lexington: University Press of Kentucky.

Larson, Kandyce, and Neal Halfon. 2010. "Family Income Gradients in the Health and Health Care Access of US Children," *Maternal Child Health Journal* 14: 332–342.

Lion, Katherine C., Ndola Prata, and Chris Steward. 2009. "Adolescent Childbearing in Nicaragua: A Quantitative Assessment of Associated Factors," *International Perspectives on Sexual and Reproductive Health* 35, 2: 91–96.

Lundquist, Jennifer H., and Douglas S. Massey. 2005. "Politics or Economics? International Migration During the Nicaraguan Contra War," *Journal of Latin American Studies,* 37, 1: 29–53. https://doi.org/10.1017/S0022216X04008594.

Lutz, Helma. 2011. *New Maids: Transnational Women and the Care Economy.* New York: Zed Books.

Macaulay, Neill. 1998. *The Sandino Affair.* Chicago: Quadrangle Books.

Macintosh, Fiona. 2016. *Rosa of the Wild Grass: The Story of a Nicaraguan Family.* Rugby, UK: Practical Action/Latin America Bureau.

MacMillan, Harriet L., Jan E. Fleming, David L. Streiner, Elizabeth Lin, Michael H. Boyle, Ellen Jamieson, Eric K. Duki, Christine A. Walsh, Maria Y. Wong, and William R. Beardslee. 2001. "Childhood Abuse and Lifetime Psychopathology in a Community Sample," *American Journal of Psychiatry* 158: 1878–1883.

MacMillan, Harriet L., Masako Tanaka, Eric Duku, Tracey Vaillancourt, and Michael H Boyle. 2013. "Child Physical and Sexual Abuse in a Community Sample of Young Adults: Results from the Ontario Child Health Study," *Child Abuse and Neglect* 37, 1: 14–21.

Martí i Puig, Salvador, and Eduardo Baumeister. 2016. "Agrarian Policies in Nicaragua: From Revolution to the Revival of Agro-exports, 1979–2015," *Journal of Agrarian Change* 17: 381–396.

Massey, Douglas S., Joaquin Arango, Graeme Hugo, Ali Kouaouci, Adela Pellegrino, and J. Edward Taylor. 1993. "Theories of International Migration: A Review and Appraisal," *Population and Development Review* 19: 431–466.

Mendes, Neuza, Fátima Palma, and Fátima Serrano. 2014. "Sexual and Reproductive Health of Portuguese Adolescents," *International Journal of Adolescent Medicine and Health* 26, 1: 3–12.

Menjívar, Cecilia. 2000. *Fragmented Ties: Salvadoran Immigrant Networks in America.* Berkeley: University of California Press.

———. 2011. *Enduring Violence: Ladina Women's Lives in Guatemala.* Berkeley: University of California Press.

Menjívar, Cecilia, and Leisy J. Abrego. 2012. "Legal Violence: Immigration Law and the Lives of Central American Immigrants," *American Journal of Sociology* 117, 5 (March): 1380–1421.

Menjívar, Cecilia, and Sarah M. Lakhani. 2016. "Transformative Effects of Immigration Law: Immigrants' Personal and Social Metamorphoses Through Regularization," *American Journal of Sociology* 121, 6 (May): 1818–1855.

Miller, Valerie. 1982. "The Nicaraguan Literacy Crusade." In *Nicaragua in Revolution*, edited by Thomas W. Walker, pp. 241–258. New York: Praeger.

Mohapatra, Sanket, Dilip Ratha, and Elina Scheja. 2010. "Impact of Migration on Economic and Social Development: A Review of Evidence and Emerging Issues." Background paper prepared for the Civil Society Days of the Global Forum on Migration and Development. Migration and Remittances Unit, World Bank.

Molé, Noelle. 2010. "Precarious Subjects: Anticipating Neoliberalism in Northern Italy's Workplace," *American Anthropologist* 112, 1 (March): 38–53.

Molyneux, Maxine. 1981. "Women's Emancipation Under Socialism: A Model for the Third World?" *World Development* 9, 9/10: 1019–1037.

———. 1986. "Mobilization Without Emancipation? Women's Interests, State, and Revolution." In *Transition and Development: Problems of Third World Socialism*, edited by Richard R. Fagen, Carmen Diana Deere, and José Luis Coraggio, pp. 280–302. New York: Monthly Review Press.

Montalto Monella, Lillo. 2018. "Are Hate Crimes on the Rise in Italy?" Euronews, July 31.

Montoya, Rosario. 2002. "Women's Sexuality, Knowledge, and Agency in Rural Nicaragua." In *Gender's Place: Feminist Anthropologies of Latin America*, edited by Rosario Montoya, Lessie Jo Frazier, and Janise Hurtig, pp. 65–88. London: Palgrave.

———. 2003. "House, Street, Collective: Revolutionary Geographies and Gender Transformation in Nicaragua, 1979–1999," *Latin American Research Review* 38, 2 (June): 61–93.

Moser, Caroline, and Cathy McIlwaine. 2000. *Urban Poor Perceptions of Violence and Exclusion in Colombia: Conflict Prevention and Post-Conflict Reconstruction.* Washington, DC: World Bank.

Mullen, Paul E., J. L. Martin, J. C. Anderson, and Sarah E. Romans. 1996. "The Long-Term Impact of the Physical, Emotional, and Sexual Abuse of Children: A Community Study," *Child Abuse and Neglect* 20, 1: 7–21.

Namy, Sophie, Catherine Carlson, Kathleen O'Hara, Janet Nakuti, Paul Bukuluki, Julius Lwanyaaga, Sylvia Namakula, Barbrah Nanyunja, Milton L. Wainberg, Dipak Naker, and Lori Michau. 2017. "Towards a Feminist Understanding of Intersecting Violence Against Women and Children in the Family," *Social Science and Medicine* 184 (July): 40–48.

New York Times. 2019. "For Central Americans, Fleeing to Europe May Beat Trying to Reach the U.S." June 9.

Norman, Rosana E., Munkhtsetseg Byambaa, Rumna De, Alexander Butchart, James Scott, and Theo Vos. 2012. "The Long-Term Health Consequences of Child Physical Abuse, Emotional Abuse, and Neglect: A Systematic Review and Meta-Analysis," *PLoS Medicine* 9, 11: e1001349. https://doi.org/10.1371/journal.pmed.1001349.

Notari, Dalmazia. 1998. *Donne da Bosco e da Riviera: Un Secolo di Emigrazione Femminile dall'alto Appennino Reggiano (1860–1960).* Bologna: Parco del Gigante.

Ollenburger, Jane C., and Helen A. Moore. 1992. *A Sociology of Women: The Intersection of Patriarchy, Capitalism, and Colonization.* Englewood Cliffs, NJ: Prentice Hall.

Olsson, Ann, Mary Ellsberg, Staffan Berglund, Andrés Herrera, Elmer Zelaya, Rodolfo Peña, Felix Zelaya, and Lars-Åke Persson. 2000. "Sexual Abuse During Childhood and Adolescence Among Nicaraguan Men and Women: A Population-Based Anonymous Survey," *Child Abuse and Neglect* 24, 12: 1579–1589.

Omi, Michael, and Howard Winant. 1986. *Racial Formation in the United States: From the 1960s to the 1980s.* New York: Routledge and Kegan Paul.

Orsini-Jones, Marina, and Francesca Gattullo. 2000. "Migrant Women in Italy: National Trends and Local Perspectives." In *Gender and Migration in Southern Europe*, edited by Floya Anthias and Gabriella Lazaridis, pp. 125–144. Oxford, UK: Berg.

Parreñas, Rhacel Salazar. 2005. *Children of Global Migration: Transnational Families and Gendered Woes.* Stanford, CA: Stanford University Press.

———. 2015. *Servants of Globalization: Migration and Domestic Work.* Stanford, CA: Stanford University Press.

Passel, Jeffrey S. 2005. "Unauthorized Migrants: Numbers and Characteristics." Background Briefing Prepared for Task Force on Immigration and America's Future. Pew Hispanic Center, June 14.

Paulson, Susan. 2016. *Masculinities and Femininities in Latin America's Uneven Development.* New York: Routledge.

Pereda, Noemí, Georgina Guilera, Maria Forns, and Juan Gómez-Benito. 2009. "The International Epidemiology of Child Sexual Abuse: A Continuation of Finkelhor (1994)," *Child Abuse and Neglect* 33, 6 (June): 331–342. http://www.sciencedirect.com/science/article/pii/S0145213409000970.

Phizacklea, Annie. 1998. "Migration and Globalization: A Feminist Perspective." In *The New Migration in Europe: Social Constructions and Social Realities,* edited by Khalid Koser and Helma Lutz, pp. 21–38. Houndmills, UK: Macmillan.

Pineda-Lucatero, A. G., Benjamín Trujillo-Hernández, Rebeca O. Millán-Guerrero, and Clemente Vásquez. 2008. "Prevalence of Childhood Sexual Abuse Among Mexican Adolescents," *Child: Care, Health and Development* 35, 2: 184–189. http://onlinelibrary.wiley.com/doi/10.1111/j.1365-2214.2008.00888.x/full.

Pojmann, Wendy. 2006. *Immigrant Women and Feminism in Italy.* Burlington, VT: Ashgate.

Polanczyk, Guilherme Vanoni, Maria Lucrécia Zavaschi, Silvia Benetti, Raquel Zenker, and Patrícia Wainberg Gammerman. 2003. "Sexual Violence and Its Prevalence Among Adolescents," *Revista de Saúde Pública* 37, 1 (February): 8–14.

Pratt, Geraldine. 2012. *Families Apart: Migrant Mothers and the Conflicts of Labor and Love.* Minneapolis: University of Minnesota Press.

Prevost, Gary, and Harry E. Vanden. 1997. "Introduction." In *The Undermining of the Sandinista Revolution,* edited by Gary Prevost and Harry E. Vanden, pp. 1–8. New York: St. Martin's Press.

Putnam, Frank W. 2003. "Ten-Year Research Update Review: Child Sexual Abuse," *Journal of the American Academy of Child and Adolescent Psychiatry* 42, 3: 269–278.

Queirolo Palmas, Luca, and Andrea T. Torre. 2005. *Il Fantasma delle Bande: Genova e i Latinos.* Genoa, Italy: Frilli.

Quintana, M. E., and R. Cajina. 1992. "Diagnóstico: Abuso Sexual Contra Menores." Centro Nicaragüense de Promoción de la Juventud y la Infancia. Dos Generaciones, Managua, Nicaragua.

Ramírez, Clemencia, Angela María Pinzón-Rondón, and Juan Carlos Botero. 2011. "Contextual Predictive Factors of Child Sexual Abuse: The Role of Parent-Child Interaction," *Child Abuse and Neglect* 35: 1022–1031.

Repak, Terry. 1995. *Waiting on Washington: Central American Workers in the Nation's Capital*. Philadelphia, PA: Temple University Press.

República de Nicaragua. 1977. *Población de Nicaragua: Compendio de las Cifras Censales y Proyecciones por Departamentos y Municipios, Años 1971–1980*. Boletín Demográfico, Oficina Ejecutiva de Encuestas y Censos (July).

Reuters. 2017. "Births in Italy Hit Record Low in 2016, Population Ages." March 6.

Reygadas, Luis, and Fernando Filgueira. 2010. "Inequality and the Incorporation Crisis: The Left's Social Policy Toolkit." In *Latin America's Left Turns: Politics, Policies, and Trajectories of Change*, edited by Maxwell A. Cameron and Eric Hershberg, pp. 171–191. Boulder, CO: Lynne Rienner.

Roberts, Dorothy E. 1992. "Racism and Patriarchy in the Meaning of Motherhood," *American University Journal of Gender, Social Policy and the Law* 1, 1: 1–38.

Rodriguez, Robyn Magalit. 2010. *Migrants for Export: How the Philippine State Brokers Labor to the World*. Minneapolis: University of Minnesota Press.

Romero, Mary. 2002. *Maid in the U.S.A.* New York: Routledge.

———. 2011. *The Maid's Daughter: Living Inside and Outside the American Dream*. New York: New York University Press.

Romero, Mary, and Zulema Valdez. 2016. "Introduction to the Special Issue: Intersectionality and Entrepreneurship," *Ethnic and Racial Studies* 39, 9: 1553–1565.

Sadowski, H., Judith Trowell, I. Kolvin, T. Weeramanthri, M. Berelowitz, and L. H. Gilbert. 2003. "Sexually Abused Girls: Patterns of Psychopathology and Exploration of Risk Factors," *European Child and Adolescent Psychiatry* 12, 5 (October): 221–230.

Safilios-Rothschild, Constantina. 1990. "Socio-economic Determinants of the Outcomes of Women's Income-Generation in Developing Countries." In *Women, Employment and the Family in the International Division of Labour*, edited by Sharon Stichter and Jane Parpart, pp. 221–228. Houndmills, UK: Macmillan.

Scheper-Hughes, Nancy. 1992. *Death Without Weeping: The Violence of Everyday Life in Brazil*. Berkeley: University of California Press.

Schickedanz, Adam, Benard P. Dreyer, and Neal Halfon. 2015. "Childhood Poverty: Understanding and Preventing the Adverse Impacts of a Most-prevalent Risk to Pediatric Health and Well-Being," *Pediatric Clinics of North America* 62, 5: 1111–1135.

Schwartz, Elaine. 2016. "A Demographic Disaster," *Econlife* (September 15). https://econlife.com/2018/06/italys-aging-population/.

Sciortino, Giuseppe. 2004. "Immigration in a Mediterranean Welfare State: The Italian Experience in Comparative Perspective," *Journal of Comparative Policy Analysis* 6, 2 (August): 111–129.

Segreti, Giulia. 2018. "Italy Migrants Fear Uncertain Future After Election." Reuters, March 5.

Smith, George P., II. 1991. "Incest and Intrafamilial Child Abuse: Fatal Attractions or Forced and Dangerous Liaisons?" *Journal of Family Law* 29: 833–878.

Sniderman, Paul M., Pierangelo Peri, Rui J. P. de Figueiredo Jr., and Thomas Piazza. 2002. *The Outsider: Prejudice and Politics in Italy.* Princeton, NJ: Princeton University Press.

Solari, Cinzia D. 2017. *On the Shoulders of Grandmothers.* New York: Routledge.

Solomon, Jennifer C. 1992. "Child Sexual Abuse by Family Members: A Radical Feminist Perspective," *Sex Roles: A Journal of Research* 27, 9/10: 473–485.

Southerland, Nancy E. 1985. "Post-Earthquake Urban Reconstruction in Managua, Nicaragua." MA thesis, University of California at Berkeley.

Speak, Clare. 2018. "As Racist Attacks Increase, Is There a 'Climate of Hatred' in Italy?" *The Local*, August 2.

Speizer, Ilene S., Mary Goodwin, Ghazaleh Samandari, and Maureen Clyde. 2008. "Dimensions of Child Punishment in Two Central American Countries: Guatemala and El Salvador," *Revista Panamericana de Salud Pública* 23, 4 (May): 247–256. https://doi.org/10.1590/S1020-49892008000400004.

Stahler-Sholk, Richard. 1990. "Stabilization Policies Under Revolutionary Transition: 1979–1990." PhD dissertation, University of California at Berkeley.

———. 1997. "Structural Adjustment and Resistance: The Political Economy of Nicaragua under Chamorro." In *The Undermining of the Sandinista Revolution*, edited by Gary Prevost and Harry Vanden, pp. 74–113. London: Macmillan.

Stanley, Flavia. 2015. "On Belonging, Difference, and Whiteness: Italy's Problem with Immigration." PhD dissertation, University of Massachusetts at Amherst.

Stephens, Beth. 1989. "Changes in the Laws Governing the Parent-Child Relationship in Post-Revolutionary Nicaragua," *Hastings International and Comparative Law Review* 12, 1 (Fall): 137–171.

Sternberg, Peter. 2000. "Challenging Machismo: Promoting Sexual and Reproductive Health with Nicaraguan Men," *Gender and Development* 8, 1: 89–99.

Stevens, Evelyn P. 1973. "Machismo and Marianismo," *Society* 10, 6 (September): 57–63.

Stoltenborgh Marije, Marinus H. van Ijzendoorn, Eveline M. Euser, and Marian J. Bakermans-Kranenburg. 2011. "A Global Perspective on Child Sexual Abuse: Meta-analysis of Prevalence Around the World." *Child Maltreatment* 16: 79–101.

Stoltz Chinchilla, Norma. 1990. "The Evolution of Revolutionary Popular Feminism in Nicaragua: Articulating Class, Gender, and National Sovereignty," *Gender and Society* IV, 3 (September): 370–397.

Sunkel, Guillermo. 2006. "El papel de la familia en la protección social en América Latina." *Serie: Políticas Sociales* 120, División de Desarrollo Social, CEPAL. April.

Swann, William B., Jr. 1996. *Self-Traps: The Elusive Quest for Higher Self-Esteem.* New York: Freeman.

Telles, Edward. 2014. *Pigmentocracies: Ethnicity, Race and Color in Latin America.* Chapel Hill: University of North Carolina Press.

Thomson Salo, Frances. 2010. "Parenting an Infant Born of Rape." In *Parenthood and Mental Health: A Bridge between Infant and Adult Psychiatry*, edited by Sam Tyano, Miri Keren, Helen Herrman and John Cox, pp. 289–300. Chichester, UK: Wiley.

Tognetti Bordogna, Mara, and Annalisa Ornaghi. 2012. "The 'Badanti' (Informal Carers) Phenomenon in Italy," *Journal of Intercultural Studies* 33, 1: 9–22. https://www-tandfonline-com.libproxy.berkeley.edu/doi/full/10.1080/07256868.2012.633312.

Torche, Florencia. 2014. "Intergenerational Mobility and Inequality: The Latin American Case." *Annual Review of Sociology* 40: 619–642.

Townsend, Janet, Emma Zapata, Jo Rowlands, Pilar Alberti, and Marta Mercado. 1999. *Women and Power: Fighting Patriarchies and Poverty.* London: Zed Books.

Trotz, Alissa. 1996. "Gender, Ethnicity and Familial Ideology in Georgetown, Guyana: Household Structure and Female Labour Force Participation Reconsidered," *European Journal of Development Research* 8, 1: 177–199.

Türken, Salman, Hilde Eileen Nafstad, Rolv Mikkel Blakar, and Katrina Roen. 2016. "Making Sense of Neoliberal Subjectivity: A Discourse Analysis of Media Language on Self-development," *Globalizations* 13, 1: 32–46.

United Nations, Department of Economic and Social Affairs, Population Division. 2019. *World Population Prospects 2019.* Online Edition, Rev. 1.

———. 2020a. *International Migrant Stock 2020*. POP/DB/MD/STOCK/Rev.2020. https://www.un.org/development/desa/pd/content/international-migrant-stock, accessed May 31, 2021.

———. 2020b. *International Migration 2020 Highlights*. ST/ESA/SER.A/452. https://www.un.org/development/desa/pd/content/publications.

Uyangoda, Nadeesha. 2018. "What Being a Person of Color in Salvini's Italy Feels Like." Al Jazeera, June 13.

Valdez, Zulema. 2015. *Entrepreneurs and the Search for the American Dream*. New York: Routledge.

Valladares, Eliette, and Rodolfo Peña. 2006. "Informe sobre abuso sexual de niñas, niños y adolescentes, 2005." Centro de Investigación en Demografía y Salud (CIDS), UNAN-León.

Van Wunnik, Lucas. 2011/2013. "The Multinational Firm in the Maquiladora Industry of Nicaragua (2007 versus 1998): More of the Same," *Annales de Géographie* 679: 266–297. https://doi.org/10.3917/ag.679.0266.

Veenema, Tener Goodwin, Clifton P. Thornton, and Andrew Corley. 2015. "The Public Health Crisis of Child Sexual Abuse in Low and Middle Income Countries: An Integrative Review of the Literature," *International Journal of Nursing Studies* 52, 4 (April): 864–881.

Vianello, Francesca Alice, Claudia Finotelli, and Elisa Brey. 2019. "A Slow Ride Towards Permanent Residency: Legal Transitions and the Working Trajectories of Ukrainian Migrants in Italy and Spain." *Journal of Ethnic and Migration Studies*. https://doi.org/10.1080/1369183X.2019.1590187.

Vilas, Carlos, M. 1986. *The Sandinista Revolution: National Liberation and Social Transformation in Central America*. New York: Monthly Review Press.

Vukelich, Donna. 1994. "Welcome to the Free Trade Zone," *Revista Envío* 150 (January). http://www.envio.org.ni/articulo/1741.

Wade, Peter. 1997. *Race and Ethnicity in Latin America*. London: Pluto Press.

———. 2008. "Race in Latin America." In *A Companion to Latin American Anthropology*, edited by Deborah Poole, pp. 177–192. Malden, MA: Blackwell.

———. 2013. "Articulations of Eroticism and Race: Domestic Service in Latin America," *Feminist Theory* 14, 2: 187–202.

Walby, Sylvia. 1990. *Theorizing Patriarchy*. Oxford, UK: Blackwell.

Walsh, Shannon Drysdale, and Cecilia Menjívar. 2016. "Impunity and Multisided Violence in the Lives of Latin American Women: El Salvador in Comparative Perspective," *Current Sociology* 64, 4: 586–602.

Walter, Knut. 1993. *The Regime of Anastasio Somoza, 1936–1956*. Chapel Hill: University of North Carolina Press.

Waters, Mary C., and Reed Ueda, with Helen B. Marrow. 2007. *The New Americans: A Guide to Immigration Since 1965*. Cambridge, MA: Harvard University Press.

Welsh, Sandy, Jacquie Carr, Barbara MacQuarrie, and Audrey Huntley. 2006. "'I'm Not Thinking of It as Sexual Harassment': Understanding Harassment Across Race and Citizenship," *Gender and Society* 20, 1: 87–107.

Williams, Harvey. 1982. "Housing Policy in Revolutionary Nicaragua." In *Nicaragua in Revolution*, edited by Thomas W. Walker, pp. 273–290. New York: Praeger.

———. 1987. "The Social Impact in Nicaragua." In *Reagan vs. the Sandinistas: The Undeclared War on Nicaragua*, edited by Thomas W. Walker, pp. 247–264. Boulder: Westview Press.

Williams, Robert G. 1986. *Export Agriculture and the Crisis in Central America*. Chapel Hill: University of North Carolina Press.

———. 1994. *States and Social Evolution: Coffee and the Rise of National Governments in Central America*. Chapel Hill: University of North Carolina Press.

Williamson, John. 1990. "What Washington Means by Policy Reform." In *Latin American Adjustment: How Much Has Happened*, edited by John Williamson, pp. 7–20. Washington, DC: Institute for International Economics.

Wilson, Tamar Diana. 2013. "Violence Against Women in Latin America," *Latin American Perspectives* 41, 1: 3–18.

Winters, Paul, Alain de Janvry, and Elisabeth Sadoulet. 2001. "Family and Community Networks in Mexico-U.S. Migration," *Journal of Human Resources* 36, 1 (Winter): 159–184.

Wonderlich, Stephen A., Ross D. Crosby, James E. Mitchell, Kevin M. Thompson, Jennifer Redlin, Gail Demuth, Joshua Smyth, and Beth Haseltine. 2001. "Eating Disturbance and Sexual Trauma in Childhood and Adulthood," *International Journal of Eating Disorders* 30: 401–412. https://doi.org/10.1002/eat.1101.

World Bank. 2012. "Better Jobs in Nicaragua: The Role of Human Capital," Report #72923. Human Development Department, Latin America and the Caribbean (January).

Yarris, Kristin E. 2017. *Care Across Generations: Solidarity and Sacrifice in Transnational Families*. Stanford, CA: Stanford University Press.

Zatz, Marjorie S., and Nancy Rodriguez. 2015. *Dreams and Nightmares: Immigration Policy, Youth, and Families*. Berkeley: University of California Press.

Zavella, Patricia. 1987. *Women's Work and Chicano Families: Cannery Workers of the Santa Clara Valley*. Ithaca, NY: Cornell University Press.

———. 2017. "Intersectional Praxis in the Movement for Reproductive Justice: The Respect ABQ Women Campaign," *Signs* 42, 2 (Winter): 509–533.

Zhao, Xiaojian. 2016. "Immigration to the United States After 1945." *Oxford Research Encyclopedias: American History.* https://doi.org/10.1093/acrefore/9780199329175.013.72.

Zong, Jie, Jeanne Batalova, and Jeffrey Hallock. 2018. "Frequently Requested Statistics on Immigrants and Immigration in the US." *Migration Information Source: The Online Journal of the Migration Policy Institute*, (February 8).

Index

Abrego, Leisy, 141, 211n4, 217n61,
217n62, 231n81, 237n71, 240n117,
245n7, 245n8
abortion, 225n101, 231n81
Africa, female migrants from, 23–24
agency, 1–2, 11–14, 79
agentic orientations, 13
aging population, of Italy, 20
agrarian reform, 39
Agricultural Workers' Union (ATC),
38
agro-industry, in Nicaragua, 8
Albania, emigration from, 18
amnesty, process of, 142–143
AMNLAE, 73, 74–76
Ana: as caregiver, 26–27; challenges of,
185, 201; children's well-being and,
192–193; disadvantages of, 200;
discrimination toward, 163–164,
168, 202; educational role of, 175–
176; education of, 46–48; emigration by, 14–17, 125–130, 206; faith

of, 230n72; family of, 36–38, 87,
220n8, 220n10; family separation
by, 156–157; financial provisions by,
146–147, 152–153, 237n74; in Germany, 50–51, 125–126; government
viewpoint of, 77; grandchildren of,
187; harassment of, 222n45; home
environment of, 184–185; home
of, 171–172; immigration status of,
144; in Italy, 127, 129–130, 205–206;
land invasion experience of, 38–
40; legal violence toward, 245n8;
life changes of, 105–106; long-
term plans of, 166; in Managua,
47–48; mother's actions toward,
119; objective of, 25; physical abuse
of, 101, 102–103; in Portugal, 128;
pregnancy of, 39, 47; property of,
72; sacrifices of, 169; sexual abuse
of, 47, 49–50, 96–101, 123; troubled
relationships of, 114–118; venereal
disease of, 104; visa of, 140; work

GLOBALIZATION
IN EVERYDAY LIFE

As global forces undeniably continue to change the politics and economies of the world, we need a more nuanced understanding of what these changes mean in our daily lives. Significant theories and studies have broadened and deepened our knowledge on globalization, yet we need to think about how these macro processes manifest on the ground and how they are maintained through daily actions.

Globalization in Everyday Life foregrounds ethnographic examination of daily life to address issues that will bring tangibility to previously abstract assertions about the global order. Moving beyond mere illustrations of global trends, books in this series underscore mutually constitutive processes of the local and global by finding unique and informative ways to bridge macro- and microanalyses. This series is a high-profile outlet for books that offer accessible readership, innovative approaches, instructive models, and analytic insights to our understanding of globalization.

CPSIA information can be obtained
at www.ICGtesting.com
Printed in the USA
JSHW052145250222
23396JS00003B/5